A Skills-based Approach

Painting
is a Class Act

Years 1 and 2

Meg Fabian

Brilliant
PUBLICATIONS

We hope you and your pupils enjoy using the ideas in this book. Brilliant Publications publishes many other books for teaching art and design. To find out more details on any of the titles listed below, please log onto our website: www.brilliantpublications.co.uk.

Painting is a Class Act, Years 3–4	978-1-905780-30-3
Painting is a Class Act, Years 5–6	978-1-905780-31-0
Drawing is a Class Act, Years 1–2	978-1-903853-60-3
Drawing is a Class Act, Years 3–4	978-1-903853-61-0
Drawing is a Class Act, Years 5–6	978-1-903853-62-7
100+ Fun Ideas for Art Activities	978-1-905780-33-4
Preschool Art	978-1-897675-49-6
Discovering Great Artists	978-1-903853-16-0
The Big Messy Art Book	978-1-903853-18-4

Acknowledgements

I would like to thank the following primary schools for their permission to include in the publication examples of work by children in their schools. This work has been done over a number of years. Wherever work is named, permission was sought for inclusion.

Primary schools

Berrynarbor V.C. Primary School	East Worlington School
Chawleigh Primary School	Filleigh Community Primary School
Clovelly Primary School	Witheridge C of E Primary School

Individual pupil list

Aiden-Thomas Cabourne	Diane Stubbs	Kyle Hettmann	Richard Grasske
Alanah Stenning	Elaine Pearce	Leanne Stevens	Robert Cooke
Andrew Loat	Ellena Meadows	Linda Dixon	Robert Peacock
Ashley Clarke	Ellie Budden	Lorna Lewis	Shani Cooke
April Britton	Evie Peacock	Lucy Clements	Shona Gregory
Ashley Stephens	Giles Gellay	Madeleine Nichols	Simone Charles
Beth James	Gwyneth Goldring	Maggie Ashworth	Sophie Warren
Bethany James	Holly Ashworth	Margaret Gellay	Sophie Dixon
Bianca Roberts	Holly Peacock	Mathew Jones	Spike Hutchings
Bob Rush	Holly Victoria	Max Hardwick	Sue Rodgers
Briony Steel	Jack Davies	Max Wild	Tim Grimshire
Buddy Morris	Jack Muirhead	Meg McClavers	Toby Short
Charlotte Green	Jade Tanton	Megan Harrop	
Chloe Gregory	James Latham	Millie Becklake	
Colin Adams	Joe Blackford	Nat Beeston	
Connor Norden	Jonathan Hussain	Nicky Loat	
Damian Hopkins	Jordan Wilde	Oliver Coulham	
Daniel Huxtable	Katy Sparks	Oliver Squire	
Daniel Rodgers	Kelly White	Phillip Searle	

Published by Brilliant Publications
Unit 10
Sparrow Hall Farm
Edlesborough
Dunstable
Bedfordshire
LU6 2ES, UK

Website: www.brilliantpublications.co.uk

General information enquiries:
Tel: 01525 222292

The name Brilliant Publications and the logo are registered trademarks.

Written by Meg Fabian
Designed by Bookcraft Limited
Front cover designed by Brilliant Publications

© Text Meg Fabian 2010
© Design Brilliant Publications 2010

Printed: ISBN 978-1-905780-29-7
eBook: ISBN 978-1-85747-125-3

First printed and published in the UK in 2010

Foreword

Being able to paint is a life-enhancing skill and the development of painting skills has benefits far beyond the art lesson. Painting:

* helps children to express themselves
* helps to promote high standards in other areas of the curriculum
* raises children's self-esteem and confidence
* gives children an understanding and awareness of colour which can be life enhancing.

This book will be invaluable to non-specialist teachers as it clearly:

* sets out the development of painting skills
* offers guidance on progression
* provides ideas to support classroom activities.

Meg Fabian is the ideal person to write this book. She is a specialist with a passion for art and has been instrumental in raising children's standards and confidence in art across a range of North Devon schools.

Phil Creek
Adviser for Art and Design
Devon Education Services

Contents

	Type of lesson	Time needed	Page
Basic skills			
Introducing powder paint			28
Investigating paintbrushes and making different brush strokes	Key Skill	30 min	31
Investigating paintbrushes and making different brush strokes	Using Skill	30 min	32
Naming the primary colours	Key Skill	10 min	33
Painting in primary colours	Using Skill	45 min	34
Powder paint handling	Key Skill	30 min	35
Painting a picture in powder paint	Using Skill	1 hour	36
Naming paint colours	Key Skill	30 min	37
Getting to know the colours and comparing blues (or reds or yellows)	Using Skill	30 min	38
Making a colour lighter without using white (changing tone in colour)	Key Skill	30 min	39
Making a colour lighter without using white (changing tone in colour)	Using Skill	30 min	40
Making a collage using work from a previous lesson	Using Skill	45 min	41
Colour mixing			
Background information			44
Colour mixing tips			45
Mixing secondary colours: purples (or greens or oranges)	Key Skill	45 min	46
Mixing and using secondary colours: green (lesson can be adapted for orange or purple)	Using Skill	1 hour	47
Changing the colours by adding a little paint at a time	Skill	Roughly 1 hour	48
Recording colour mixing	Skill	45 min	49
Earth colours and making browns	Skill	30 min	50
Painting in browns (and other earth colours)	Using Skill	1 hour	51
Painting in secondary colours and browns (and using different tones of colours)	Using Skill	2 hours	52
Using a range of colours in a painting	Using Skill	2 hours	53
Creating skin tones	Skill	30 min	54
Painting a self-portrait using skin tones	Using Skill	Roughly 1 hour	55
Colour matching	Key Skill	Roughly 1 hour	56
Colour theory			
Background information			58
Keys aspects of colour theory			60
The colour wheel	Key Skill	30 min	61
Painting in complementary colours	Using Skill	1 hour	62
Colour and mood	Skill	45 min	63
Colour families	Key Skill	2 hours	64
Considering relationships between colours	Skill	2 hours	65

A skills-based approach to painting

For children as young artists, painting can be a means of personal expression, a way to express ideas and feelings.

All artists experiment with colour and use materials in a personal way. This book aims to enable teachers to support children in this same process of discovery and exploration.

The use of paint needs to be taught to children; they need to be led to an awareness of colour and how it can be mixed and used in order for them to grow in confidence and in understanding in the handling of paint. They should know it can be applied in layers or changed, and that its surface can be flat or textured. They should know that different qualities of paint may be used for different purposes.

Younger pupils will generally paint without inhibition, but as children progress through the school they will need direct teaching in order for them to master the media and to develop skills. The originality, the individual vision and inspiration will come from them. However formally they are taught, their creativity will not be impaired and they will still evolve their own style and have their own ideas.

How the skills-based approach works

Painting is essentially about colour and paints and the way in which these are controlled and used. In this book, these aspects are taken apart and pared down to their basic elements. They have been separated initially into simple lessons which show children how particular types of paint behave and the different ways in which colours can be mixed and used.

The skills acquired should be used in a context as soon as possible, not only for purposes of consolidation, but also so that children will be able to see how these skills can be used in a painting and how they will increase the effectiveness of their work.

Elaine Pearce, Year 2 (in the style of Paul Klee)

The skills and experiences should build over time to help children develop the confidence and competence they need to create the effects they desire. They should to be able to express their own ideas and feelings effectively in paint and colour. Confidence in the process and in themselves is essential if they are going to gain the benefits of being able to take pleasure in it and communicate through this medium.

One way to achieve this confidence is to help children achieve control over the paints and the tools. They should also be encouraged to see opportunities to change and develop their work when they use these skills in the context of a painting.

Children need to realize that adult artists also had to learn and practise basic techniques and that they themselves are now involved in the same process.

Learning to paint is as difficult as learning any other complex discipline. One way we can help children not to be overwhelmed with the task is to limit the choices of media and colours, and to be specific about the focus of the painting session.

Paints have different properties and children should be given experience of a wide range, although they should not be introduced to too many at once because this will confuse them. It is to be recommended that the school has one staple paint medium that will be used consistently throughout the school, with other painting media being used alongside this as appropriate.

Which paints?

Although there are lessons which specify ready-mixed paint, particularly for younger children, in this book the staple paint is powder paint. The reasons for this are covered in more detail in the introduction to the chapter on powder paint. However, in most of the lessons, ready-mixed paint can be used in place of powder paint if that is the preferred medium of the class teacher or the school. Other painting media are also introduced, as can be seen on the contents page.

Looking at the work of other artists to see how they have dealt with colour and paint is an integral part of this approach to the teaching of painting. It helps children to recognize that they are young artists struggling with the same essential elements of painting – colour, shape, tone, texture and movement – as all adult artists, past and present.

When looking at works of art, they can be told, 'This is what artists do. They look at each other's work for inspiration and solutions, and they take ideas and change them. This is what they have always done; it is why artists often like to work and live near other artists. A creative person can take an idea and turn it into something which is his or her own.'

Few children in a school will become professional artists, but an appreciation of art and of colour is life-enhancing.

Andrew Loat, Year 2

Progression

In an ideal world, there would be consistency and continuity in the approach to painting throughout the school. The order of the content of the art curriculum will vary according to the school's own planning, but the principle behind the teaching in this book is that the skill/medium/technique is introduced and taught and is then used in a painting context as soon as possible. This could be the same day, the next art session, or whenever is appropriate to the skill.

Children will need regular opportunities to experiment with a new medium so that they have a chance to examine its potential. Successful use of a new skill or medium boosts a child's self-esteem and builds confidence to experiment.

Whereas there are some media that are more age-appropriate than others (for example, oil painting is generally better saved for older Key Stage 2 children), it is as well, where possible, to give all ages the opportunity to experiment with different media and materials. Older junior children can make stunning mono prints from finger paintings, whilst young infants respond well to the challenge of painting with tiny brushes.

Painting should be tackled in terms of what is possible and appropriate to the medium. Learning about paint is a gradual process, beginning in school at foundation stage and developing in complexity as understanding grows.

This should be enhanced from the earliest years by the introduction of works of art. Children should be invited to respond and to develop a vocabulary of response. The questioning from the teacher should become more probing and specific as the years go by, starting with simple questioning about what the children can see and what they like or don't like about a work of art, and progressing to such thoughts as 'what the artist's intention might have been'.

Examples of a range of questioning in response to works of art is to be found on pages 88–89 in the chapter on Using works of art.

Children's development in painting

Children first use colour at an intuitive and emotional or convenience level, because they like it, because it looks right or because it was handy and there was some left.

Children tend to express what they know rather than what they see, which is why skies tend to be blue at the top of the page and grass green at the bottom, with an area of white left in between. The appearance of a yellow quarter section of a sun in the top right- or left-hand corner is really just a symbol which the child knows will be recognized and 'read' by whoever views the painting. They become quite surprised if they are questioned about why they put it there and when they last saw a sun like this.

This schematic approach to painting a scene should really not appear later than Year 3, unless the child is very immature, as then it is really just a form of laziness. As they mature, they become more aware of the complexity of the visual environment and the problems of interpreting the 'real' world.

When children become aware of the difference between the images they paint and those they see around them, they can lose satisfaction with what they have produced and it becomes important to them that their images are acceptable to others as well as themselves.

As young children develop an awareness of space, the random earlier daubs are replaced by a more considered representation. At this stage there is no concept of scale and the child

Jack Muirhead, reception (a flower elf)

exaggerates and distorts to emphasize things of personal significance and importance. As co-ordination increases, children extend their range of symbols and execute paintings with more detail, together with a diminishing size of their work.

Experience and progression of skills

Foundation Stage
* Explores making a variety of marks on papers
* Uses a variety of tools to spread paint, eg straws, sponges, fingers
* Explores mark-making using thick brushes
* Creates patterns using different tools and colours
* Experiences painting flat and upright
* Blot paintings
* Paints on different 2-D and 3-D surfaces
* Paints on a variety of papers, coloured and shaped
* Experiments with haphazard colour mixing with ready-mixed paint
* Simple wax resist, crayons/candles and paint
* Experiences the effect on paint of adding water, glue, sand, sawdust, etc

* Paints for fun and exploration
* Has a go at representing something observed, remembered or imagined using colour/tools
* Expresses opinions about own paintings and paintings of other children
* Looks at and makes simple responses to works of art
* Mono prints from finger paintings
* Learns names of primary and secondary colours

Year 1
* Continues with experimentation
* Gains greater control over range of applicators used
* Alters the consistency by adding water
* Extends colour vocabulary: brown, light blue, dark blue, etc
* Introduced to names of paint colours, eg brilliant blue, crimson, vermilion, lemon yellow, etc
* Adds white to colours
* Experiences mixing secondary colours
* Uses different brushes for different painting jobs

Sophie Warren, Year 1

* Uses colour and marks to express mood
* Explores using thin and thick paint to create light and dark tones of colours
* Paints to express feelings and moods via choice of colour and strokes
* Starts to lay out and clear up equipment
* Describes own paintings, comments on achievements
* Encouraged to make positive comments about artwork of peers
* Thinks about backgrounds
* Paints to illustrate, narrate and record
* Uses wax resist with oil pastels and Brusho®
* Creates blot paintings
* Experiences powder paint handling
* Uses Brusho® (powdered watercolour)
* Introduced to colour theories: hot/cold/happy/sad colours
* Uses sketch books
* Recognizes and names primary and secondary colours

Year 2

* Paints in a range of brush sizes
* Uses different brushes within one painting
* Learns to mix and control powder paint
* Paints colour washes in Brusho®
* Experiments with combining secondary colours to make browns
* Makes a range of greens and oranges with different reds, blues and yellows
* Learns how to mix and match colours

* Looks at brush strokes and colours used in works of art
* Learns about cave paintings and the materials used
* Makes simple paints from natural objects, eg earth, chalk, blackberries, etc
* Looks at art from other cultures
* Paints to express mood, feelings and expression
* Extends responses to works of art and knowledge of famous artists
* Recognizes key works of art, eg the Mona Lisa
* Uses a work of art as a starting point
* Begins to recognize that paintings are from long ago by looking at the costumes and/or style
* Wax resist with oil pastels and Brusho®, adding scraffito
* Blown paint/ink pictures
* Paints from first-hand experience, eg portraits, plants, occasions, etc
* Uses ready-mixed paint
* Uses ready-mixed paint to paint 3-D objects, both self-made and found
* Uses a sketch book to record colour mixing and collect visual information to use in paintings and to write comments about works of art (their own and of other artists)
* Paints in pearlescent and metallic paints
* Works in a variety of scales
* Works individually and in groups

Year 2 pupil

Resources

In an ideal world, a well-stocked art cupboard might contain:

Different types of paint
* Finger paints
* Ready-mixed
* Powder paint
* Tempera paint (blocks and tablets)
* Watercolours: powdered (Brusho®)
* Watercolours: tablets
* Metallic
* Pearlescent
* Cromar
* Marbling

Drawing media
* Watercolour pencils
* Water-soluble crayons
* Charcoal
* Oil pastel
* Art (chalky) pastels
* Felt tips
* Permanent ink pens

Brushes
* Long- and short-handled stiff-bristled brushes in different sizes and tips
* Soft brushes in various sizes
* Decorator brushes in various sizes

Papers
As well as the usual paper that a primary school keeps:
* Cartridge paper, ready-cut in various sizes
* Kitchen paper
* Junior art paper
* Blotting paper

Sundry items
* Paint wells (for powder paint)
* Sketch books
* Palettes (various types to suit the paint being used)
* Water pots
* Protective clothing
* Painting storage racks (for drying)
* Masking tape

Technical painting terms
The painter's materials are called 'media' and include, for example, oils, watercolours, acrylics, etc.

These media are applied to a 'support', such as canvas, wood, paper, using a variety of tools such as brushes, palette knife and fingers. Below the surface of a painting there may be other layers of paint, usually called an 'under-painting', and beneath the painting there may also be an 'under-drawing'.

Explanation of other painting terms can be found in the glossary on pages 115–117.

More detailed information about each resource such as colours, sizes, quantities, types available etc and advice follows.

Specific information about each type of paint is on pages 12–13 and there is more about powder paint on pages 28–29.

Aiden-Thomas Cabourne, Year 2

Paints

Finger paints

These usually come ready-mixed in re-sealable pots; they are available in bright colours, in black and white and with glitter.

Ready-mixed

This comes in squeezy bottles in a wide range of colours. The range of colours is very useful for younger pupils but, as the children progress through Key Stage 1, they should gradually be limited to using the six basic colours and black and white, as this will encourage them to mix their own shades rather than use the colours straight from the bottle. The basic colours are vermilion and crimson red, brilliant and cyan blue, and lemon and brilliant yellow.

Ready-mixed paint is excellent for younger children, as powder paint is more difficult to mix, but it is also very useful for larger-scale work for all ages and for painting models.

As with most paints, it is advisable to order double the quantity of white and yellow. Various substances can be added to it to create different textures in paintings. There is more about this in 'texture' on pages 17–18.

Ashley Stephens, Year 1 (finger painting in Aboriginal style)

Metallic paint

It is better to buy this in ready-mixed form as the powdered variety can be difficult to mix up. There are two grades of ready-mixed paint: Meltdown paint, which is more expensive but is suited to smaller-scale work and is excellent for painting small clay models; and less expensive varieties which are not so glorious when dry but which are quite suitable for general use and for younger children.

Pearlescent

These water-based paints have a lovely shimmer and add a different dimension to a painting. They are also useful for painting models, and particularly for clay models if the school does not have a kiln to fire glazes.

Cromar

These are translucent water-based paints that can be used on any surface but are ideal for use on glass or plastic.

Tempera (block) paint

Tempera comes in solid blocks and needs to be thoroughly moistened before use. The blocks – flat cylindrical tablets that fit into a palette – need to be of a good quality, otherwise it is difficult to make paint of a covering consistency. They have limited use when colours need to be mixed as they generally end up with other colours over the top and have to be cleaned before they can be used next time. No lessons in this medium are included in this book.

Although they are difficult to keep clean, the blocks are quick to set out and not messy to clear up, so they can be useful when the classroom has no sink. Younger children do not find them daunting. However, they are not sufficient to be the only paint available.

Powder paint

Powder paint is the best painting medium in the primary school. It allows full and sensitive colour mixing and is reasonably priced. It comes in dry form and children can mix it themselves, but the process needs to be taught. The best aspect of powder paint is that it is possible to mix an almost limitless range of colours. It is not necessary to stock more than six colours plus black and white.

The downside of using powder paint is that it can be difficult for children to mix a large amount of a blended colour, and they need to develop their skills in using it. They will also need direct teaching and support to get the right consistency. There is more about this in the chapter on basic skills (pages 28–29).

Watercolour

This comes in three forms: tablet, tube and powder. However, the powdered form is the easiest for Key Stage 1 children to use. There is no reason, though, why Year 2 children shouldn't have a little go with watercolours from tablets, and there are larger tablets available for younger children. The more difficult skills, like laying a wash and layering colours, should really be left for Key Stage 2.

The tablets can be bought separately or ready placed in tins which have a lid that can be used for colour mixing.

The powder is very versatile and is excellent for large washes, wax resist and for use on fabrics, especially batik. The most common brand is Brusho®. It is not colour-fast and will wash out.

It can be mixed with water to any density of colour and can be stored in screw-top jars for later use. It can also be sprinkled directly onto damp paper for an unusual effect. It comes in small tubs and will stain the skin under your fingernails, so it is advisable to wear latex gloves when mixing it.

Watercolours become translucent when applied thinly.

Poster paint

This water-based paint comes in small pots or tubes and does not really do anything that good quality ready-mixed paint does not.

Fabric paint

There are a variety of fabric paints available from different suppliers. There are colour-fast varieties and also some that come in crayon form. Some need ironing to make them colour-fast. They come in all colours, including fluorescent and pearlescent types.

Acrylic paint

Acrylic paint is a thick, creamy paint sold in large tubes or pots. Acrylics can be diluted with water but have a plastic base which forms a waterproof skin. The paint peels off skin but does not come out of clothes, and for this reason it is not really suitable for Key Stage 1 use unless the children are closely supervised.

Stencilling on torn paper, group work, Years 1 and 2

Acrylic paint can be built up in layers, can be over-painted once dry without mixing colours, and can be used to create texture. It can be applied with a brush or a palette knife.

Particular care has to be taken when using acrylic paint as it is also a strong adhesive. Paintbrushes need to be cleaned immediately after the painting session has finished or they will set rock hard and have to be thrown away.

Gouache
Gouache is an opaque watercolour; the pigment is thickened with white chalk. It is not really necessary in primary school unless a particular project requires it, although it is a useful medium for graphic design. It comes in tubes.

Ink
Brusho® (powdered watercolour) can be used in place of ink if it is mixed with only a small amount of water. Some bottled inks are unsuitable for use with children, so the labels should be read with care.

Marbling inks
Marbling inks are special oil-based colours. They float on the surface of water, and paper can be laid on top to pick up the patterns of the swirling colours. They are relatively foolproof and children love the effects created. However, the children need to wear protective clothing.

Drawing media

Watercolour pencils
These are artists' quality coloured pencils. Lovely colour blending effects can be achieved with them and the children's drawings can be wet with a brush so the colours move. They are particularly useful in plant studies.

Tim Grimshire, Year 1 (watercolour pencils)

Water-soluble crayons
These are used in the same way as watercolour pencils.

Felt tips
Most felt-tip pens can be used as described for watercolour pencils. They are also interesting to use to show colour separation when spots of colour are drawn onto wet blotting paper and left for the colours to spread and separate.

Permanent ink pens
These generally come in three thicknesses and the thicker points can be round- or chisel-ended.

These are excellent for drawing over paintings (examples of this can be found on pages 38 and 41). They work well over watercolours, but care needs to be taken when using them over thick powder paint or ready-mixed paint, because the pen points can clog, and they do not work well over wet paint. Permanent pens are also good for drawing before painting as the ink does not run when paint is applied over drawings.

Charcoal
Charcoal drawings can be wet with a brush and the black will move to make shades of grey. This is a classic medium and has a long history.

Artists' pastels
Chalky pastels can be used in the same way as charcoal. Using sepia or burnt sienna pastels can give an 'old look' to a painting. This might be appropriate when studying artists such as Leonardo da Vinci, for example.

Brushes
It is important to offer the children a range of brushes, both small and large. House painting brushes are also useful for covering large areas and for certain techniques such as spatter painting. Brushes need to be looked after and washed out after use; and never stored brush-end downward in a container. This is particularly important with short-handled watercolour brushes as these are virtually unusable once the ends have become bent. Store brushes which are to be used for acrylics separately.

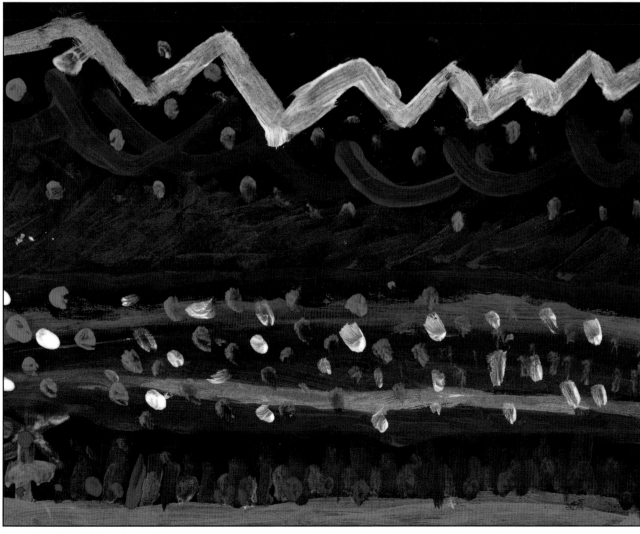

Experimenting with brush strokes

Children need to be taught good brush techniques, ie how to hold them just above the ferrule (metal band) with a similar hold to pencils, and not to scrub with them, which splays the hairs. This shortens their life (the brushes not the children, although if I catch them at it…!!).

Children should also be encouraged not to leave their brushes standing in water pots, but to rinse them and lay them across their palettes or on the table, even when the lesson is paused for further information and teaching. It is prudent to make this the normal practice so it becomes second nature. Brushes' points, particularly watercolour brush points, become misshapen when left standing in water.

Different brush strokes can be made with different ends. A range of good brushes in different sizes is good for children to experiment with mark making in paint.

General-use brushes: ready-mixed paint, powder and acrylics

Hog hair is the cheapest option and adequate for most uses; the downside is that they tend to be softer and can lose their hair. Synthetic hair is also available. This is more expensive, but it keeps its shape well and is more economical in the long run.

Brushes are generally long-handled and are available in a range of thicknesses from size 4 to size 18. Short-handled brushes are excellent for Key Stage 1 as the longer-handled ones can be rather unwieldy for younger children. However, long-handled brushes are easier to store upside-down in blocks or pots as the handles are slimmer.

For general use, the round ends are adequate, but it is good to have a few sizes of flat-ended brushes as well for painting with textured paint. A brush with a square end will produce a different effect from a round one. In order to gain confidence in the use of a range of brushes, it is good to encourage pupils to experiment with their differing effects.

Watercolour brushes

The best brushes, like the best paints, tend to be the most expensive. The cheaper brushes are really not worth bothering with; buy the best you can afford if the children are going to have

Stencilling on torn paper, group work, Years 1 and 2

Holly Peacock, Year 2

a serious go with watercolours. Otherwise there are various other small 'soft brush' options, sometimes known as pony-hair, which are adequate for most Key Stage 1 general use.

A range of sizes is again important; sizes 4–12 are useful. The larger ones are good for washes and the small to medium for detail.

Watercolour brushes need to be looked after and should be kept separately and stored with care – never brush-end downward in a pot.

Brush storage

There are ready-made brush stands available from different suppliers. It can be a bit fiddly to put the brushes in some of them, but this can always be done by an art monitor. Otherwise, cleaned brushes can be stored flat in trays or wooded ends down in pots in their different sizes.

Children should be encouraged to choose the most appropriate brush for the job in hand, particularly in terms of size. Frequently, children will try to cover large areas with a tiny brush or try to paint in minute detail with a large brush. If a range of brush sizes is available to them on their table from the onset of the session, they will be more likely to independently choose the best one for their purpose.

Other methods of applying paint

It is important to point out that brushes are not the only method of applying paint to a surface. Most children enjoy inventing and making their own painting implements. Children should have the opportunity to experiment with such things as fingers, rags, strips of card, rollers and sponges.

Sponges, for example, offer endless opportunities for painting experiments. Rough textures and special effects can be achieved when paints of different consistencies are applied with natural or synthetic sponges of various degrees of coarseness.

Cotton buds are useful as they are easy to hold, are absorbent and they keep their shape well. They are especially useful for painting small, precise areas, such as petals and stamens of flowers, or for painting in the style of the Pointillists or Aborigine dot pictures.

Fur fabric can be used to apply paint, for example to create a grassy effect.

Single prints can be made from paintings while the paint is still wet, by placing a sheet of paper on top of the painting and peeling it off.

Marbles can be rolled in paint and then rolled across the paper.

Paint can be:
* Dropped or dripped onto the paper
* Thrown on as in action painting (if you are very brave, have a large space to work in and are prepared for the ensuing mess)
* Splattered on by pulling back the bristle of a stiff brush such as a toothbrush or washing-up brush
* Sprayed on with a diffuser or an aerosol can
* Blown in different directions along the page through a straw (use thin paint or ink)
* Sprinkled on as dry powder onto a wet surface
* Scraped with a variety of implements
* Lifted off with a variety of materials, leaving a paler colour.

Texture

Fabric can be pressed into wet paint to create a texture in a painting. Thick paint can be applied with a plastic or palette knife to create a rough, uneven texture which is called 'impasto'.

Various substances can be added to paint to make it thicker or textured, such as PVA, sawdust, salt, starch, flour, icing sugar, crushed eggshells, sand or Polyfilla®.

Paint applied thickly can be scraped with twigs or the ends of brushes to make lines and marks in the paint.

Bits and pieces can be dropped onto thick, wet paint, such as dry grass, sand, sawdust, tissue paper, foil, thin fabric, netting or glitter.

Paper

Shape
Artists have terms for which way round paper is to be used. 'Portrait' refers to having the long side vertical, while 'landscape' refers to the longer side being horizontal.

Quality
Good quality paper is essential if the paint is to adhere satisfactorily to the surface and if the paper is to remain flat after drying. If the paper is too thin, it may well not absorb moisture and may cockle when dry, spoiling the look of the work. Newsprint, cheap sugar paper and shiny paper are unsatisfactory and should be avoided except, perhaps, as test paper for colour mixing.

Paper is sold not only in sizes but also by weight. The weight of one square metre of paper in grams is written as GSM or g/sm: the larger the number, the stronger and firmer the paper. 70–170 g/sm is the range most school suppliers carry.

It is useful to order the paper you need in manageable sizes, unless you need the largest size for large-scale or group work. The very large sheets are difficult to store and often become damaged when other paper is removed or replaced. Separate packs of A1, A2, A3 and A4, ready-cut in the weight you need, are useful. Larger pieces have to be cut to size and there is not always enough time to fiddle about. As art is such a resource-heavy subject, collecting and setting out a range of media before a lesson can be daunting. Locating the guillotine, finding a space to put it on and cutting up the paper can be the last straw.

Sketchbooks should be of the best quality paper that the art budget can run to. Not only is this better for drawing on, it will hold the paint and means that children can work directly into their books when necessary.

Chloe Gregory, Year 2

Types of paper

Kitchen paper

Thin, cheap paper, also known sometimes as 'fish and chip' paper, is not an ideal surface for paint. It goes soggy quickly, it cockles, and the colours disappear into it. It can be acceptable for early years work, but only because these children do so many paintings, sometimes consisting of just a few brush strokes. In this case it would be too expensive to use good quality cartridge paper all the time.

Junior art paper

Junior art paper is slightly lighter and cheaper than cartridge paper and is adequate for general use. However, if a lot of paint or paint with high water content is being used, cartridge is better.

Cartridge

Cartridge paper is so called because it was made strong and firm in order to make cartridges for gunpowder. 115 g/sm is a good medium weight for general use, while 135 g/sm is better for acrylics and watercolours.

Pre-prepared backgrounds

Backgrounds should not always be white, nor always plain. It is good to give the children the opportunity to paint on coloured, patterned and textured surfaces.

Backgrounds can be:
* Wet, damp or dry
* Screwed up and smoothed out
* Rollered, using printing or decorator's rollers, with paint or printing ink
* Collaged
* Painted
* Printed in different ways, eg screwed-up cling film, bubble wrap or fabric
* Colour-washed using thin paints or inks
* Textured, such as wallpaper, sandpaper or woodchip.

Other surfaces and finishes

Paint can be applied to many different surfaces, such as cardboard, chipboard, wood, stone, etc. Some surfaces, however, need specialist paint – ceramics and glass, for example, and also fabric if it is to be washed and the colours not fade.

Children could paint on walls, doors, benches, trees, on fabric or on plastic. Old shoes, containers and furniture can be transformed.

Clear PVA can be over-painted to make artwork waterproof (up to a point), or varnishes can be applied to make colours brighter. I have heard that furniture polish can be sprayed over powder paint paintings and then buffed to bring out the colours; however, I have not managed to achieve this effect – maybe I used the wrong polish!

Other resources

Water pots

Water pots need to be stable and stackable. The type with a wider base than top are the best, and also don't need a lid. The pots must be tall enough to hold long-handled brushes so that they don't fall out. You will need enough for one between two children and plenty of spares for other purposes, such as holding quantities of ready-mixed paint or mixed-up Brusho® (powdered watercolour).

Palettes

There are several different varieties of palettes available from suppliers, but many teachers just use old plates. It depends really upon what suits your purpose and what you personally prefer to use.

Year 2 pupil

Palettes need to be easy to wash out quickly, so curved edges to the hollows are helpful. They also need to stack and not take up too much room on the table. Unless you are lucky enough to have an art room with lots of table space for each child, you will need to consider carefully the space on the table for paints, palettes, water pots and whatever other resources are being used.

Plastic moulded palettes with nine wells are excellent for colour mixing, as they give enough space for a range of colours and are big enough to share between two. Palettes are also available with six wells.

The disadvantage of mixing paint on single flat surfaces, like plates or trays, is that it is difficult to keep the colours separated and they tend to run together.

Watercolours can be mixed in the lids of the paint boxes, on an old plate, on palettes with smaller wells; a stiff piece of shiny card will do if you are really stuck.

It is possible to buy special paper palettes for acrylics, and this may save a lot of time on clearing up.

A tip which saves water and washing-up time is to put a piece of cling film over the palette. At the end of the painting session, pull off the cling film and throw it away. This leaves the palettes clean and does not pour chemicals into the water system.

Easels
It is good for children to have the experience of working at an easel at some stage in their school life. This generally happens at lower Key Stage 1 when children have a selection of ready-mixed colours in pots along the bottom of an easel tray. While it is good to be able to stand back from your work and view it at a distance, the disadvantage is that, unless it is very thick, the paint tends to run down the paper. Once the children have dipped their brushes in the water to clean them, the paint becomes thin and watery and will dribble down the page.

Drying racks
There are several different types available, pretty much all of them fiddly and tricky in different ways. The ones with loose, moveable shelves are particularly maddening as the shelves tend to come away in your hand when you are holding a wet painting in the other. Others have shelves which, after a few years of use, tend to slope

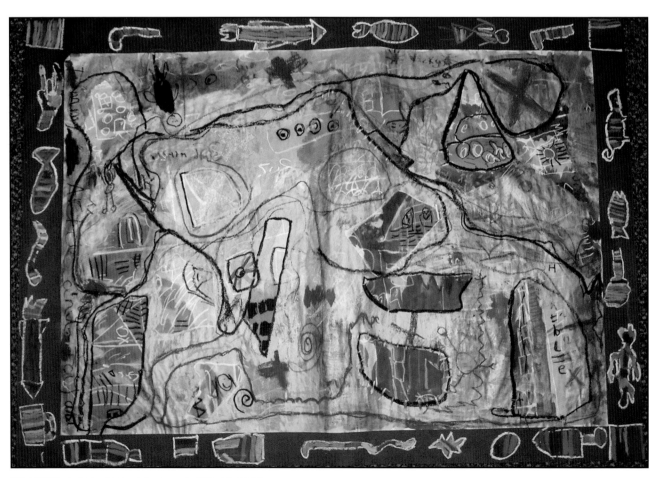

Stencilling on torn paper, group work, Years 1 and 2

downwards (children have been known to lean on them and speed this tendency), so inevitably the wet paintings all slide off the shelves. Fun!

Drying racks take up quite a bit of space in a classroom unless wall-mounted, and they can become dumping grounds; however, they are essential in order to have somewhere to put wet artwork and to stop it becoming dog-eared and damaged. If the racks are accessible to children, they can carry their own work to the rack, but this can be fraught with danger. Wet artwork often runs unless children remember to carry it horizontally, and there is always the danger of them bumping into a child who isn't wearing a painting overall, thereby smearing them with paint. This is naturally always a child who has a very particular parent!

Some drying racks have lift-up shelves, while others have pull-out shelves, and some are on wheels so they can be removed from the classroom.

Pegging artwork up on washing lines or clothes drying racks is a popular solution and can work well unless paint is wet and running.

Protective clothing

This is another area fraught with difficulty, so here are a few suggestions.

An old adult-sized T-shirt makes an excellent painting overall. It has no buttons or strings and slips on easily. It covers most of the arms and the body, and comes down to the thighs or even lower. You could purchase 30 or so new T-shirts quite cheaply, probably at no more than a pound each, whereas you could spend the whole year asking children to bring them in from home and get only a few responses.

The school could buy painting overalls or aprons for each class, but it is only worthwhile getting the better quality ones. Cheaper aprons are a waste of time as they rip or split very quickly.

Whichever way you do it, the children need to protect their clothes for most painting lessons.

Year 1 pupil

Classroom organization

The first consideration in classroom organization is, 'how many children are going to be painting at one time?' This determines how much equipment is needed. Foundation children tend to paint in smaller groups, with the activity rotating over the day or week, until everyone who should have had a go at the activity has had their turn. Year 1 and Year 2 may follow this pattern but it is quite likely that, for various reasons, there will be times when the whole class is painting at the same time.

The greater the number of children painting at the same time, the more crucial it is that the equipment is organized efficiently. Children can then achieve optimum benefit from the experience and will not have to battle against the mess and muddle that can ensue quickly when equipment is not organized with care and consideration.

Many teachers shudder at the thought of a whole class of young children all painting at the same time, but it is manageable and it does have some advantages. It provides a whole-class experience, and the shared sense of discovery and achievement can be powerful. It does 'get it over with' in one go, and with such a crowded curriculum there is no longer time for things to drag out over several weeks. Also, with smaller groups each taking their own turn to paint, the moment can pass and the activity may lose its impact, or a topical aspect may no longer apply. There are also display implications: do you wait until all the children have done it before the artwork goes up on the wall? The younger the children, the sooner they want to see their work displayed or to take it home.

The following are a few pointers that apply whatever the size of the group, and regardless of where the art materials are kept – whether they are in your classroom, stored in some central location or, if your school is big enough, in an art room.

Newspaper

If you cover tables with newspaper, two layers is best. The advantage of this is that it absorbs some spills, extra layers can be added if necessary and damp brushes can be dried on it. Newspaper can be cleared quickly away at the end of the session and, unless there have been a lot of spills, tables should not even need wiping. If the children are setting out newspaper themselves, then check that it does not poke out beyond the edges of the table. This can cause disasters in that, when anyone walks past the table, they are in danger of catching it against themselves and inadvertently swiping the whole contents of the table onto the floor.

One last point about newspapers: broadsheets do the job best. It takes less time to lay them out as the pages are bigger and there are fewer 'unsuitable' images. Even so, keep an eye out for disturbing images that might distress young children – for example, from war zones or of natural disasters. Just flip those pages over.

Setting out tables

Consider paper size before setting out the tables; if children are working with A2 or A3 paper, then fewer of them can work at a time. If it is group work on a large-scale surface, you may have to leave space around the edge of the table for materials, or place them on a table nearby.

For a table of children doing individual work, set out:
* Paper for artwork
* Enough water pots, paints and palettes positioned so that children do not have to reach across each other to get to them (this causes water and paint to land on their paintings when it shouldn't)
* A test paper for each child to try out colours and dab brushes on
* A pencil, for writing the child's name on the back of their work, if nothing else
* At least one brush per child.

As a general rule, one water pot and one palette between two children works well. This may vary according to the activity and the size of the palettes.

Consider what other resources need to be on the table, eg items to be depicted, other art media or sketchbooks and where they can be best placed. Sketchbooks take up a lot of room; if children are using these for reference, they could put them under their chairs while they are not looking at them.

Remember that children will also need protective clothing (see page 21).

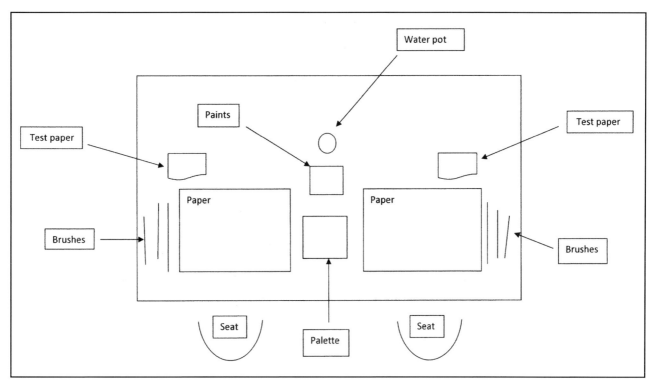

A table set out for two children

There is more specific information about setting out different media in chapters relating to that particular medium.

Changing dirty paint water

As children work more independently, they can be encouraged to change their own water when they think it needs changing. It can be explained to them that although their water may look dirty, it only needs changing if, when they put a clean brush in the water and then dab it into their test paper, it shows up as a colour rather than just a wet mark.

Consideration for others

Children should be encouraged to help set out, clear away and clean up from the earliest age, in whatever way is appropriate to that age, and they should also be taught to keep their work space clean. If this becomes messy, not only is their own artwork in danger of getting ruined but so is other children's work. They will need to be taught to look after the brushes and to consider the needs of other children who are sharing the materials.

Clearing up

Oh dear, the dreaded clearing-up time! This is not so bad if you have adult help, but for a number of reasons this may not be available.

If you do not have a teaching assistant, or you do have one but they are not free to assist, a willing parent helper is a boon. Failing all these options, however, you will just have to pack up a bit earlier and have a simple activity organized to keep the children busy whilst you deal with the clearing up.

Try this sequence of clearing-up activities:
* Have just one or two 'monitors'.
* Say, 'No one is to get up from their seats unless I have asked them to', otherwise the room will be full of children milling about with water pots, etc, getting in each other's way or getting into mischief.
* Clear up one group at a time and leave the others still working.
* Remove artwork first and put it somewhere safe. Clearing-up time is the most likely time for something disastrous to happen to it.
* Remove paints.
* Don't let any children carry powder paint around, because sooner or later they will drop it or will trip up and send it flying. It will go everywhere.
* Collect brushes and drop them into the sink (even if children have washed them, they will still generally need another wash). Leave them there while the water pots are rinsed.

* Collect the water pots next and wash them up, stacking them upside-down to drain. These take up the most room in the sink and so are best got rid of first.
* Wash the brushes and stand them to drain in a water pot or two.
* Collect palettes (or paint pots) and dump them in the sink to soak (NB see note about palettes and cling film on page 20).
* While the palettes are soaking, remove any other paint from the tables.
* Collect test papers.
* Remove newspaper.
* Send that group to wash their hands and put away their aprons, and give them their next activity.
* Wash the palettes, which, by now, will not be so difficult to clean. Children will need to be taught how to clean palettes. Getting the tap turned on at the right pressure is key to this, as is holding the palettes under running water at an angle away from themselves. Otherwise a full bore of water hits the palette and sprays right back at the child or the child next to them. This they consider to be a fine sport, so an eye needs to be kept on them.
* Repeat the clearing-up routine with the next group.

This is not as bad as it sounds. If, whenever possible, the children have something to do, it should run fairly smoothly. There will be times when they will have to just sit there patiently for a few moments with nothing to do during clearing up, but that can't be helped.

If you have no sink (poor you!). Try using three buckets:
* One with clean water to fill water pots
* One empty for dirty brushes and paint water
* One half full of water to soak palettes; better still use some kind of disposable palettes

Keeping artwork

Younger children usually want to take their work home as soon as possible, but you may want to display some of it, and you might also want to keep a few examples for school records or for your own future reference. These can be stored in large polythene window display books or in a home-made sugar paper display book.

You or the art co-ordinator might want evidence of coverage and progression for a number of reasons. A sample of artwork with a few notes attached about resources, planning, focus, etc can be valuable for future use. A glance at the artwork alone can be enough to remind you what you did and enable you to do it again at a later date.

If you want to be really organized, you could also keep labels from the display with the artwork and file it somewhere others could access it.

Year 2 pupil

Starting points and ideas for themes, topics or inspiration

Before you start painting

Backgrounds

Before you start any artwork, some consideration should be given to the background. Children should not always work on white, or even plain, paper.

The surface they work on, be it paper, card or whatever, could be coloured, patterned or textured. This might be ready-made or prepared by the children themselves.

Backgrounds can be printed, children could roll inked rollers over them in different colours, they might have been ragged (printed with screwed-up rags dipped in paint), textured, or they might be wet or dampened. Paper could be screwed up and then smoothed out again before it is worked on, or even screwed up, ironed after a first layer of paint is applied and then painted again.

It is important for children to consider backgrounds as part of their paintings, not just the white bits behind their picture.

Younger children might be encouraged to 'fill in the background with a colour', but Year 2 children should be starting to consider their backgrounds from the onset and to think about what might be in them and what colours they might be.

Discussion and observation

Painting from observation – from looking at and representing what exists, as opposed to painting abstract feelings and moods – is easier if children have the opportunity to study how something looks. Whether this is through the work or from first-hand experience depends on the subject matter.

If it is not possible for whatever reason to look at the real thing, then the Internet is an excellent resource. If you have an interactive whiteboard, open up the Google search engine and click on 'Images'. If you then type in whatever it is you want to look at, eg dragons, it will bring up an enormous selection of images for you to select and enlarge on the screen. There is usually a 'see full size image' option to click on, which will make the image larger so that all the children can see it.

Children can be directed to look at the basic shape of the subject, the colour, the surface texture, where the light falls, the darkest and lightest areas, etc.

They should also be encouraged to look at their environment and be given opportunities to express their ideas, thoughts and feelings about it.

The more children observe, handle and discuss the things they are going to paint, the more detailed their work will be. Before starting painting, encourage discussion and questions about the nature of the task, the objectives and the skills involved.

Experiences and stimuli for paintings

* Responding to excursions and outings
* Interpreting music, poetry, stories and drama
* Studying nature and man-made objects in the everyday world
* Investigating art materials
* Interpreting personal experiences, feelings and moods.

Starting-points and subject ideas

* Animals, fish, insects
* Plants: flowers, trees, grasses, etc

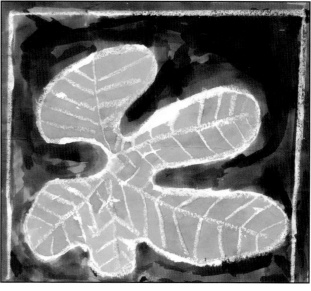

Year 2 pupil

25

- Interiors, views through windows/doors, family scenes
- Domestic objects, food and utensils, furniture, still life
- Buildings past and present, doors, roofs, windows, bricks
- Landscapes, rural and urban
- Water: sea, lakes, rivers
- Natural disasters: volcanoes, tidal waves, etc
- Portraits: self, individual, groups, miniatures
- Fantasy: dragons, fairies, magic, mystery, wizards etc
- Dreams, wishes
- The future: transport, clothes, homes
- Space: travel, planets, sun, moon, etc
- Toys, games, past and present
- Fire: candles, flames, etc
- Light, shade, shadows, contrast
- Reflection: in water, glass, on curved surfaces
- Weather: storm, rain, sun, wind, heat, cold, snow, frost
- Seasons: characteristics and colours
- Camouflage in animals, insects, birds, fish, etc
- Multicultural life and culture
- Artefacts linked to topics, history, science, etc
- Transport: cars, lorries, motorbikes, wheels, aeroplanes, trains
- Roads, road markings, traffic, street lights
- Underground: caves, creatures, tunnels
- Myths and legends
- Entertainment: circus, theatre, dance, music, puppets, fairs
- Sports and games: clothing, equipment, stars, Olympics
- Machines: cogs, chains, tools, engines, fantasy
- Advertising: magazines, television, hoardings, packaging

- Growth: animal, human, plant
- Clothing: fashion, costumes, fabrics, hats, shoes, past and present
- Past cultures: Egypt, Greece, etc
- Celebrations: birthdays, weddings, parties
- Food, drink
- Patterns: natural and man-made
- Movement: animal, human, speed, clouds, wind
- Habitats: jungle, desert, under stones, Arctic, etc
- Families: animal, human, plants, objects
- Time: clocks, watches
- Decorative arts: ceramics, weaving, jewellery.

Points for children to consider

When we ask children to make paintings, we may underestimate how many decisions have to be made and how many choices there are to be made.

When making a painting, here are just some of the points children might have to consider:

- What will the content of the painting be?
- Will the painting have a particular mood or feeling?
- What type of background is needed?
- Will the background be one colour or several colours?
- Is the background an important part of the composition or is it neutral?
- Will the surface be wet/damp or dry?
- Should the child make some kind of preliminary drawing or marks?
- Where is a good place to begin the painting?
- What brush(es) will be needed for different parts of the painting?
- Which colour to start with?
- How much paint needs to be mixed to get started?
- Is the paint mixed to the desired consistency?
- Does one area need to be dry before it is worked on, or worked next to?
- What will happen to the under-layer of paint if it is painted over?
- How will special effects be created?
- Is it better to put in small details later?
- Can a desired effect be achieved by using special brush marks?
- How does the painting look from a distance?
- Does anything need changing to improve the painting?
- Does the painting need to be finished in one session?
- Is the painting finished?

Phillip Searle, Year 2

Basic skills

Painting by Year 1 pupil

Introducing powder paint

Can't bear the thought of powder paint with younger children?

Some infant teachers feel daunted by the thought of using powder paint in class. There is no need to be, as powder paint can be used very successfully in Years 1 and 2, particularly when the handling of powder paint itself is taught as a separate lesson (see page 35). Foundation children, however, will find ready-mixed paint much easier, so powder could well be left until Year 1 to be introduced. All the colour mixing and matching lessons in this book can be done with ready-mixed paint if that is the teacher's preferred medium; it is really a matter of what the class teacher feels is most appropriate. Having said that, here is an explanation of why powder paint is a good choice.

Why powder paint?

Powder colour is by far the best choice for colour mixing because it gives children the best opportunity to control the process of mixing and changing colour. Dry colour cannot be used straight from the pot; water has to be added and this involves children with the process from the onset.

Success depends on children having been taught powder paint handling as a specific skill. If it is taught in a separate session when the focus is dealing with the medium rather than creating a painting, then children are only fighting one battle. It is worth spending time on this battle, because when the children have mastered the medium they will be better able to create the effects they want when they come to use the skill in a painting.

Having the right containers and setting out the 'painting station' in a user-friendly way makes a world of difference. Teachers often think that powder paint makes more mess and work than ready-mixed paint but it does not. Indeed, while dry powder does have its difficulties, if it is controlled through good classroom organization, it is less messy than ready-mixed paint and certainly less wasteful.

What is powder paint? An explanation that can be read to children

All paint consists of colour and something to mix it with. The mixer is called a binder. The binder mixes it together and makes it stick to the paper. Some paints are mixed together with oil, some with a kind of plastic and some with water. Paint can be bought in tubes or bottles where the colour and the binder have already been mixed up together. Ready-mixed paint is called that because it is already mixed up.

Powder paint has not yet been mixed with a binder. That has to be done by you. The binder is water. So, when you add water to powder paint, you are in fact mixing your own paint.

Oliver Squire, Year 2 (colour wash)

Organization of paint and equipment

For all colour mixing activities, only six colours are necessary. These colours are:

✳ Two reds – vermilion and crimson
✳ Two blues – brilliant blue (ultramarine) and cyan (sometimes known as sky blue; it is a turquoisey blue)
✳ Two yellows – brilliant yellow (egg yellow) and lemon yellow

These can be stored in six plastic paint wells that fit into a small tray and can be placed on the table. See the diagram on page 23. The advantage is that you can remove or change the selection of colours if you want to. Black and white are also useful as they cannot be created by mixing, although it is a good idea to dispense a little at a time as a little goes a long way.

The paint wells can be refilled from larger powder paint containers, and the easiest way to do this is to use the paint well like a scoop and dip it directly into the container. Only the most trustworthy of art monitors can be entrusted with this task!

Equipment needed for powder painting

✳ Newspaper
✳ Paper for artwork
✳ One set of paint wells between two children
✳ One water pot between two
✳ One palette between two
✳ Paint, water and palettes need to be positioned so that children do not have to reach across each other to get to them. This causes water and paint to land on their paintings when it shouldn't. See diagram
✳ A test paper for each child to try out colours and dab their brush on
✳ A pencil, for writing the child's name on the back of work, if nothing else
✳ At least one brush per child; but a selection of brushes of different sizes is better to give children the opportunity to exercise choice.

Key skills in handling powder paint

✳ Controlling the amount of water on the brush and in the palette
✳ Getting the consistency of the paint right
✳ Mixing up enough of the colour
✳ Adding enough pigment
✳ Re-mixing the colour when necessary
✳ Transferring powder to the palette on a brush.

These skills are covered in the powder paint handling lesson on page 35. Children need to revisit this activity at least once a year. Other skills will be covered in colour mixing lessons, such as adding a little of a colour at a time to change a colour/shade.

Gwyneth Goldring, Year 2

Tips for children about using palettes

❉ Remember you are sharing the palette; decide with your partner which areas on/in the palette you will each have.

❉ Don't use every part of your palette straight away, use the space sensibly.

❉ If all your spaces are full, look to see if you can reuse one area again, for example if you want an orange but there is no space free, if you have a red mixed up, then add yellow to it to get your orange, or if there is a yellow mixed up then add red to that to get orange. If you want a purple and you have a blue mixed then add red to it, and so on. You don't necessarily need to mix the colour from scratch.

There are other important skills when painting, but these apply to many different painting media, not just powder paint: for example, using the palette space sensibly; knowing when to change the water; looking after the brushes. Those aspects will need reinforcing at the beginning of most painting lessons.

Clearing up tips

❉ Washed palettes are better dried with a damp J-cloth than with a paper towel. Paper towels are not absorbent enough for the job.

❉ If the children are washing up, tell them, 'Don't turn the water on full blast and hold the palette under it or you will be sprayed with water. Always tip the palette so the dirty water runs down into the sink, not down you.'

Pitfalls of powder paint

❉ It is difficult for children to mix a large amount of a colour. If they need a lot of paint, perhaps for a group or large-scale activity, then ready-mixed paint is more appropriate.

❉ It is hard to re-mix the same colour when it has run out and it will run out quickly. Children need to try to remember how they mixed their colour so that they can achieve that shade again, particularly with browns.

❉ Children will need to be careful transferring paint to the palette from the paint wells. They tend to try to balance precarious heaps of dry powder that can be knocked, and then will sprinkle powder everywhere. The excess powder paint will also change the colour too drastically. They need to be reminded that it is best to change a shade or colour gradually with small amounts at a time.

❉ If you are mixing a lot of paint, the powder can tend to float on the surface of the water and be tricky to mix in. This is particularly true of black and the metallic powder paints. A drop of washing-up liquid in the water solves this.

❉ The colours look lovely and bright when just painted, but they lose a little of this brightness when dry. Special pieces of work could be laminated; this brings up the colours beautifully.

Year 2 pupil

Investigating paintbrushes and making different brush strokes

Time
30 min

Resources
Newspaper to cover tables

Per group of 5 or 6 children:
2 or 3 paint colours
(could be any paint except
watercolours)
2 water pots
1 palette

For each child:
3 long-handled paintbrushes: small,
medium and large bristle
1 short-handled, medium-fine soft-
haired brush
A3 piece of paper

For teacher:
One of each type of brush to show
A2 piece of paper to demonstrate the
brush marks
Something to fix paper to board

Brush information on pages 15–17

National Curriculum
4a, 2c

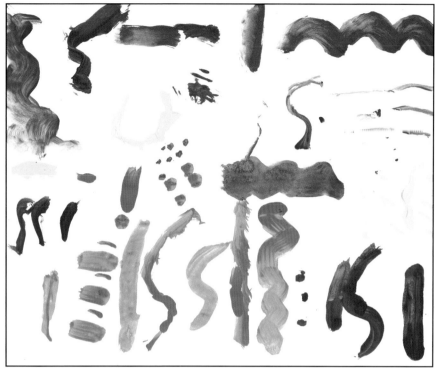

Year 1 pupil's brush strokes

Introduction
Artists use many different types of brushes, depending on what kind of paint they are using, how big or how small the painting is and what kind of effect they want to make. Today you will be looking at two different types of paintbrush and making as many different marks as you can with each type.

Practical activity
* Show children the three sizes of long-handled brushes and tell them that the bristles can be made of different materials. (See brush information on pages 15–17.)
* Ask the children to look at the long-handled brushes they have and look for indication on the brush handles as to the size.
* Explain that the metal part of the brush is called the ferrule.
* Tell the children that they should hold the brushes as they would hold a pencil. The best place to hold a brush is just above where the ferrule meets the handle (see Potential pitfall).
* Next, ask them to look at their short-handled soft brush and explain that the bristle might be made from the fur of a little animal called a sable, or it might be squirrel hair, pony hair or hog hair, or it could be a factory-made material such as nylon.
* Explain that different brushes are used for different purposes and will make different marks.
* Ask them to mix a slightly thinned solution of paint and then take a short-handled, small soft brush and paint some straight and wavy lines on the paper. Now ask them to repeat this, but press down on the brush a little so the lines are wider. Demonstrate this.
* They could try painting tiny dots, long lines, thick lines, thin lines, zigzags or big blobs. They could also try to make brush strokes of different lengths and thicknesses. Demonstrate.
* Encourage them to make as many different marks as they can.
* They should now repeat the process with the three different long-handled brushes.

Potential pitfall
Children often hold the brush handles either very close to the bristles and get paint all over their fingers, which then transfers itself to the painting, or they hold them too far along the handle, which makes it difficult for them to control the brush.

Investigating paintbrushes and making different brush strokes

Time
30 min

Resources
Newspaper to cover tables

Per group of 5 or 6 children:
2–3 paint colours (could be any paint except watercolours)
Collection of brushes in different sizes
2 water pots
1 palette

For each child:
3 long-handled paintbrushes: small, medium and large bristle
1 short-handled, medium-fine soft-haired brush
A4 piece of black paper

For teacher:
One of each type of brush to show
A2 piece of paper to demonstrate the brush marks
Something to fix paper to board

National Curriculum
2a, 4a

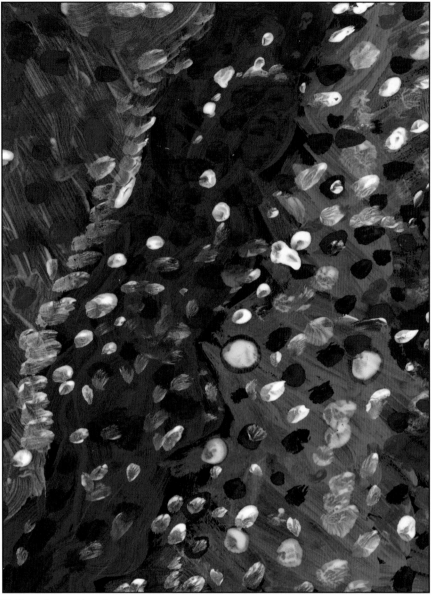

Mathew Jones, Year 2

Introduction
You have tried out making marks with different sizes and kinds of brush, and now you can paint a picture using those brushes. I don't mind what you paint: it could be a person or an animal, a painting of a house and a garden, or a field full of grass and flowers, it does not matter. What does matter is that you try to make as many different brush strokes as you can.

Practical activity
* Ask the children to pick up their long-handled brushes and look for a number on the brush handles which shows the size, and then to notice the different sizes of the bristles.
* Remind the children to hold the brushes as they would hold a pencil. The best place to hold a brush is just above where the metal bit

(the ferrule) meets the handle (see Potential pitfall below).
* Go over the different brush strokes they could make. Demonstrate: tiny dots; long lines; thick lines; thin lines; zigzags; big blobs; and brush strokes of different lengths and thicknesses.
* Encourage them to make as many different types of marks as they can in their paintings.

Potential pitfall
Children often hold the brush handles either very close to the bristles and get paint all over their fingers, which then transfers itself to the painting, or they hold them too far along the handle, which makes it difficult for them to control the brush.

Naming the primary colours

Time
10 min

Resources
A few objects in red, blue and yellow
(with no patterns or other colours on)
Felt tip pens
Paper

National Curriculum
4a

Children's collections of red, yellow and blue items

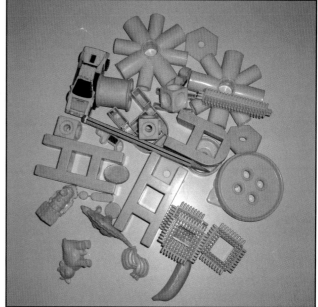

Introduction
We are going to go over the names of three colours today: red (hold up the red object), blue (hold up the blue object) and yellow (hold up the yellow object). I expect you all know the names of these colours already.

Practical activity
* Hold up the objects again in turn and ask the children to call out the colour. Reinforce the name of the colour each time.
* Divide them into three groups and say, 'You're going on a colour hunt.' Send each group off to collect items in one of the colours, eg Lego® bricks, scissors, crayons, counters, containers, plastic shapes, etc.
* Make three piles, one of each colour.
* Children could draw these in felt tips.

* Explain that red, blue and yellow are 'primary colours' and that you can have different reds, different blues and different yellows, but that you cannot make a red unless you have red, you cannot make a blue unless you have blue, and you cannot make a yellow unless you have yellow.
* Tell them that you can make a green or purple or orange by mixing two primary colours together, but that you cannot make a primary colour in this way.
* Children could then investigate the variations in different reds, blues and yellows within the pile.
* The collections of sorted colours could be labelled and left as a display.

33

USING SKILL

Painting in primary colours

Time
45 min

Resources
Newspaper
Water pots
Ready-mixed paint
Yellow, red, blue in palettes or pots
Cartridge paper
Black oil pastels
Medium paintbrushes
Examples of Mondrian's work
Information about Mondrian on page 85

National Curriculum
4a,c, 5a

Holly Ashworth, Year 1 (in the style of a Mondrian painting)

Introduction
The artist Mondrian loved to paint in primary colours. Quite a number of his most famous paintings are painted just in blue, red and yellow. We are going to do some paintings a bit like his.

Practical activity
* Children can put their paper any way round they like.
* Tell them to draw three or four straight lines from one side of the paper to the other in oil pastel. There should be a space between each line.
* They then turn the paper the other way round and draw three or four straight lines going across the other way. They should now have a grid.
* Ask children to paint three shapes in yellow, but not next to each other.
* Tell them to wash their brushes and paint three shapes in red, but not next to any other red shape. Tell them to be careful not to let the wet colours touch each other.
* Lastly paint three in blue. Again, no same colours should be next to each other.

Extension activity
Give children just two primary colours and ask them to make the third, eg give them red and yellow and ask them to make a blue. This is a bit mean, but it does reinforce the fact that you cannot make a primary colour unless you have it already. You can only make different blues if you already have a blue.

KEY SKILL

Powder paint handling

Time
30 min

Resources
Newspaper
Powder paint colours:
• 1 red
• 1 blue
• 1 yellow
Water pots
Palettes
Medium long-handled brushes
Cartridge paper/sketchbooks
Test papers
For teachers: useful information about powder paint on page 28

National Curriculum
2a, 4a

Shona Gregory, Year 1

Introduction

Today you are going to be learning how to handle powder paint. We will be practising how to mix the paint and learning how to use your palettes, when to change your water and how to paint in strong colours.

Practical activity

❋ The lesson could be started by reading to the children the information about powder paint at the start of this chapter (page 28).

❋ Explain that when children are mixing up paint, it is better not to use a delicate brush. They should use a medium long-handled brush.

❋ Remind them to hold the brush just above the ferrule (metal bit).

❋ Demonstrate the following procedure:
1. Dip the brush in the water.
2. Stroke the brush on the top of the water pot to remove surplus water.
3. Dip the brush into powder colour and transfer to the mixing palette.
4. Stir the brush around until the powder and water are blended.
5. Repeat the process until enough paint is mixed for the children's needs.
6. Test the colour on test paper with just a few dabs or lines of paint.

❋ Explain that too much water makes the paint very thin and runny, and that the thickness of the mixture should be like cream rather than milk. If the paint is mixed to a creamy thickness then the colour will be as bright

and strong as it can be – the red will be a deep strong red; the blue will be a deep strong blue, and so on.

❋ Ask the children to experiment with the thickness of the paint and to see how strong they can make a colour.

❋ Tell the children that if they can see the bottom of the palette through the paint then they have not mixed up enough to paint a strong colour, so they should add more powdered colour to it.

❋ Suggest children repeat this process with all of the colours.

❋ Next, mix an orange, a green and a purple. Tell the children to do this by adding powder paint into an existing mixed colour in their palette, rather than by using a new area of the palette. For example, if they want orange, add red to a yellow or yellow to a red. This is good practice for future painting sessions and will reduce the queue at the sink to wash palettes.

❋ Explain that they should wash their brushes between colours, always wiping the brush on the top edge of the water pot afterwards to control the amount of water going into the paint mixture.

❋ Water should be changed when it is dirty. Tell the children that they can test if the water needs changing by putting a cleaned brush in the water and dabbing a few watery marks on their test paper. If the dabs are not coloured, then the water doesn't need changing.

USING SKILL

Painting a picture in powder paint

Time
1 hour

Resources
Newspaper
Full set of powder paint colours (2 reds, 2 blues, 2 yellows – see page 29)
Water pots
Palettes
Medium long-handled brushes
Black permanent pens, medium-tip or black oil pastels
Cartridge paper A3
Test papers
If possible, a copy of Kandinsky's 'Composition VIII' (1925) or his painting 'Yellow, red, blue' (1925) or similar paintings of his
Information about Kandinsky on page 84

National Curriculum
2a, 4a,c, 5a

Sophie Dixon, Year 2

Introduction
You have been learning how to use powder paint and how to paint in strong bright colours, so today you are going to try to use those skills in a painting. We are going to borrow some shapes and colours from some paintings by the Russian artist Kandinsky. He loved bright colours, so he is a good artist for us to look at.

Practical activity
* Show children some of Kandinsky's pictures and point out the bright colours and the shapes of the contrasting black lines.
* Ask the children to describe some of the types of lines, shapes and colours they can see.
* Tell the children to draw the following series of black lines; ask them all to draw at the same time, and wait until they have completed the first set before they all complete the second set and so on:
  * a long wavy black line right across the paper
  * two or three arcs anywhere on the page
  * two or three circles of different sizes
  * a long straight line and shorter straight line at a different angle

* some sets of three straight parallel lines (demonstrate on the board) in different places on the page
* some rectangles, some with a chequer pattern
* some black lines crossing the arcs.
* Take some suggestions and ideas from Kandinsky's paintings.
* Remind children of steps 1–6 from the powder paint handling lesson on the previous page, and demonstrate the process.
* Ask them to mix a bright yellow and paint some of the background.
* Then add a little red to the yellow to make a bright orange and paint some other areas.
* They could then add some more red to the orange and paint in some other areas in a bright strong red.
* Suggest that they carry on with different colours until they have filled in every area of the picture with lovely bright strong colours.
* They could make a little book to record the process.

Naming paint colours

KEY SKILL

Time
30 min

Resources
Newspaper to cover tables

Per pair of children:
6 powder paint or ready-mixed colours:
- 2 reds: vermilion and crimson
- 2 blues: brilliant blue and cyan
- 2 yellows: brilliant and lemon yellow
1 water pot
1 palette

For each child:
1 medium long-handled brush
Cartridge paper/sketchbooks

For the teacher:
A2 piece of paper to demonstrate the colours
Masking tape

National Curriculum
2a, 4a

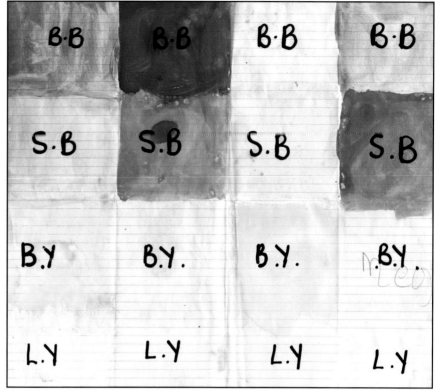

Meg McClavers, Year 1

Introduction
Paint colours have their own special names, so you need to learn these names and get used to using them. There are lots of different shades of reds, blues and yellows, and grown-up artists have names for them all. If they go into an art shop to buy a colour, they will say exactly which red or blue they want. For now, though, we only have to learn the names of two blues, two reds and two yellows.

Practical activity
- Put out one set of the two yellows in front of each pair of children and ask them to look at the two yellows and notice the difference.
- Ask them how they would describe the yellows and in what ways they are different.
- Tell them the darker yellow is called Brilliant Yellow and that it is a bit like the colour of an egg yolk.
- Emphasize this by painting a patch of brilliant yellow paint on the large piece of paper and writing 'Brilliant Yellow' on it in brilliant yellow paint. Tape the paper to the board with masking tape.
- Ask the children to paint a patch of brilliant

yellow. Younger children could paint a big 'BY' next to it, while older children could label the colour 'Brilliant Yellow'.
- Explain that the other lighter yellow is called 'Lemon Yellow'.
- Emphasize this in the same way as before.
- Repeat this process with the two reds, explaining that the deeper red is called 'Crimson' and the lighter, more orangey red is called 'Vermilion', each time asking children to notice the difference between the two colours.
- Next introduce the two blues.
- Explain that the darker blue is called 'Brilliant Blue' and the lighter blue is called 'Cyan' (you might prefer to give it a different name such as sky blue).
- Emphasize as before.
- Run over the names of the colours at the end of the session. Children will need reminding of these colour names almost every time they paint. It may seem to take a long time to sink in, perhaps because they do not use these names in any other context.

Getting to know the colours and comparing blues (or reds or yellows)

USING SKILL

Time
30 min

Resources
Newspaper to cover tables

Per pair of children:
Powder paint or ready-mixed colours:
- 2 reds: vermilion and crimson
- 2 blues: brilliant blue and cyan
- 2 yellows: brilliant and lemon yellow
1 water pot
1 palette

For each child:
1 medium long-handled brush
A2 cartridge paper
Test papers
Permanent ink pen

For the teacher:
A piece of paper to demonstrate the colours
Masking tape

National Curriculum
2a, 4a

Ellie Budden, Year 1

Introduction
Today we are going to look at and paint in these two different blues and you are going to mix some new blues.

Practical activity
* Put the two different blues in front of the children and discuss how they are different.
* Remind children of the names of the two blues.
* Revise how to dip the brush in the water and stroke it on the side of the pot to remove excess water.
* Demonstrate painting a patch of one of the blues on the A2 paper and write the name of the blue next to it. Tape this to the board.
* Ask children to paint a little dab of this blue on their test papers.
* Repeat this with the other blue.
* Next, demonstrate transferring a little of one blue into the palette and adding a little of the second blue to it, then mixing the two blues

together. Paint a patch of this on the A2 paper for the children to see.
* Tell the children to do the same thing and paint a dab on top of their test papers.
* They could make up a name for the new blue.
* Now give each child a piece of cartridge paper and ask them to cover it with squares and rectangles of as many different blues as they can mix.
* Remind them to try out the colours on their test papers first.
* When the paintings are dry, children could write or draw patterns over them in permanent pen.
* This whole activity can be repeated with the two reds and the two yellows. When placed on the wall together, they make an attractive display and the labelling can reinforce the names of the colours.

Making a colour lighter without using white (changing tone in colour)

Time
30 min

Resources
Newspaper to cover tables

Per pair of children:
Powder paint or ready-mixed colours
(any strong colour)
1 water pot
1 palette

For each child:
1 long-handled brush
A5 cartridge paper or sketchbooks
Test paper

For teacher:
An A2 piece of paper to demonstrate
the colours
Masking tape to fix it to the board

National Curriculum
2a, 4a

Colin Adams, Year 2

Introduction
Today you are going to learn how to make colours lighter. One way is to add white paint, but we are going to do it a different way: we are going to make colours lighter by using less paint and a bit more water.

Practical activity
※ If children are using powder paint, then tell them to mix up whichever colour has been chosen for this exercise; otherwise, start with some of the chosen colour in a palette. For the purposes of this lesson, we will assume you are using brilliant blue, but cyan (sky blue), crimson or vermilion would also be good choices.
※ If children are using powder paint, remind them that the paint needs to be at least the consistency of cream if it is to give its full value. If necessary, run over the mixing and use of powder paint (page 35).
※ Next, children should make a dab of paint on the test paper to check that the colour is as strong and deep as it can be. This demonstrates just how strong the colour can be.
※ Now tell them to paint a short broad line in the strongest, deepest tone of blue at the top of the page.
※ Next, ask the children to wash their brushes

and then dab their wet brushes in the paint mixture and try out a dab on their test papers to see what happens when they use a little less paint and a little more water. The colour should come out a slightly lighter tone. Demonstrate this.
※ Explain that they will need to control the amount of water so that the paint is a light tone but not too runny. This might require some practice.
※ Encourage them to experiment in making different tones of blue and trying them out on their test papers.
※ Now ask the children to paint a line of slightly lighter blue just beneath the first and darkest line.
※ Next, they should paint a slightly lighter blue line below that, and so on down the page. Older or more able children could be challenged to make four or more tones of blue, while less able or younger children might aim for three.
※ This technique could then be practised with another colour, and later the paintings could be used to make a collage (see page 41) or as a background (see next lesson).

USING SKILL

Making a colour lighter without using white (changing tone in colour)

Time
30 min

Resources
Newspaper to cover tables

Per pair of children:
Powder paint or ready-mixed colours:
- 2 reds: vermilion and crimson
- 2 blues: brilliant blue and cyan
- 2 yellows: brilliant and lemon yellow
1 water pot
1 palette

For each child:
1 long-handled brush
A4 cartridge paper or sketchbooks
Test paper

For teacher:
Flowers or pictures of flowers

National Curriculum
2a, 4a, 5a

Colin Adams, Year 2

Note
The flower painted in this lesson was cut out when it was dry, and stuck on the work from the lesson on page 39

Introduction
You have been practising making colours lighter or darker by using different amounts of water and paint. Now you are going to do this in a painting. Try to use as many tones of the same colour as you can. You might wonder what I mean by tone in colour. If you look at a black and white photocopy of a coloured picture, you will see that it is made up of different shades of grey and black. These show the different tones (lightness and darkness) that the colours had.

Practical activity
※ Ask the children to mix up whichever colour has been chosen for this exercise.
※ Ask the children to think of a subject to paint. A flower has been painted here as the class were looking at plants in science.
※ Next, the children should use their fine brushes dipped in a pale mixture of their colour to sketch out their picture in a very, very pale tone.
※ Encourage them to test their colour on their test paper before they paint their subject.
※ In this lesson it was suggested to the children

to make the tips of the petals the darkest part of the flower and to make the colour paler as they got nearer the stalk.
※ The children then painted the area nearest the stalk first in a pale crimson, again testing their colour out before they used it.
※ Next, they painted the tips of the petals in deep crimson and blended the two tones together with clean wet bushes, making sure their brush strokes went along the petals towards the centre.
※ If children are using powder paint, remind them that the paint needs to be at least the consistency of cream if it is to give its full value, and always to test out their colour on their test papers before using it.
※ Lastly, they could add a little purple or orange to add interest to the petals, and mix a green to paint the stalk or leaves. They could look at real flowers or pictures of flowers with dramatic markings, such as orchids or lilies with markings in a contrasting colour.

Troubleshooting
If any child has painted a deep colour where they wanted a pale one, then some of the colour can be removed if the painting is quickly blotted with a tissue.

Making a collage using work from a previous lesson (page 39)

USING SKILL

Time
45 min

Resources
Newspaper to cover tables
Glue sticks
Scissors

For every child:
Poly envelope
A3 paper for background.
Pencil
Their dry artwork from the lesson on page 39
Broad-pointed permanent pen

For the teacher:
A2 paper to demonstrate
Blu-Tack®
Access to the work of the Swiss artist Paul Klee, such as 'Legend of the Nile', where he makes black drawings over colour in one range

National Curriculum
2a, 4a, 5c

Year 2 pupil

This pupil has used two different blues and painted in thick lines in different tones of those blues. When the painting was dry it was cut into strips crossways across the painted lines. The strips of colour were then glued down to make a background for a drawing.

Introduction
We are going to use most of the coloured stripes you painted yesterday/last week to make collages, and it will help you to see the difference between the different tones of each colour.

Practical activity
❋ Show the children the collage illustrated here and discuss how the different tones (you could say 'lights' and 'darks' for younger children) of colours really show up when they are cut up and broken down into little squares.
❋ Explain that they are going to make something similar.
❋ Ask the children to fold their painted striped papers so that the folds run across the stripes of colour. Younger children may need help with this. Demonstrate if necessary.
❋ Check that the children have folded them in the right direction. Someone will almost certainly have folded them the wrong way!
❋ Now tell the children to cut along the folds to make four strips.

❋ Ask them to write their names immediately on the back of each strip and to put the strips in their envelope as they do so. If this is not done, it will very quickly become impossible for children to tell whose strips of colours are whose.
❋ Repeat this with any other painted stripes if they have them.
❋ They should now have at least four strips of paper with short colour-change stripes going across each (or eight if they have painted two colours).
❋ Tell the children to take out all the strips and arrange them on the background paper, top to tail (darkest to lightest alternately), side by side. Different colours could be alternated.
❋ Demonstrate this by using Blu-Tack® to fix a set on the board for the class to see.
❋ The children can then glue their arrangements down.
❋ Now show the children some Paul Klee pictures, if you can access them, or show the collage illustrated with this lesson.

Lesson continued on next page.

❋ Ask them to think of something that would look good over the coloured background. In the example on page 41 a boat was drawn, as it fitted with a water topic.

The more colours that have been tried out in the previous lesson, the more colourful the collage will be and the more different ideas the children might have for the over-drawings.

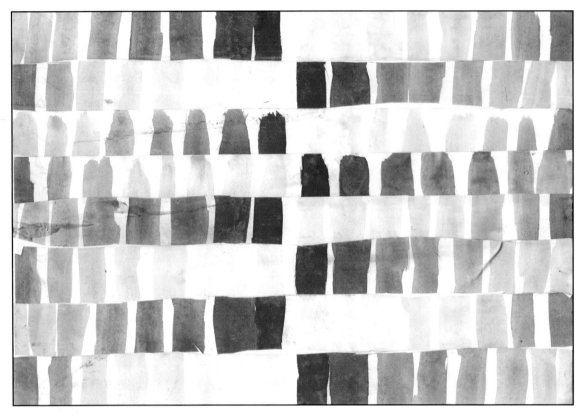

Robert Peacock, Year 1

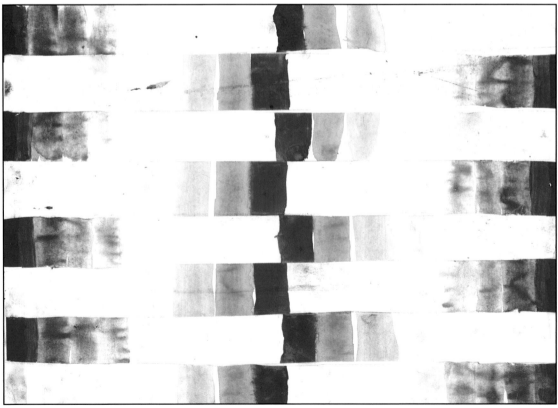

Tiff Choo, Year 2 (painting from the lesson on page 39 cut and glued down, ready for over-drawing)

Colour mixing

Year 2 pupil

Background information

Even in the early years, children need to be introduced to mixing and making their own colours.

Paint provides the best and most flexible medium for exploring colour. For general painting, powder paints give children the best opportunity to do this effectively – but ultimately this is a matter of personal choice by the teacher, and the principles of colour mixing will hold good for all types of paint.

Ready-mixed liquid paints are the best paints for colour mixing for foundation and younger Year 1 children, as younger children will find powder paint more of a struggle to manipulate. The introduction to powder paint handling is covered separately on page 35.

When using ready-mixed colours, it is still important to encourage colour mixing. To provide a brush in each pot of ready-mixed colour is to deny pupils a learning opportunity.

Myriads of colours can be mixed from the three primaries: red, blue and yellow. Children are often amazed at the seemingly endless possibilities.

It is recommended in the early stages of painting that only primary colours are available, along with white so that children can discover for themselves the effect of combining pigments. Black should be withheld in these early stages of mixing; it is difficult to control, and adding too much can destroy other colours and may dishearten children who are learning to mix.

Year 2 pupil

Colours can be mixed in different ways. There is the usual mode of mixing paint in a palette of some kind, but younger children will enjoy rubbing two colours between their palms and creating mixed-colour handprints, or dipping their brush in more than one colour and stroking the brush across the paper to create a multi-coloured semi-mixed mark.

Subject matter

Often, when we think of making a painting, we ask the children to make paintings of things or situations, such as 'a boat on the sea' or 'me and my mum'. In these early experiments with colour, 'content free' ideas are the best. Simply introduce the paints to the children as a means of finding out about the colours. They can paint lines, circles, squares or patches of colours without worrying about the subject matter. This leaves them free to enjoy colour for its own sake.

Crucial to the teaching of painting is recognition that the careful matching, mixing and application of colour requires time.

Mixing and using paint also needs much time for the preparation and for introductory activities – so much so that at the end of the allotted time there may be little to show other than a mass of apparently meaningless splodges of colour and marks. However, time spent on such activities is never wasted. It provides children with invaluable information to store in their visual memory, so that when they are engaged in a painting activity they have some reference on which to draw.

Colour mixing is one of the most significant aspects in learning how to use paint, and it invites children to discriminate between many qualities of shade and tint. Suddenly their paintings will come alive as this full range of colours is at their disposal.

The skill of mixing paint will require development over a number of years. There is a great deal to learn, and each stage needs to be carefully developed and built on in the future.

Children's descriptive language of colour can be developed side by side with the skills of colour mixing, and they should be encouraged to have a personal response to colour and start to be able to relate it to mood and atmosphere.

Colour mixing tips

Mixing their own colours will help children to develop an awareness and appreciation of colour, and that is a life-enhancing ability which should not be undervalued.

Colour mixing tips
* Crimson is the best red for mixing purples.
* Vermilion is the best red for mixing oranges.
* Cyan and lemon yellow make vivid greens.
* Brilliant blue (ultramarine) and brilliant yellow make natural greens.
* Black and yellow make olive greens.

Black
* Brilliant blue, crimson, vermilion and brilliant yellow make a near black.
* A pure black cannot be mixed.
* Black added to colours darkens colours but also dulls them.

White
* White lightens colours but can also dull them.

* Touches of other colours added to white will make different types of white.

Brown
* Different combinations of the three primaries make different browns.
* Green and red make brown.
* Vermilion and blue make a kind of brown.
* Yellow and purple make a grey/brown.

Skin tones (all need slight adjustments to match)
* A little of crimson or vermilion with a lot of white and a touch of yellow and the teeniest touch of blue will make a pale skin tone.
* Warm brown and some white make a darker skin tone. Small touches of other colours will vary the shade.
* Cream can be made with white and brilliant yellow and a touch of red.
* Crimson and white make good pinks but not good skin tones.

Year 2 pupil

Mixing secondary colours: purples (or greens or oranges)

KEY SKILL

Time
45 min

Resources
Newspaper to cover tables

Per pair of children:
Powder paint or ready-mixed colours:
- crimson + brilliant blue (for the best purples)
- cyan + lemon yellow (for the brightest greens)
- brilliant yellows + vermilion (for the most vivid oranges)
1 water pot
1 palette

For each child:
1 medium long-handled brush
A3 cartridge paper
Test paper
Permanent pen

For the teacher:
A3 piece of paper to demonstrate the colours
Masking tape
Access to Paul Klee's 'Signs in Yellow' (1937) or similar Klee work

National Curriculum
2a, 4a

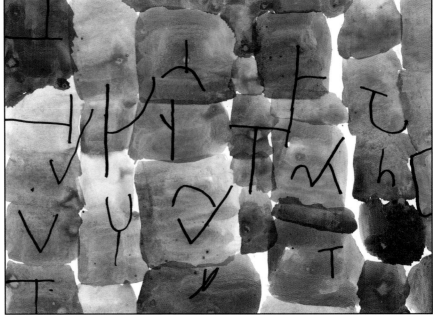
Joe Blackford, Year 1

Introduction
Today we are going to mix purple (or orange or green) for ourselves. We are not going to use purple that has been made up for us already, we are going to make our own purples. Purple is a secondary colour and it is made by mixing two primary colours together.

Practical activity
※ Ask the children if they know which two primary colours are mixed together to make purple.
※ Explain that any red and blue will make a purple, but some reds and blues make better purples than other reds and blues.
※ Tell them that crimson and brilliant blue make lovely purples, but vermilion and cyan (sky blue) make a rather browny-purple.
※ Remind children how to dip their brush in the water and stroke the brush on the side of the pot to remove excess water.

※ Ask them to experiment with mixing up different purples and to paint little dabs of purple on their test papers.
※ Write on the board for them to copy onto their test papers, 'Red and blue make purple.' The test papers can be stuck in their sketchbooks for them to refer back to.
※ Next, demonstrate how they can make different purples by using different proportions of red and blue. Show them how to make a violet-purple by using more blue than red and how to make a mauve-purple by using more red than blue. Paint patches of different purples on A3 paper and tape the paper to the board so they can see.
※ Now they can cover their cartridge paper with patches of different purples so that they can compare the different shades.
※ When the paintings are dry, they could look at Paul Klee's pictures and draw over their pictures in a similar style with permanent ink pens.
※ This lesson can be repeated for oranges and greens. The completed work will make a lovely display.

USING SKILL

Mixing and using secondary colours: green (lesson can be adapted for orange or purple)

Time
1 hour

Resources
Newspaper to cover tables
Flowers of different colours (or pictures of them)

Per pair of children:
Powder paint or ready-mixed colours:
- cyan + brilliant blue
- lemon + brilliant yellow
- crimson + vermilion red
1 water pot
1 palette

For each child:
1 medium long-handled brush
Cartridge paper
Test paper

For the teacher:
A3 piece of paper to demonstrate the colours
Masking tape

National Curriculum
2a, 4a

Daniel Huxtable, Year 2

Introduction
We are going to mix lots of different greens today and make a lovely background for our paintings of flowers.

Practical activity
* First, working on their cartridge paper, the children can paint a series of flowers dotted about the page in bright colours. These could be in orange or purple if they know how to mix these secondary colours, or in any bright colours they like.
* While the paintings are drying, talk to them about green and ask them to point out green objects in the room. They could think of other things that are green. If the school has a garden or grassed area, they could go out and look at all the different greens on the trees and in the hedges and grass.
* Ask the children which two primary colours they think make green.
* Explain that cyan (sky blue) and lemon yellow make the brightest greens, and brilliant blue

and either of the yellows make the more natural-looking greens.
* Ask them to experiment mixing up different greens and to paint little dabs of these colours on their test papers. These can be stuck into their sketch books as a colour mixing reference and they could annotate them, 'yellow and blue makes green.'
* Remind children how to dip their brush in the water and stroke the brush on the side of the pot to remove excess water.
* Demonstrate how they can make different greens, not just by using different blues and yellows but also by using different proportions of yellow and blue. Show them how to make a light green by using more yellow than blue, and a darker green by using more blue than yellow. Paint patches of different greens on A3 paper and tape the paper to the board so they can see.
* Now they can fill in the background of their flower paintings with lots of different greens, they could make brush strokes that look like grass or patches of green that look like light and shade.

SKILL Changing the colours by adding a little paint at a time

Year 1 pupils

Time
Roughly 1 hour

Resources
Newspaper to cover tables

Per pair of children:
Powder paint or ready-mixed colours:
- cyan + brilliant blue
- lemon + brilliant yellow
- crimson + vermilion red
1 water pot
1 palette

For each child:
1 medium long-handled brush
A3 cartridge paper or resource sheet 1
on page 118
Test papers

For teacher:
A2 paper to demonstrate and tape to
fix to the board

National Curriculum
2a, 4a,b

Introduction

*Today you are going to learn a very useful painting skill, one
that most painters have to master. It is the skill of changing
one colour slowly into another colour. It is quite good fun
to make a yellow turn gradually into a red or a blue turn
gradually into a red. We are going to paint some brightly
coloured scarves.*

Practical activity

❋ Tell the children to mix up some vermilion
and paint a short stripe of vermilion, leaving
a space at the top of the page for the tassels
of the scarf. Show the children the illustration
above so they can get the idea of how to
set it out on the page – or you could use
resource sheet 1 on page 118.

❋ Demonstrate painting the stripes.

❋ Next, tell them to add a little amount of
brilliant yellow to the vermilion, transferring
the paint onto the tip of the brush.

❋ Test the new colour out on the test paper to
make sure it is a slightly different colour. If
the colour hasn't changed, tell them to add
a tiny bit more brilliant yellow and test it out
again. Tell the children that they should test
the colour on their test papers before they
use it, to make sure it is the colour they want.

If the colour has changed too much, they
need to add a bit more vermilion back into
the mixture.

❋ Now they should paint a stripe of the new
colour, just below the vermilion stripe.

❋ You may need to demonstrate each step.

❋ Next, children should add a little more
brilliant yellow to the same mixture. They
need to test the new colour first on the test
paper and, if it is a bit more orange than the
last colour made, paint the new colour next
to the previous stripe.

❋ They should continue down the paper, aiming
not to get to pure brilliant yellow before the
end of the scarf. Year 2 should manage at
least five or six colour changes between one
primary and the other, while younger children
may only achieve three or four.

❋ Now repeat the activity with cyan (sky blue)
and lemon yellow and make another stripy
scarf.

❋ Children could also do a brilliant blue to
crimson scarf if there is enough time.

❋ Older children could go on to experiment with
other combinations of primaries: crimson
and lemon yellow, cyan and brilliant yellow,
vermilion and lemon yellow and so on.

❋ When they have finished, ask the children
to paint some multi-coloured tassels on the
ends of the scarf, or they could draw them on
with felt tips or pencils.

SKILL

Recording colour mixing

Time
45 min

Resources
Newspaper to cover tables

Per pair of children:
Powder paint or ready-mixed colours:
- cyan + brilliant blue
- lemon + brilliant yellow
- crimson + vermilion red
1 water pot
1 palette

For each child:
1 medium long-handled brush
Copy of resource sheet 2 on page 119
Pencil
Test paper

For the teacher:
A3 piece of paper to demonstrate
the process, and tape to stick it up
A3 paper with a painted patch of
each colour being used and its name

National Curriculum
2a, 4a

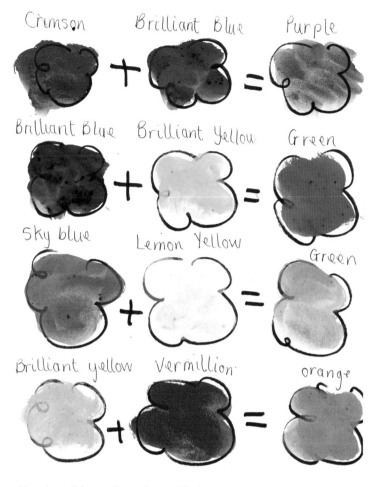

Year 1 pupil (recording colour mixing)

Note
Resource sheet 2 (page 119) can be used in different ways. Younger children could write, or the teacher could write, before the sheets are photocopied: 'red' over one cloud, 'blue' over the next and 'purple' over the last, so the colour sum reads red + blue = purple, or whatever colour mix is required.

Alternatively, the specific colour could be written in: ie lemon yellow + sky blue = green. Another way for older children is to have one page just for one colour, for example a crimson page. All five of the first clouds would be crimson and then the second cloud could be a different colour in each case:

crimson + brilliant blue = purple
crimson + sky blue = purple
crimson + lemon yellow = orange
crimson + vermilion = bright red
crimson + bright yellow = orange

Introduction
Today you are going to mix your own colours to do some colour sums. It will help you remember how to mix colours so that you can make them again. Sometimes it is hard to remember how you made a particular colour.

Practical activity
✳ If powder paint is being used, then revise its mixing and use (page 35).
✳ Ask children to mix up and paint their first colour in the first cloud.
✳ Next, tell them to mix up a little of the second colour and paint in the second cloud. Demonstrate this.
✳ Now tell the children to mix the two colours together, test the colour on their test papers and then paint in the third cloud. Demonstrate.
✳ Those who are writing in the colours should write them in as they go along, or they will be likely to forget.
✳ The work should be stuck in their sketchbooks for future reference.
✳ This activity can be repeated for mixing browns using different reds and greens.

SKILL

Earth colours and making browns

Time
30 min

Resources
Newspaper to cover tables

Per pair of children:
Powder paint or ready-mixed colours:
- cyan + brilliant blue
- lemon + brilliant yellow
- crimson + vermilion red
1 water pot
1 palette

For each child:
1 medium long-handled brush
Cartridge paper/sketchbooks
Test paper

For the teacher:
A3 paper to demonstrate and tape to fix it up

National Curriculum
2a,c, 4a, 5a

Jonathan Hussain, Year 2

Note
Earth colours include all browns, brown-greens, copper, black, rust, oranges, cream, stone.

Introduction
Today you are going to mix some colours that are called 'earth colours'. I expect you can work out what one of them will be! Earth can be different kinds of brown though. In some parts of the country the earth is a reddy-brown, and in others it is a very dark brown, almost black. It can even be a yellowy-brown, especially where there is a lot of clay in it, such as in London.

Earth colours are natural colours – colours that you might find in the woods in the autumn. All kinds of brown and browny-greens, the colours of leaves and the colours of stones are earth colours. You are going to have a go at mixing up your own browns. It isn't difficult. Can anyone guess which colours you mix together to make brown?

Practical activity
* Discuss with the children their different ideas about how they could make brown.
* Explain that there are two ways, but both ways are really the same thing.
* One way is to mix red and green. The other

way is to mix all three primaries – red, yellow and blue. Demonstrate by first making a green and then add vermilion.
* It could be pointed out to older children that mixing red and green is the same thing as mixing all three primaries, since you make green by mixing blue and yellow.
* Explain that you can make different kinds of brown by adding a bit more of one of the primaries, or a bit less.
* Give them time to experiment in mixing all the primaries and paint dabs of their various colours.
* Younger children could start by mixing green and then adding red, while older ones should try out the different colours and try to make a collection of different browns: some that are nearly orange and some that are nearly green.
* They could then see if they can make a very, very dark brown – almost black. This can be done by mixing varying amounts of vermilion, brilliant blue and a little yellow. Children generally really enjoy trying to mix black; it is impossible to mix a pure black, but a near black can be managed with experimentation.

USING SKILL

Painting in browns (and other earth colours)

Time
1 hour

Links
Science
Seasons

Resources
Newspaper to cover tables

Per pair of children:
Powder paint or ready-mixed colours:
- cyan + brilliant blue
- lemon + brilliant yellow
- crimson + vermilion red
1 water pot
1 palette

For each child:
1 medium long-handled brush
Cartridge paper
Test paper
A pencil
A black permanent pen

For the teacher:
A few autumn leaves or pictures of autumn leaves

Possible extras:
Some gold and green metallic pens
Gold, copper or bronze ready-mixed paint

National Curriculum
2a, 4a, 5a

Bianca Roberts, Year 2

Note

This lesson can be done in the same session as the one on the previous page. Earth colours include all browns, brown-greens, copper, black, rust, oranges, cream, stone.

Introduction

You have mixed earth colours already, and now you are going to paint a picture of autumn leaves using those colours.

Practical activity

❋ If necessary, go over which colours are earth colours and revise mixing browns.

❋ Children should examine the leaves and discuss the patterns on them.

❋ Ask them to draw some leaf outlines scattered across the page. Children will need to be told not to make the leaves too small as they are going to be painting them.

❋ Next, they should mix up some oranges and paint a few leaves.

❋ Then they need to add blue to these oranges to make some browns and paint a few more leaves in different browns – or they could make a new brown from scratch.

❋ Next ask them to experiment and try to mix a few other earth colours: greens, greeny-browns, rusty colours (pale brown makes a good stone colour, and with a touch of yellow makes a cream).

❋ Remind children how they tried to mix black and ask them to mix up the darkest colour they can and then paint the background with it.

❋ When the paint is dry, the children should draw around the outline of the leaves and draw in the vein patterns.

❋ For further decoration, they could add dabs of metallic paint to the leaves.

❋ Lastly, draw some leaves on the dark background with metallic pens.

Painting in secondary colours and browns (and using different tones of colours)

USING SKILL

Time
2 hours

Resources
Newspaper to cover tables

Per pair of children:
Powder paint or ready-mixed colours:
- cyan + brilliant blue
- lemon + brilliant yellow
- crimson + vermilion red
1 water pot
1 palette

For each child:
1 medium long-handled brush
1 fine long-handled brush
A3 cartridge paper
Colour mixing work from earlier lesson
Test paper

For the teacher:
A3 piece of paper to demonstrate the colours
Masking tape
Access to Paul Klee's 'Red and White Domes' or one of his Tunisian works

National Curriculum
2a, 4a, 5a,d

Lorna Lewis, Year 2

Introduction
You have learned how to mix oranges and purples and you have also learned how to make a colour lighter without using white. Today you are going to do a painting in which you will do all of those things, and you are going to make your own browns.

Practical activity
* Revise the three primary colours and how to mix orange and purple.
* Suggest that the children look back at previous colour mixing work.
* Remind children how to dip their brush in the water and stroke the brush on the side of the pot to remove excess water.
* Children could mix a few oranges and purples and test them on their test papers.
* Remind the children how to make brown by mixing all three primaries together. They should try this out and record their mixing.
* Suggest that today they could make a good brown that will go well with the other colours by mixing purple and yellow. Give them time to try this out.

* Revise the technique of painting in different tones (page 39).
* Show the children the painting by Paul Klee if you have it. You could tell them that it was when Paul Klee saw the wonderful colours of Tunisia that he decided to be an artist. If not, say that they are making a painting of a village a bit like Bethlehem, with square houses and domed roofs. You could fold the paper into squares to make the sizing easier for them.
* Tell them to paint lots of squares in different oranges, purples and browns, but not right to the top of the paper. These are the houses.
* Ask the children to try to paint a light, dark and medium house of each colour and to try mixing some purples and oranges together to make new subtle colours.
* While the houses are drying, they should paint some semicircles on top of the highest houses with a fine brush in a dark tone and fill the dome in with a lighter tone of any colour except purple.
* Next they should mix a soft, misty purple and paint in the night sky.
* Lastly, the children could mix a dark brown and paint some small rectangles for doorways and windows.

USING SKILL

Using a range of colours in a painting

Time
2 hours

Resources
Newspaper to cover tables

Per pair of children:
Powder paint or ready-mixed colours:
- cyan + brilliant blue
- lemon + brilliant yellow
- crimson + vermilion red
1 water pot
1 palette

For each child:
1 medium long-handled brush
1 fine long-handled brush, for figures
Cartridge paper (with circles or squares ready drawn if necessary)
Test paper

For the teacher:
Access to Wassily Kandinsky's 'Colour Studies' or Robert Delaunay's 'Circular Forms'

National Curriculum
2a, 4a, 5a,d

Joe Blackford, Year 2

Introduction
You have learned how to mix lots of different colours, and today you are going to use as many of those wonderful colours as you can all in one painting.

Practical activity
* Children could either have one big circle, quartered, with a series of concentric circles inside it, as in this illustration, or concentric squares as in the Kandinsky painting.
* Revise mixing secondary colours if necessary.
* Remind children to test colours on their test papers before they use a colour, in case it isn't the colour they want.
* Children then mix their own colour and paint one section of the picture, then mix another and paint with that, and so on. Discourage using unmixed colours.
* Tell them to think about whatever colour they use and where they are going to put it in the painting.

* They could paint wet colour against wet colour and let the colours merge at the edges, as in the Kandinsky painting, or keep the colours separate.
* Suggest they just really enjoy using as many wonderful colours as they can. In this context, they do not have to think about the composition, just the colours.
* Tell them to mix up and paint one or two browns as well if they want to, and suggest they try making some pastel colours by adding white.
* Emphasize how gorgeous colours can be by using phrases like 'sizzling scarlet' and 'juicy purple', 'glowing orange' and 'sunshine yellow'. They might like to suggest some names of their own.
* In this example, children added some small colourful paintings of themselves and their best friends on separate pieces of paper and stuck them on later.

SKILL Creating skin tones

Time
30 min

Resources
Newspaper to cover tables

Per pair of children:
Powder paint or ready-mixed colours:
- cyan + brilliant blue
- lemon + brilliant yellow
- crimson + vermilion red
- white
1 water pot
1 palette

For each child:
1 medium long-handled brush
A4 cartridge paper or sketchbook
Test paper

For the teacher:
A3 piece of paper to demonstrate the process, and tape to stick it up

National Curriculum
2a, 4a, 5a

Year 2 pupil

Note
This activity is more appropriate when the children have covered most of the colour mixing lessons, as it will require all their colour mixing skills. Also, some forethought needs to be given in consideration of the vocabulary that will be used to describe different skin colours. The lesson may also work better if it is done with a small group at a time, as the children will need support with recording what colours they used.

Introduction
Today you are going to try to mix up a skin colour; you will try to mix your own skin colour, but if there is time you might mix up other people's skin colours too. This will be very useful when you paint portraits. A portrait is usually a picture of a person, although you can have animal portraits, too.

Practical activity
* Tell the children that they might need to mix quite a few colours together to make a skin colour. Go over these pointers in mixing skin tones and explain that they all need slight adjustments to match:
  - A little of crimson or vermilion with a lot of white and a touch of yellow and the teeniest touch of blue will make a pale skin tone

- Warm brown and some white make a darker skin tone; small touches of other colours will vary the shade
- Cream can be made with white and brilliant yellow and a touch of red
- Crimson and white make good pinks but not good skin tones
- Mouths are not usually bright red unless the person is wearing lipstick

* Demonstrate how to mix at least one of the skin tones and show how the children can adjust the colour by adding more of one colour or another. Also remind them how to make a colour lighter without using white (page 39).
* Ask the children to look at their hands and try to mix their own skin tone.
* They should paint dabs of the different skin tones they have mixed on their paper.
* Help them to record what colours they have used.
* At the end of the session, children could put a tick or a smiley face next to the colours they think are the best match for their own skin tones.
* If there is time, they could try to mix other skin tones or try to mix hair and eye colours.

Painting a self-portrait using skin tones

USING SKILL

Time
Roughly 1 hour

Resources
Newspaper to cover tables

Per pair of children:
Powder paint or ready-mixed colours:
• cyan + brilliant blue
• lemon + brilliant yellow
• crimson + vermilion red
• white
1 water pot
1 palette

For each child:
A choice of brush sizes
A mirror
A4 cartridge paper or sketchbook
Skin tone mixing recordings from
previous session
HB pencil
Test paper

For the teacher:
A3 piece of paper to demonstrate the
process, and tape to stick it up

National Curriculum
2a, 4a, 5a

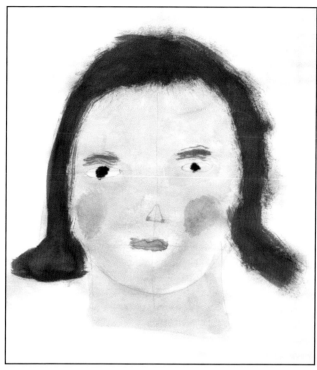

Millie Becklake, Year 2

Note
I usually allow a set time for children to be silly with mirrors – say 5 minutes – to get it out of their system.

Introduction
Today you are going to use your skills in mixing and matching skin tones to paint a self-portrait. You will be using the skills of mixing skin tones that you have already practised, so you will need to look back at the recording you did when you mixed those colours.

Practical activity
※ Children should have a good, long look at their faces in their mirrors.
※ They should note face shape, hairline and expression.
※ Next they should lightly mark out the overall shape of their head and neck, filling the paper. Then lightly draw in eyes, nose, mouth and mark where the hair will be. Younger children will need help with this.

※ Explain that the focus is painting the skin tones; it doesn't really matter if their drawings don't look much like themselves. Detail can be put in later with a fine brush if there is time.
※ Tell the children to look at their colour mix recordings from the last session.
※ Ask them to re-mix their skin tone and to paint a light version (less paint, more water) of this colour right across the face and neck of their drawing, just leaving the eyes and hair unpainted.
※ Next they should add a little more crimson to the mixture and paint the ears, neck and the cheeks a slightly deeper colour.
※ Encourage the children to try to mix a natural mouth colour, using maybe a blend of the two reds and a touch of brilliant yellow; they could try out a little brilliant blue as well. Try some dabs of colour to see which looks most natural, then paint the mouth in a watered-down version of this colour, varying the tone to create highlights. No bright red mouths!
※ Hair and eyes can be painted next, leaving the white paper for the whites of the eyes, and then the background.
※ Detail, texture and pattern can be added last with a fine brush.

55

Colour matching

KEY SKILL

Time
Roughly 1 hour

Resources
Newspaper to cover tables

Per pair of children:
Powder paint or ready-mixed colours:
- cyan + brilliant blue
- lemon + brilliant yellow
- crimson + vermilion red
1 water pot and 1 palette

For each child:
1 medium long-handled brush
1 finer brush for painting the fairy
A3 cartridge paper
A smaller piece of paper for the fairy
Test papers

For the teacher:
A few flowers, or pictures of flowers
Access to some of Cicely Mary
Barker's 'Flower Fairy' pictures

National Curriculum
2a, 4a,b,c, 5a

Year 2 pupil (a flower fairy hiding in a flower)

Introduction

Today you are going to practise something that might be very useful to you in life, whether you become a grown-up artist or not. It is the skill of colour matching. What we mean by colour matching is finding or making a colour that is as similar as possible to another one. This is easy, of course, when the colour comes straight from the pot, but it is not so easy when you have mixed your own colour up and have to make it again exactly the same. Nor is it easy to match a colour that is as near as possible to one that someone else has mixed up. This can be a bit tricky, but the best way to do it is to look at the colour very carefully and try to work out what kind of colour it is that you are trying to match. If it is an orange, for example, you could ask yourself questions like: 'Is it a dark orange or a light orange?' 'Is it a yellowy orange or an orange that is nearly red?' Just use your eyes to help you judge the colour.

Practical activity

* Show the children the flower fairy pictures and point out how the artist has matched the colours of the fairies/elves very closely to the colours of the flower they live in.
* Tell them that they are going to paint some flowers and then some fairies/elves to live in them.
* Children should now choose a colour for their flower. Older children could make their own colour, while younger ones could use an existing colour from the pot. However, both age groups could paint in lighter and darker tones of their chosen colour (see the lesson on making a colour lighter without using white on page 39).
* Discuss flower and petal shapes, showing children the flowers or pictures of flowers.
* Having chosen and mixed their colours, the children should paint a large simple flower shape filling up most of the page.
* Next, children should paint in the petals and the centre of the flower.
* They could also paint some leaves and the background.
* Now ask them to paint a tiny fairy/elf using their fine brushes on the small piece of paper.
* Tell them that the colour of the fairy/elf should be the same colour as the fairy's flower so that he/she cannot be seen. Say it is their job to make sure the fairy/elf is nearly invisible to keep him/her safe.
* If the children have their colour still mixed up in their palettes, this will be easy, but remind them to think about whether the tone of the fairy/elf is much lighter or darker than the flower itself. If the fairy/elf is too dark or too light, he/she will still show up and be in danger of being seen. This will encourage them to notice tone as well as colour when matching.
* When the pictures are dry, the fairy/elf should be cut out and glued onto the flower so that it is hard to spot.

Colour theory

Damien Hopkins, Year 2

Background information

Without light there is no colour. Our main natural source of light is the sun.

The rainbow

If we take white light and pass it through a prism, we get a band of colours; you call it a rainbow, but scientists call it a spectrum. If it rains when the sun is out, the light of the sun shines through the rain. Each drop of rain acts like a little prism and breaks up the white light into all the colours of the rainbow. A rainbow is a spectrum.

In the rainbow, the colours are not separate and you cannot tell where one colour ends and the next begins. Scientists have separated the colours of the rainbow and arranged them into a circle. It is called the colour wheel.

Primary colours

The three primary colours are red, blue and yellow. They are called primary colours because they cannot be made from any other colours. You cannot make a blue by mixing other colours together. You can make different types of blue by adding other colours to a blue, but you cannot make a blue unless you have a blue in the first place. It is the same for red and yellow.

From these three primary colours we can mix all the rest. From red and blue and yellow you can make hundreds of different colours.

If you mix roughly the same amounts of red and blue and yellow paint together in a paint pot, you get a kind of muddy brown.

Secondary colours

Orange, green and purple are called secondary colours because they are made by mixing two primary colours together.

Blue and red make purple, red and yellow make orange, and blue and yellow make green.

The colour wheel

Colour wheels are a useful way of showing the effects of mixing paints.

The colours always go round the wheel in the same order, but some colour wheels have more colours than others. In the simplest colour wheel, there are six colours: three primaries and three secondaries. The colours are always arranged so that the primary colours are next to a secondary colour.

One half of the wheel has colours that look warm (red, orange, yellow) and the other half has colours that look cool (blue, green, purple.)

The colour wheel

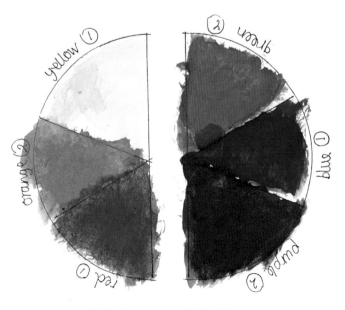

Hot colours   **Cold colours**

Complementary colours

Each colour on the colour wheel has another colour which sits directly opposite it on the wheel. These pairs of colours are called complementary colours, and when they are put next to each other they look very bright and they stand out in your painting. You could think of them as 'opposite colours'.

Complementary pairs of colours are red and green, blue and orange, purple and yellow.

Earth colours

Browns, greys, blacks, rusty reds are called earth colours.

Hot and cold colours

Some colours are thought of as either 'hot' or 'cold' colours.

Pinks, some purples, reds, yellows, warm browns and oranges are considered warm or hot colours.

Some bluey-purples, blues, greens and greys and blacks are considered cold colours.

Colour moods

Different colours are associated with different feelings, although not everyone feels the same way about colours.

These are some general feelings:
* Red = anger, danger, heat
* Blue = sadness, loneliness, cold
* Yellow = happiness
* Purple = poison, royalty
* Green = envy, spring
* White = innocence, cold, winter
* Black = strength, night time

Colours have different symbolism in different cultures.

How artists use colour theory to create certain effects

If an artist wants to give the illusion that something is near in their picture, or far away, there are two ways they can do this. One way is to paint things bigger if they are near to you, and smaller if they are far away.

However, there is another way. If the artist wants something to appear to be in the far distance of their picture, they could also use cool, pale colours such as soft blues or very pale purples – misty colours. If, on the other hand, they want something to seem nearer or to stand out, they could use warm, strong colours, such as bright reds or vivid oranges.

If they want to create a powerful or dramatic effect, they might well use two complementary colours together. If they want a peaceful, calm image, they might use lighter tones of harmonious colours.

Tone in colour

A colour can be made lighter or darker in tone in two ways:

The first way is by adding white gradually. This will make a colour lighter and lighter by degrees. Black can be added in the same way, to make it darker.

The second way is achieved by changing the amounts of paint and water. A little paint and a lot of water makes the colour look pale, while more paint and less water makes a deeper version of the same colour.

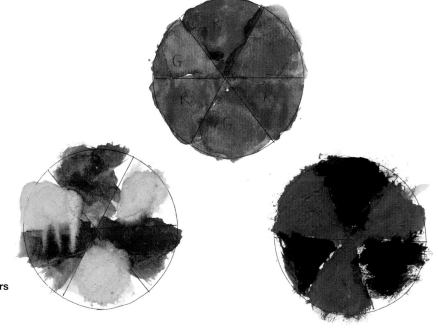

Complementary colours

Key aspects of colour theory

Primary colours

red   blue   yellow

Secondary colours

green   orange   purple

Tertiary colours

Tertiary colours are made by mixing all three primaries and are mostly variations of brown.

Complementary colours

red + green   blue + orange   yellow + purple

Complementary colours contrast.

Harmonious colours

Harmonious colours are close to each other on the colour wheel. They appear to blend when close to each other.

Earth colours

browns   black   greys   rusty-reds   orangey-browns

Warm colours

pinks   red-purples   reds   oranges   yellows   browns

Warm colours advance (seem closer) in a picture.

Cool colours

blues   greens   blue-purples   greys   black   green-yellows

Cool colours recede (seem further away) in a picture.

The colour wheel

KEY SKILL

Time
30 min

Resources
Newspaper
Ready-mix paint:
Red, blue, yellow
Orange, green purple in pots or palettes
Thin brushes
Water pots
Photocopies of resource sheet 3 (page 120)

National Curriculum
4a

Year 2 pupil

Introduction
You remember the primary colours? (Ask the children to name them.) Today we are going to learn about secondary colours. Can anyone guess what they are?

Practical activity
❋ Name the secondary colours and explain that they are made by mixing two primary colours together.
❋ Ask children which two primary colours do they think are used to make green? Orange?
❋ Ask them how they would make purple. Go back and forth over this a few times until it seems to have sunk in.
❋ Show the class the colour wheel illustrated above and explain that the colours go around it in a particular order. It goes: primary, secondary, primary, secondary and so on.
❋ Point out that each secondary colour is between the two primaries that create it; so orange is between red and yellow, green is between blue and yellow and purple is between red and blue.
❋ Give them a blank colour wheel each and tell them to paint in each section, starting with yellow, then orange, and so on around the wheel (start with yellow because yellow will be the most spoilt if anyone puts an unwashed brush in it after using another colour).
❋ Remind the children to wash their brushes carefully between each colour.
❋ When the colour wheels are dry, they should be stuck into their sketchbooks for future reference. They may need to refer to them when they colour mix, or if they forget how to mix secondary colours.

Extension activity
If there is time, with any remaining paint, the children could attempt to paint a rainbow. Tell them whatever mnemonic the school uses to remember the colour order. 'Read Out Your Green Book In Verse' is a good one, or children may have mnemonics of their own. They could devise one for themselves.

Explain that indigo is a very deep purply blue and that they could try to make it by mixing blue and purple.

Painting in complementary colours

USING SKILL

Time
1 hour

Resources
Newspaper to cover tables
Oil pastels

Per pair of children:
Powder paint or ready-mixed colours:
• cyan + brilliant blue
• lemon + brilliant yellow
• crimson + vermilion red
1 water pot
1 palette
Oil pastels (optional)

For each child:
1 medium long-handled brush
Cartridge paper
Test paper
If they have them, colour wheels from
previous lesson

National Curriculum
2a, 4a, 5a

Lucy Clements, Year 2

Note
Complementary colour pairs are: red/green, blue/
orange, yellow/purple.

Introduction
*You have painted some colour wheels, and now we are
going to paint a colourful picture using some colours from
that wheel. Do you remember that some colours are called
primary colours (red, blue, yellow) and some colours are
called secondary colours (orange, green, purple)? Well, there
are pairs of colours that are called 'complementary' colours.
Complementary colours contrast; that means they seem very
bright when they are put next to each other.*

Practical activity
❋ Tell the children to look at their colour wheels.
❋ Ask them which colour is opposite
red (green), and explain that green is
complementary to red. Now ask them what
colour is opposite blue (orange) and then
what is opposite yellow (purple).
❋ If necessary, revise mixing secondary colours
(page 46).

❋ Ask the children to choose which pair of
complementary colours they want to use,
or, to make organization and support easier,
select a pair of complementary colours for
each table.
❋ Tell children to mix up and paint lots of
squares of different colours (reds or blues
or yellows, whichever primary is chosen; in
this example it was reds) but to leave some
spaces for the complementary colour.
❋ Next they should wash their palettes and mix
up different versions of their complementary
colour (in this case, different greens).
❋ Now tell the children to paint in the remaining
spaces with squares of this colour.
❋ When the paint is dry, they could use oil
pastels to draw patterns on top of their
colours with the complementary colour, eg
red oil pastels on green squares and green oil
pastels on red squares.
❋ When the pictures are finished, ask the
children to notice how the colours seem
really bright together.

Colour and mood

SKILL

Time
45 min

Resources
Newspaper
Ready-mix paint in 2 different blues or
2 different reds in pots or palettes
Water pots
Medium brushes
Cartridge paper
Scrap paper for testing colours
Yellow paint for extension activity

National Curriculum
2c, 4a

Alanah Stenning, Year 2

Introduction

Artists use colours in different ways. Sometimes they want to show how they feel in their paintings. Perhaps, they might be angry or very happy and they want you to look at their picture and understand their feelings. Sometimes they want to create a special effect. Some colours are thought to be cold colours and some warm; some colours are thought to be sad or happy or mysterious.

Practical activity

❋ Ask the children which colours they think might be cool/cold colours and which they think might be hot/warm.

❋ Brainstorm expressions like 'red for danger', 'seeing red', 'red hot' or 'blue with cold' or 'to get the blues'.

❋ Explain that blue, green and bluey-purple are considered cold colours and that red, orange and yellow are considered warm colours.

❋ Demonstrate that by folding a colour wheel in half they can show warm colours on one side and cool on the other.

❋ Half the class could paint in blues and half in reds; ask them to paint a cool/sad picture or a hot/angry one. If they paint a face, they should be able to create the effect that it is a sad/cold person or a hot/angry one.

❋ Tell them to try to do this without resorting to painting tears or big smiles as it should be the colour that tells the story (however, they might not be able to resist it).

Extension activity

Children could try painting in a whole range of cool colours or a whole range of warm colours with a subject of their own choice.

Colour families

KEY SKILL

Time
2 hours

Resources
Newspaper to cover tables

Per pair of children:
Powder paint or ready-mixed colours:
• cyan + brilliant blue
• lemon + brilliant yellow
• crimson + vermilion red
1 water pot
1 palette

For each child:
1 medium long-handled brush
1 fine long-handled brush, for figures
Cartridge paper
Test paper

For the teacher
A copy of a rainbow

National Curriculum
2a, 4a, 5a,d

Evie Peacock, Year 2

Introduction

Artists know that some colours go well together and other colours do not. Sometimes they use colours that do not go together so well because they want to make a dramatic effect, and sometimes they use colours that go well together to make a more peaceful effect. Colours that go well together are called harmonious colours because the colours are rather like musical notes; when they are put together they make a beautiful effect. Everyone has different ideas about which colours look good together, but there are some generally accepted rules of colour which artists use and this is called 'colour theory'. Today you are going to mix and paint some harmonious colours – groups of colours that go well together. We could call them 'colour families'.

Practical activity

❋ Show the children the colour wheel and explain that colours which are close together, in a continuous run, on the colour wheel (or in the rainbow), generally go well together and harmonize.

❋ Tell children they are going to paint some unusual rainbows in different colour families.

❋ Suggest that they choose and mix up three colours that are close together, eg crimson, purple and brilliant blue.

❋ Ask the children to paint an arc of each colour (the order of the colours does not matter as the overall effect will be harmonious anyway).

❋ Next, they should add a few more arcs of colours made by mixing these three colours together. This should create a rainbow of reds and purples and blues.

❋ Now the children could choose another three colours that are close to each other, such as crimson, vermilion and brilliant yellow, and create a rainbow with these in the same way as the first rainbow.

❋ They could continue until there is no room left on the paper, or they could have a new piece of paper for each rainbow.

❋ Finally, they could mix a blue for the sky and paint the background.

Considering relationships between colours

Time
2 hours

Resources
Newspaper to cover tables

Per pair of children.
Powder paint or ready-mixed colours:
- crimson + vermilion red
- cyan +brilliant blue
- brilliant + lemon yellow
1 water pot
1 palette

For each child:
1 medium long-handled brush
1 fine long-handled brush, for figures
Cartridge paper folded or drawn into
9 or 12 squares for older children
and 6 or 4 squares for younger ones.
Test paper

For the teacher:
Access to Wassily Kandinsky's
'Farbstafel' or Terry Frost's 'Orchard
Tambourines'

National Curriculum
2a, 4a, 5a,d

Megan Harrop, Year 1

Introduction

You have learned how to mix lots of wonderful colours and you know how to mix up and paint with strong bright colours, but today you are going to think about how colours look when they are placed next to each other. We could call this thinking about colour relationships. Just as you change when you are with different people, so colours seem to change when they are with other colours. They look different. Everyone has different ideas about what colours look good together.

Practical activity

- Quickly revise mixing secondary colours if necessary.
- Remind children to test colours on their test papers before they use a colour in case it isn't the colour that they want.
- Suggest that children choose any colours to start with and paint circles in the middle of a few of the squares.
- When three or four squares have different coloured circles in the middle, they could start thinking about painting a ring of colour around the centre colours.
- They do not necessarily need to wait for

the colour to dry before they paint the next colour; they might enjoy the effect of wet colours blending a little as they do in the Kandinsky painting, or they might prefer to wait for colours to dry and achieve a crisper colour contrast as in the Frost picture.
- Tell them that they must think carefully about whatever colour they use and think how it looks next to its neighbouring colour.
- Suggest they ask themselves these kinds of questions:
  - 'How does this colour look next to this colour?'
  - 'Do I like those colours together, what other colour might look better?'
  - 'What colour shall I use next and how will it affect the other colours?'
- As children are painting, they should try to think of individual relationships between colours and the effect of the whole painting as it grows.
- They should continue until the paper is covered.
- In this example, children added some colourful over-drawings in oil pastels.

Watercolours

Beth James, Year 2

Background information

Watercolours are made of finely powdered pigments (colours) to which gum has been added to bind them together. The gum dissolves easily in water and helps to fix the colour to the paper. The colours are pure and translucent and can be built up in layers.

A brief history

Many people think that watercolour painting was invented in the 18th century, but in fact it was a fully developed art form long before that. The ancient Egyptians were using watercolours to illustrate their Books of the Dead two thousand years before the birth of Christ. Medieval illustrators were highly skilled in the craft and the earliest of them used 'pure' (meaning 'transparent') watercolour, while later ones added other substances to make the paint more solid and to create a base on which gold leaf was laid.

The British artist JMW Turner (1775–1851) worked a great deal in watercolours and the medium remained popular right through the Victorian era. Edward Hopper (1882–1967) and others continued the tradition in America, while Edward Burra, David Jones and Paul Nash were perhaps the major English exponents. The Swiss artist Paul Klee (1879–1940), a founder member of the Bauhaus, produced his most significant work in the medium.

Character of the medium

The chief characteristics of watercolour paint are its transparency and pureness of colour. The whiteness of the paper shines through and gives the colours light. The paint should be used thinly and the painter can build up the picture in layers. It is this quality of the paper shining through the transparent pigment that gives pictures in watercolours the sparkle and brilliance that sets them apart from other types of painting.

Mistakes can be difficult to correct. Only delicate colours can be washed out with a clean wet brush or a piece of sponge or cotton wool.

In watercolour, only the paper is white; white paint is generally not used. The artist starts with the most delicate colours and adds by over-painting.

Paint

The paints can be purchased in tablets of colour, powdered or in tubes.

Brusho®

Powdered watercolour, which is generally known as 'Brusho®' and mixed with water, is excellent for use with Key Stage 1 children, and it is quite versatile. It can be used for wax relief, colouring-in drawings, as the colour for batik and for general painting.

A flood of gorgeous colour over a quick drawing in bold permanent black pen can look stunning and can be done very quickly. Washes can be laid with it, as with conventional water colours, and younger children enjoy the brilliant colours and the way they blend and mix on the paper.

Nicky Loat, Year 2

Brusho® can be applied quite freely with a large brush or used for delicate work with a finer brush.

Brusho® that has been mixed up and is surplus at the end of the lesson can be stored in clear glass or plastic jars for use another time. It is very useful to keep a range of colours ready mixed up to save time.

Colours

Brusho® comes in a wide range of jewel-like colours and it is not very expensive. It is a good idea to stock as many colours as you can. The yellow and the black tend to get used the most, so it is best to order more of these colours.

Brushes

Watercolours are best applied with soft flexible brushes. If the art budget allows, buy some good brushes and keep them especially for watercolours or delicate work. The best watercolour brushes have sable hair and are very expensive, but squirrel hair makes a more reasonably priced substitute.

For most work in Brusho®, long-handled hog-hair brushes are fine. There is more information about brushes on pages 16–17.

Paper

Watercolours should be painted on a heavier weight paper than is used for general painting. Proper watercolour paper comes in different thicknesses and with different textures, but heavier cartridge paper will do fine. 190 g/sm (90 lb) or above won't wrinkle too much when painted on.

Dry, damp or wet paper

Generally, watercolours are painted on wetted paper. The paper may just be a little damp or it can be quite wet – it depends on the effect desired. The wetter the paper, the looser and freer the effect will be, and colours will blend and blur into each other. Damp paper allows for a bit more control, and dry paper will leave sharp edges which cannot be removed or dried. It is good for children to experiment with these different effects.

Year 1 pupil (painting a wash, page 71)

Making blot pictures with powdered watercolour (Brusho®)

SKILL

Time
20 min

Resources
Newspapers for the tables

Per group of children:
3 or 4 colours of Brusho®, ready-mixed in pots with two or three paintbrushes in each pot

For each child:
Several pieces of cartridge paper, folded in half

National Curriculum
2a, 4a, 5a

Bethany James, Year 1

Introduction
You are going to make some blot pictures in Brusho®. Brusho® is powdered watercolour paint. The lovely thing about watercolour paint is that the colours are very bright and clear, because the white of the paper shines through them. We call that 'transparent colour'. You will be putting splodges of different colours on one side of the paper and, when you fold and press them, the colours will mix together as you will see.

Practical activity
* Explain to the children that they must always put the brush back into the pot they took it from or the colours will get muddled up – particularly the yellow!
* Point out that they will have to work fast before the Brusho® has a chance to dry or soak into the paper.
* Tell them to paint some big splodges of colours, slightly overlapping, on one side of the paper.

* Next tell them (they may need help with this) to quickly fold the paper in half and press down on it. Explain that this will help the colours to mix.
* They may like to have several goes at this using different colour combinations, and they could try doing it on wetted paper to see the difference.
* The resulting pictures may well look like fantastic creatures, which the children will like. Point out the places where the colours have mixed and the new colours that have been created.
* If the pictures are laminated, it really brings the colours out.

Allowing the colours to mix on the surface of a painting

SKILL

Time
20 min

Resources
Newspapers for the tables

Per group of children:
A lot of yellow and a little red Brusho®, ready-mixed in pots
Smaller amounts of a third colour of Brusho® if required
Two or three big paintbrushes in each pot
Box of mixed coloured oil pastels

For each child:
A3 piece of cartridge paper

National Curriculum
2a, 4a, 5a

Shani Cook, Year 1

Introduction
You are going to paint with Brusho® today. Brusho® is powdered watercolour paint. The lovely thing about watercolour paint is that the colours are very bright and clear, because the white of the paper shines through them. We call that 'transparent colour'. You will do a drawing first in oil pastels and then add some lovely colours in all the spaces. You will see the colours mixing together as you paint with them.

Practical activity
❋ Ask the children to do a big bold drawing in oil pastels. This could be topic-led, or the playground makes quite a good subject, or it could be of friends and family.
❋ When the drawings are finished, the children can then paint Brusho® in the background.
❋ Explain to the children that they must always put the brush back into the pot they took it from or the colours will get muddled up – particularly the yellow.

❋ Encourage them to paint the colours on freely and to have plenty of Brusho® on the brush, adding more if they want.
❋ It does not matter if there are pools of wet paint on the painting, except that it will have to be allowed to dry flat and not carried around wet.
❋ Encourage the children to notice where the colours have mixed and the lovely soft watery blend they have made.
❋ Point out that the brightness comes because the white of the paper shines through the paint.

Potential pitfall
It may be necessary to mix up extra yellow and have it handy. However many times you tell them not to, someone will inevitably put a red or green brush in the yellow!

Painting a wash (activity in two sessions)

KEY SKILL

Time
1st session: 30–40 min
2nd session: 5 min per child

Resources
Session 1
A4 white paper
A4 black sugar paper cut in half longways
Scissors and glue sticks
Twigs, fir tree cuttings
Black felt tips

Session 2
Several layers of newspaper
Sponge or cotton wool
Normal blue, weak purple, pink or yellow Brusho®, ready-mixed in pots
Clean water in a water pot
1 decorator-size paintbrush in each pot
Some glitter and small silver stars
Glue stick

For the teacher:
Some pictures of night skies, sunrises, sunsets, etc

National Curriculum
2a, 4a, 5a

Robert Cooke, Year 1

Note
The first session can be done with the whole class, but the second is better done individually and can be done on another day. The photocopying can be done in between sessions.

Introduction
You are going to paint with Brusho®, which is powdered watercolour paint. The lovely thing about watercolour paint is that the colours are very bright and clear, because the white of the paper shines through them. Watercolour paints are perfect for painting skies, and that is what you are going to do. You will be using a very big brush and painting very fast from side to side of the paper in blues and purples to make it look like an evening sky.

Practical activity
Session 1
* Show the children the illustration above and on page 68. Explain that the 'hills' were made by cutting and sticking black sugar paper.
* Give them their piece of black sugar paper.
* Tell them to draw a wavy line across it to look like hills and to cut it out along the line.
* Next, tell the children to stick the black paper down on to the white background.
* Children should now stick on some twigs or fir cuttings to be the trees across the foreground so they are silhouetted against the sky.
* Now they should draw some figures or animals walking along the horizon. In these examples, the children have drawn shepherds and sheep.
* These pictures now need to be photocopied ready for session 2.

Session 2
* Show the children some pictures of evening skies.
* Damp the paper with a sponge or cotton wool.
* Tell the children to:
  * Paint a broad stripe of deep blue across the top of the paper.
  * Very quickly paint the next stripe across the paper with just water. The water stripe should overlap the lower edge of the blue stripe and the white paper so that the blue is diluted and spreads downwards a little.
  * Very quickly choose another colour and paint a stripe so that it blends at the edges with the pale blue.
  * Use the water brush to wash the colour down to the black horizon.
* When the pictures are dry, the children could add glitter and silver stars.

USING SKILL

Painting drawings with watercolours (Brusho®)

Time
45 min

Resources
Per group of children:
4 or 5 colours of Brusho®, ready-mixed up in pots with two or three medium/ fine brushes in each pot
(see note below)
1 water pot
Some very fine brushes in case children need them

For each child:
Children's own drawings done in fine pens and photocopied or drawn in permanent ink

National Curriculum
2a, 4a, 5a

Nat Beeston, Year 2

Note

It can be difficult for children to work out which colour is which when the Brusho® is in coloured water pots, as the darker colours look very similar, so place a piece of white paper beneath each pot and paint some of the colour from that pot onto the paper. The children can glance at the paper to check the colour inside the pot. If you were really organized (and I have never done this), you could laminate the paper and use it next time.

Introduction

You are going to add some watercolour paint (Brusho®) to your drawings. Because watercolours let the paper show through, you will still be able to see the lines of your drawings through the colours.

Practical activity

※ Ask the children to think about what parts of their drawings they want to add colour to.

※ Remind them that if two wet colours are next to each other they may mix. That is OK if they want the colours to mix but, if they do not, they should wait a little while as Brusho® dries quite quickly.

※ Tell the children to use the larger brushes for larger areas like the sky and smaller brushes

for smaller areas. Remind them to put the correct brush back in the correct colour. If they need to keep the brush for any reason, they must wash it in the clean water pot before putting it in a different colour.

For the painting illustrated, children:
※ looked at Russian babushka nesting dolls;
※ drew patterns from the dolls in their sketchbooks;
※ looked at pictures of Russian palaces;
※ designed their own palace for their dolls, in their sketchbooks;
※ drew the dolls first and then drew their palace in the background.

When the painting was dry, they drew silver stars with metallic pens on the sky.

Potential pitfall

Keep back some spare Brusho® in each colour. As children tend to put brushes back in the wrong pots (it doesn't matter how many times you remind them) the colours get mixed; the yellow is particularly vulnerable.

Sprinkling dry powdered watercolours (Brusho®) onto wet paper

 SKILL

Time
1 hour

Resources
Newspapers for the tables
Glue sticks
Scissors
Latex gloves (see Pitfall)

Per group of children:
Light green Brusho®, mixed in pots
A few medium brushes in each pot
Some deeper green Brusho® in powdered form
1 or 2 water pots

For each child:
A3 white cartridge paper
Black fine-line pen, water-based (not permanent)
Green felt-tip pen
Postcard-size piece of watercolour paper
1 fine brush

For the teacher:
Pictures of sheep

National Curriculum
2a, 4a, 5a

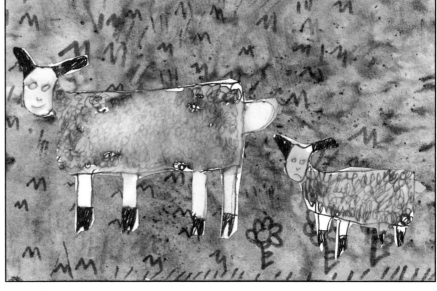

Ashley Clarke, Year 2

Note
This activity can be done without any over-drawings, just for the sake of the lovely effects. Different colours could be sprinkled onto wet paper, which could be pre-coloured or just white.

Introduction
You are going to try out sprinkling dry watercolour powder onto wet paper; you will find it interesting to see what happens. You will use special thick paper which is meant just for watercolour paints. Watercolours, as you might guess from the name, have more water in them than other paints, so extra-thick paper is needed to soak up the water. You will sprinkle the powder onto wet paper and this paper will become the background to your picture.

Practical activity
❋ Show pictures of sheep to the children. (The children who did the work illustrated lived in a rural area and were able to observe sheep from the playground. Some of the pictures were displayed upside-down so that the

sheep had their legs in the air, as there had been an outbreak of foot-and-mouth disease!)
❋ Tell the children to draw some sheep in fine-line pen on ordinary art paper. Suggest drawing them from different angles, from the side, the front, walking, grazing, etc.
❋ Encourage them to add texture for the sheep's wool and details, such as faces, tails and legs.
❋ Ask the children to choose one or two of their favourite drawings and to wet their fine brushes and then paint over the surface of the sheep drawings with a little water so that the colour runs a little. The sheep should go grey, but the lines of the drawing will still show through. In this example, the sheep went green – we were not expecting that – it may have been the make of pen.
❋ Next, they should leave these drawings to dry and paint their pieces of watercolour paper all over with the light green Brusho®.
❋ Immediately, while the paint is wet, tell the children to pinch some powdered dark green Brusho® in their dry fingertips and sprinkle a little, here and there, over the paper. They will enjoy watching the changes.
❋ When the paper is dry, the children could draw lines in green felt pens for grass, cut out their sheep and glue them onto the background.

Potential pitfall
The dry Brusho® powder may temporarily stain fingers, so you might want to use Latex gloves.

SKILL Painting on wet paper

Time
10 min per child

Resources
Newspapers for the tables
Spare newspapers
Masking tape or sponge

Per group of children:
Different colours of Brusho®, ready-mixed in pots
Two or three big paintbrushes in each pot
Fine felt tips in different colours (optional)

For each child:
A4 piece of very thick cartridge paper or blotting paper

National Curriculum
2a, 4a, 5a

Jack Davies, Year 1

Note
It is good for children to try painting on different surfaces. Painting on wet paper can be quite exciting as the paint changes while the children watch.

Introduction
You are going to paint on wet paper today. You can do this with any paints but you will be using Brusho®. Brusho® is powdered watercolour paint and it is ideal for this activity as it is quite thin paint and it will spread well. When you paint on wet or damp paper, the colours run and spread together. They look a bit blurry when they are dry but the effect can be lovely.

Practical activity
One method of wetting paper is as follows:
* Soak a piece of paper in water.
* Press the paper between two pieces of newspaper to remove excess water.
* Lay the paper on the table and tape it down with masking tape. This will stop it wrinkling when it is dry.

Alternatively, you could use this simpler method:
* Wet the paper thoroughly with a wet sponge; give it a moment or two to soak in before painting.
* Now tell the children to paint a picture or pattern on the paper. The paint will quickly spread out on the damp paper and will continue to spread out until the paper is dry.
* When the pictures are dry, they could be drawn over using fine felt-tip pens in similar colours. For example, if children had painted a flower, details such as stamen, petal outlines, stalks and buds could be drawn on top. In the artwork illustrated above, Jack drew in leaf veins and serrated leaf edges.

SKILL   Wax resist and powdered watercolours (Brusho®)

Time
An afternoon

Link
Science

Resources
Newspapers for the tables
Oil pastels

For three or four children:
Green Brusho®, mixed in a pot

For each child:
A3 white cartridge paper
1 medium long-handled brush

For the teacher:
Bunch of mixed flowers or pictures of flowers
A3 paper to demonstrate and tape to fix it to board

National Curriculum
2a, 4a, 5a

Year 2 pupil

Note
Brusho® is excellent for wax resist work. It is thinner and more translucent than powder or ready-mixed paint, so the drawing shows through better.

Introduction
You are going to draw some beautiful flowers and then you're going to do something a bit surprising to your drawing, but I will tell you about that later. First, let's concentrate on drawing the flowers.

Practical activity
* Draw the children's attention to the fact that flowers can be very different in shape as well as in colour, and that the petals can be very different shapes as well.
* Tell them to choose an oil pastel and draw a rough circle which will be the flower centre. Ask the children to use the same colour to draw petals all the way around the circle.
* Now tell them to rub the petals, from the outside of the petal down to the centre. The oil pastel colour will smudge down the petal to make a paler version of the original colour. You may need to demonstrate this. Younger children could just colour in the petals solidly. Repeat this with different colours of

oil pastels until the paper is covered with flowers as in the illustration above.
* Next, ask the children to colour in the flower centres with either yellow, pale green, light orange or brown oil pastels, depending on the flower. They could add some dots in red or orange to represent stamen. Green stalks and leaves should be added to the flowers, and insects could be drawn in the spaces.
* Now explain to the children that they are going to paint in green watercolour paint over their pictures. Older children could try to go round the flowers if they want to. The oil pastel is thinner on the petals, but it won't really matter if they go over it as the petals will then be tinged with green, which will look quite effective anyway.
* Younger children can paint green Brusho® all over their picture, and the flowers and leaves will reappear where the oil rejects the paint.
* When the paintings are dry, more leaves and stalks can be added with different-coloured green oil pastels. If the stalks and leaves go right across some of the flowers, it will look as if some flowers are in front of others. This will help to create an illusion of depth and distance.

SKILL # Collage using papers created using wax resist and Brusho®

Time
2 sessions of 1 hour each

Resources
Newspapers for the tables
Oil pastels
Scissors (2nd session)
Glue sticks (2nd session)

For a group of 3–4 children:
Several different very strong colours
and black Brusho®, mixed in a pot,
with three or four brushes in each pot

For each child:
Several pieces of A5 white paper
Bright-coloured paper for background
(2nd session)

For the teacher:
Some examples of the work of the
illustrator Brian Wildsmith

National Curriculum
2a, 4a,c, 5a

Oliver Coulham, Year 1

Introduction

You are going to make a picture out of cut-up coloured paper.
This is known as a 'collage'. You can make a collage out of
anything: cut-up magazine pictures, bits of fabric, odds and
ends of anything. Today you are going to make your own
coloured papers to cut up. If you look at the illustrations of
Brian Wildsmith, you can see lots of examples of lines of one
colour, with other colours behind them. He might have painted
the colours first and drawn the lines on afterwards, or he
might have done the lines first in one colour and then painted
over the top. That is the way we are going to try.

Practical activity

Session 1

* Show children some pictures by Brian
  Wildsmith and point out the way he used
  lines and colours.
* Tell them to choose a colour (say, red or blue
  or brown) and scribble lots of lines to and fro
  across the paper, using different reds, blues
  or browns in oil pastels.
* Now they should do the same thing with
  another family of colours on another piece of
  paper.
* This should be repeated until they have three
  or four different pieces of paper, all with
  coloured scribbles on (each child can have
  their own choice of colours).

* Now tell the children to paint over each piece
  of paper with Brusho® that is the same colour
  as the scribbles, eg yellow over yellow, green
  over greens, etc. The black could go over any
  colour or over grey, white or black oil pastel
  scribbles.

Session 2

* Place a pile of the children's coloured papers
  in the middle of each group. This does not
  have to be the work of each child in that
  group – the coloured papers are to share.
* The children can now decide which exotic
  animal or bird to depict. The illustrated
  example was meant to be a peacock.
* They should think about the overall shape of
  the creature and what colours they want to
  use. The colours do not need to be life-like,
  and the creature could be an imaginary one
  such as a dragon.
* Next, the children should cut out the
  coloured papers into the shapes they want
  and arrange them on their backgrounds, but
  they should not stick them down yet.
* The children should, at this stage, consider
  what to add, take away or move. They can
  make longer legs or necks, bigger heads, etc.
  Once they have settled on the image they
  want, they should then stick it down before
  someone opens a door and it all blows away!
* Lastly, they could add small detail using tiny
  scraps of paper, such as eyes, teeth, beaks,
  etc.

History of painting

Year 2 pupils

Introduction to cave paintings

The earliest paintings have been found in caves all over the world and many date from at least 20,000 years ago. Prehistoric people lived at the entrances to these caves and the paintings have been found deep inside them. There are many pictures of the animals the people hunted, such as bison, horses, stags and even woolly rhinoceroses. From these paintings, we know about such extinct animals as the mammoth. There are various theories about why they were painted, but some historians think they were part of the hunting ritual and would bring good luck in a hunt. Other experts think that the caves where the paintings are found might have been places of worship.

Some famous caves in France were discovered by accident. Some boys were out for a walk with their dog, and the dog disappeared down a hole in the hillside. One of the boys went to search for him. The ground beneath the boy's feet gave way and he tumbled into a cave, followed by his friends. They lit matches to see where they were, and were amazed to find hundreds of animals painted on the walls.

The prehistoric artists used earth and rocks to make a kind of reddish-brown, as well as a yellowy-brown called ochre. They used chalk out of the earth for white and powdered burnt sticks for black. They mixed the colours with clay, and added water or animal fats to make them liquid. The paints were kept in hollowed-out bones, which were plugged at one end. The artists painted with their fingers or used brushes made of twigs with chewed ends. Pads of fur and moss were also used, and they worked by the light of animal fat lamps.

They only had a few colours to paint with. These colours were, in fact, the only colours any artists had to work with for thousands of years. They just had:
* Black
* White
* A kind of dark mossy green
* A muddy brown
* A reddish-brown
* A yellowy-brown

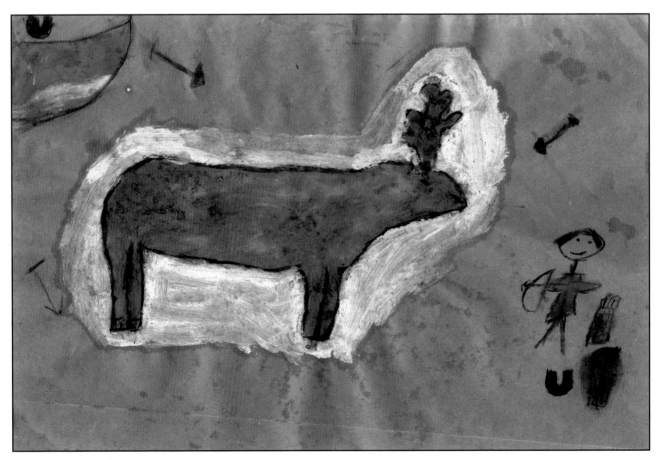

Jordan Wilde, Year 2

ACTIVITY Cave paintings

Time
1 hour

Links
History

Resources
Newspaper to cover tables

Per pair of children:
Brown, vermilion, black and white
ready-mixed paint
1 water pot
1 palette

For all children:
A piece of charcoal
Protective clothing
Sketchbook and pencil
A3 brown or stone-coloured paper

For the teacher:
Access to images of cave paintings of
horses, deer, bison and wild boar

National Curriculum
2a,c, 3a, 4a,c, 5a,d

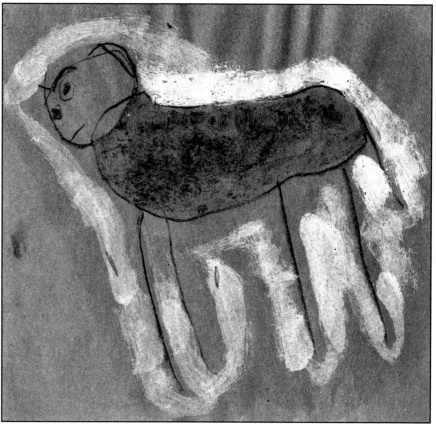

Year 1 pupil

Note
This lesson works very well if the children make their own paints, but it also can be done using school charcoal, brushes, chalk, brown pastels or paint. It does have more impact when the children make their own materials, but it is messy and time-consuming. Ironically, the end results often look better when they have used shop-bought products. The home-made variety can look like a pig's breakfast, but the children love doing it.

Introduction
Read the information on cave paintings on page 78 to the children. Tell them that they are going to make some paintings similar to those found in the caves.

Practical activity
* Look at the images of cave paintings and discuss the colours and the content. Remind the children why the cave people painted animals, and what their homes might have been like.

* Children should now look at images of cows and horses, etc and sketch some in their sketchbooks. If the real thing is nearby, that would be perfect,

* Next, using charcoal, they should draw, using their charcoal on their brown paper, one large cow, deer or horse in the middle of the page.

* Tell the children to paint or colour the background white. This should make the animal stand out as it is on brown paper.

* Ask them to colour the animal in brown.

* Now children could try adding a little white or vermilion to the brown to make different browns and paint some patches of these new colours on the animal.

* When the picture is dry, they could add detail with their charcoal, such as cracks on the wall, fur, horns or markings on the animal, along with hunters and arrows, etc.

Older children could add a little yellow to the brown to try to make an ochre colour.

ACTIVITY Using early religious art: images of the mother and child

Time
2 hours

Links History/RE/Christmas

Resources
Newspaper to cover tables
Gold paper/Scissors/Glue sticks

Per pair of children:
Ready-mixed paint
Brilliant Blue and Gold
1 water pot
1 palette
Skin tone crayon

For each child:
1 fine and 1 larger brush
Sketchbook or paper
1 fine-line black pen
A3 white paper
A4 brown suger paper cut to shape
as in the illustration

For the teacher:
Access to some pictures of triptychs
or diptychs (see note). And/or some
examples of paintings of Mary and
the baby Jesus from the 14th or
15th century, such as Masaccio's
Madonna del Solletico
A doll and some cloth (blue if
possible)

National Curriculum
2a, 4a, 5a,d

Holly Victoria, Year 2 (photocopied sheet music has been torn and placed behind Mary and the angels)

Note
A triptych is a folding altarpiece with three hinged
panels. Similarly, a diptych has two panels and a
polyptych has several panels. Good examples of
these are the Wilton Diptych and Giotto's Bologna
Polyptych. A Google search will bring up many more.

Introduction
*Long ago, most paintings were done for either very rich
people or for the church. Most ordinary people could not read,
so the paintings and the stained glass in a church were very
important because they could tell the people stories from
the Bible. Most churches would have at least one painting,
and that would usually be of either Jesus on the cross or his
mother Mary. Sometimes paintings would be folded up and
taken to another church or castle. They were very valuable,
because the paintings often had real gold in them and a blue
paint that was as expensive as gold. We are going to do a
painting of Mary and Jesus today, in blue and gold.*

Practical activity
❋ Show children the pictures of altarpieces, or
of the holy mother and child.
❋ Ask them what they think the gold circles
behind the figures' heads are. Explain, and point
out the patterns (if there are any) on the halos.
❋ Ask a child to pose with a toy and some cloth
over their head as Mary, and tell the children
to have a few goes at drawing her.
❋ When the children have had a little practice,
tell them to draw a mother and baby on their
white paper. The paper size will depend
on whether it is to be a single painting or a
triptych. They could also draw some angels
playing music for the side panels.
❋ Next, they should colour in the face and any
skin showing with the skin-tone crayon, and
then paint the robe and dress blue.
❋ While that is drying, they should paint the
background of their brown paper in gold,
leaving a space for a border.
❋ They could draw wooden carving patterns
around the border as a frame.
❋ Next, children should cut out a circle of gold
paper and draw patterns on it. This will go
behind Mary's head as a halo, so it will need
to be the right size.
❋ Now they can cut out the Mary and baby and
glue the halo on behind the head and the
whole figure down on the gold background.
The angels go on the side panels.
❋ The side panels can fold in to meet at the
middle like a wardrobe door. These make
unusual Christmas cards.

Using works of art

Sue Rogers, Year 2 (in the style of Georgia O'Keeffe)

Artists and art movements

Children gain confidence through the ability to handle and control a substance as complex as paint, and by being able to express and communicate ideas through painting. Learning about the way artists, past and present, have used paint, can extend the range of possibilities for children in their knowledge and in their thinking.

Studying the works of an artist, whether famous or relatively unknown, is often an excellent way of trying out the techniques favoured by various art movements.

It is essential to have access to a good supply of materials, such as prints of paintings by your chosen artists. These do not have to be expensive items – they can be old calendars, cut up and laminated, birthday or Christmas cards, or even old art books which are too tatty to use in the library, cut up and laminated.

Shops that sell remaindered books are an excellent source of art books, but be careful to go through them and make sure there are no unsuitable images. I do not mean nudes, as these are part of classical art history and children need to get used to seeing these without sniggering, but there can be really unsuitable images, including those that are violent, disturbing or erotic. For example, check before you consider using any books on Klimt, because of his erotic drawings.

If you have an interactive whiteboard in the class or art room, a brilliant way to share larger images of works of art with children is to use the Internet. Open up Google and click on 'Images', then type in either an artist or the subject you want, and then click 'search' again. You will be presented with a number of thumbnail images and, if you click again on these, you will get a larger image. Some will have 'see full size image' written below, and you can click on this to bring the picture up full size.

The National Gallery's website has a wonderful zoom facility whereby you can zoom in on any area of the picture and see it in detail. Try it with Fra Filippo Lippi's Annunciation and you can even see the tiny slit in the skirts of the stomach area where the spirit of God is about to enter. Or, try Canaletto's 'Stonemason's yard', where you can zoom in and show the children where the fallen toddler is weeing himself in surprise. They will like that!

Charlotte Green, Year 2 (in the style of Kandinsky)

Particularly useful artists to use with children

Paul Klee (Swiss, 1879–1940)
Used in Basic skills (page 41)
Used in Colour mixing (page 46)
Used in Colour theory (page 52)

Paul Klee's work has been used in several places in this book; he is a wonderful artist to use with children as his work has a childlike quality. He was fascinated with children's artwork and children relate well to this quality, which makes his work accessible to them and non-threatening.

Klee worked on colour mixing in a progressive series of works as part of his teaching at the Bauhaus design school in West Germany. Many of his experiments were carried out in the form of beautiful small watercolours, painted in many overlapping layers of transparent colour, mostly based on just two colours. Many of his paintings show a range of colours juxtaposed, and these are excellent for children to look at when learning about colour mixing or colour relationships.

Henri Rousseau (French, 1844–1910)
Rousseau is particularly useful to use if children have been studying wild animals, green colour mixing or jungles. Children might like to know that he never went to the jungle or ever saw any wild animals or jungle plants, except in the zoological gardens in Paris. His style is slightly naive, which makes it easy for children to relate to.

Georges Seurat (French, 1859–1891)
Seurat's experimentation with colour – and in particular his idea that the colours could be painted separately in small dots or dashes and the eye of the viewer would do the colour mixing – makes him an interesting artist to work with when children are studying either the art movement to which he belonged ('Pointillism') or colour mixing and colour theory.

Georgia O'Keeffe (American, 1887–1986)
Used in Using works of art (page 91)

Georgia O'Keeffe's large dramatic paintings of flowers, often painted in single colours or just two colours, are ideal for children to look at when they are painting for any reason in a restricted palette (perhaps because they are investigating a range of one colour or are experimenting with simple colour mixing). Her paintings have tremendous mood and impact.

Claude Monet (French, 1840–1926)
Used in Using works of art (page 93)

Monet is an inspirational artist to tell children about. He would paint the same scene over and over again to capture it in different lights, times of day, weather conditions and seasons. Children can be shown his series of paintings of haystacks or cathedrals or of the famous gardens at Giverny – all paintings of the same scenes but in different colours. They can look at his works if they are studying subtle differences in colours, and also if they are concentrating on brush strokes. It is easy for them to see these in many of his paintings.

Vincent Van Gogh (Dutch, 1853–1890)
Van Gogh's vigorous brush marks are clear for children to see. They can see the passion and mood of his paintings and discuss his vivid use of colour. Children are often interested to hear that Van Gogh was quite weak at drawing when he started but he worked and worked to improve. They might also like to hear about his powerful emotions, to know that he tried to cut off his own ear, that he loved the colour yellow and that Don McLean's song 'Vincent' ('Starry starry night … ') was written about him. Films have also been made of his life story.

Maggie Ashworth, Year 2 (in the style of Georgia O'Keeffe)

Franz Marc (German, 1880–1916)

Marc's use of strong bold colours, often combined with black, are dramatic and appealing to children – particularly his paintings of animals.

Marc Chagall (Russian, 1887–1985)

Chagall painted many dream-like paintings which feature stories, family scenes such as weddings and parties, and other aspects of his life in Russia. The slightly childlike folk quality of many of his pictures appeals to children and is a good source for paintings on a dream theme.

Gustav Klimt (Austrian, 1862–1918)

Used in Using works of art (page 92)

Klimt's work is a glorious mixture of colours, patterns and textures. He uses gold, golden yellows and brilliant jewel-like colours in his works, and the subject matter is often heavy with symbolism. While a lot of his works are semi-erotic (check for this before you use any books on his work), there are a number of works that are inspirational for children to work from, eg 'The tree of life', 'Portrait of Adele Bloche-Bauer 1' and his 'Apple tree', 'Poppy field' and 'Sunflower'.

Kelly White, Year 2

Wassily Kandinsky (Russian, 1866–1944)

Used in Basic skills (page 36)
Used in Colour theory (page 65)

Kandinsky's use of brilliant colours and often non-figurative compositions make him an excellent artist to use with even very young children, especially when they are just concentrating on working in colour. His work is distinctive and children can easily recognize it. He worked in a group of artists in a movement called 'The Blue Rider', which included Paul Klee, Franz Marc and August Macke, all of whom are wonderful artists to use with children. He was possibly the first 'abstract' artist.

Robert Delauney (French, 1885–1941)

Used in Colour mixing (page 53)

Delauney was a pioneer of abstract art who painted some compositions which were of pure colour in concentric circles. These are a good starting-point for children when mixing and painting colours as the composition is not daunting, and you can explain to the children that he was experimenting with different colour combinations.

Friedrich Hundertwasser (Austrian, 1928–2000)

Used in Using works of art (page 90)

Hundertwasser's work is extraordinary; he was an architect as well as a painter. It is very difficult to describe his work, as his paintings are full of brilliant colours and lines and often include houses in the compositions. He, rather like the Catalan architect Gaudi, loved to soften the contours of buildings with curved edges and organic forms. Children respond well to his colourful and unusual paintings and they are a good vehicle for wax resist pictures because of his use of line and colour.

Pablo Picasso (Spanish, 1881–1973)

Picasso is an inspirational artist to use with children because of the enormous range of his work, which includes not only painting but also ceramics, sculpture, collage and graphics. They need to understand that he could draw superbly by the age of 15 and spent the rest of his life experimenting and pushing artistic boundaries. One of the aspects of Picasso that is so inspiring is the sheer force of his creativity and the fact that he was still trying new styles and ideas in his 90s.

Joseph Turner (British, 1775–1851)

Turner is probably one of Britain's best-known painters, along with Constable. Turner was a master at painting light and the energy of the elements. Children might like to hear that the inspiration for a painting called 'Snow storm' arose when he was tied to the mast of a boat for four hours during a terrible storm, and he later painted this picture based on his experience. He is an excellent artist for children to study when they are using watercolours and are trying to get a feeling of lightness and brightness, particularly in skies.

Amadeo Modigliani (Italian, 1884–1920)

Modigliani is probably the archetypal 'bohemian' artist who loved, lived and drank well but not wisely. He was passionate, romantic, good-looking and died young. He was also a brilliant artist. His work is very distinctive as his portraits tend to have elongated faces and necks. He was much influenced by African sculptures and masks. Children might like to hear that in a fit of passion and depression, he threw many of his sculptures in the river Seine in Paris.

Piet Mondrian (Dutch, 1872–1944)

Used in Basic skills (page 34)

A lot (but not all) of Mondrian's works are easily recognizable as he uses similar pictorial elements in them: the straight line, the horizontal line, the primary colours, red, yellow and blue and the non-colours black, grey and white. For this reason, he is excellent to use as a starting-point for work on learning the primary colours. Simple Mondrian-like paintings are easily achievable by even quite young children. This work can be combined with maths, in the study of right angles, rectangles and squares. He was part of an art group known as 'De Stijl'.

Jackson Pollock (American, 1912–1956)

Used in Other techniques (page 109)

Jackson Pollock was a pioneer of an art movement called 'Action painting'; he would throw, spray, trickle or splatter the paint on top of the surface of the canvas layer upon layer, building up a highly patterned and textured surface. He would even ride a bike over it. The

April Britton, Year 2 (in the style of Friedrich Hundertwasser)

action involved in the making of the painting was as important as the look of the final artwork. Children will enjoy using some of his techniques: different colours of paint can be dribbled from squeezy bottles onto the paper and toy cars can be run through the paint. This works as well with very young children as it does with older ones.

Cicely Mary Barker (English, 1895–1973)
Used in Colour matching (page 56)

Cicely Mary Barker is famous for her paintings of flower fairies. She was an illustrator and was greatly influenced by Pre-Raphaelite art.

Too delicate to attend school, she was educated at home where she spent a lot of time alone reading and drawing. Her flower drawings were always botanically accurate and her models for the fairies were mainly children who attended her sister's Nursery school. The pictures of flower fairies are lovely to use with children to show them how well the artist has matched the colours of the fairies to the flower.

Bob Rush, Year 2

Some art movements of the 19th and 20th century

Here are some art movements that you might want to refer to at some point with your pupils. Many of them are mentioned at some point in this book.

Fauves (based in Paris in the 1900s)
Known as the 'wild beasts', they used brilliant colour, often not as seen in nature. Their subject matter was really colour itself. Artists include André Derain.

Pre-Raphaelites (mainly French and British, 1848 onwards)
They painted very realistically, often depicting romantic scenes from medieval England, from Shakespeare, legends and poems. Children may enjoy hearing the stories behind the paintings: the Arthurian legends or 'The Lady of Shalott'. The Pre-Raphaelites are much scorned by art snobs.

Impressionists (Europe, 1860s onwards)
The Impressionists, as the name suggests, were interested in capturing an impression – a fleeting moment of light and atmosphere. They were revolutionary at the time in showing loose brush marks and not tight realism, and their paintings met with violent negative responses from the established art world. The most famous artists involved in the movement were Monet, Renoir, Manet, Sisley, Degas and Cézanne.

Post-Impressionists (Dutch and French, 1880s)
Some artists turned away from the ideas of the impressionists and went their own way. The most famous of these were Paul Gauguin and Vincent Van Gogh, two artists who had a turbulent friendship and greatly influenced each other's work.

Cubism (Europe, end of 19th century)
This movement abandoned traditional methods, perspective and vision, portraying a subject from several viewpoints, searching and emphasizing its geometric forms. Cézanne was the first cubist and he was joined by others such as Picasso and Braque.

Abstract painting (Europe, end of 19th century onwards)
This is generally considered to be non-representational art, ie it does not attempt to represent nature or any recognizable subject matter. Kandinsky was the artist who made the first step towards complete abstraction.

Another sub-group of artists who could also be called abstract artists were known as 'De Stijl', a movement that was formed in Holland in 1917. Their paintings contained mainly horizontal and vertical lines, and the most famous exponent was Mondrian.

Surrealism (Europe, 1923 onwards)

This was an art movement which stressed the importance of the irrational and the subconscious. Surrealist paintings are often quite strange and can be disturbing to children. The most famous exponent is the Spanish artist Salvador Dali.

Dada (Switzerland 1914)

The Dadaists were a group of artists who wanted to produce art that shocked people, just as the First World War, which was then starting, was shocking. The name Dada was chosen at random, but it is in fact a French word for a child's rocking horse. The Dada artists were very anti-art, and had their own ideas of art that were not the same as those of the rest of society. Marcel Duchamp was an artist working in this movement. He liked to take ready-made objects and exhibit them as art in galleries. His most famous work in this genre, the children might like to hear, was a urinal.

Action painting (USA, 1950s)

These paintings were sometimes painted using the hands directly on the canvas, or by throwing or dribbling the paint onto the canvas. The artwork was as much about the actual movement and the physical involvement of the artist as it was about the way the painting looked. Children generally thoroughly enjoy having a go at this!

Pop art (USA, 1960s)

In the 1960s, the music of the Beatles was heard throughout the world. Art could also become 'pop' like music. Pop artists welcomed the images we see today, such as cans of Coke, advertisements and comic books. The artists working in this movement used the mass production of their age to produce their work, which often includes repeated images. These reflect posters and the rows of products that could be found on supermarket shelves (supermarkets themselves were new in the 1960s). Iconic images from films and television were often taken and altered. Andy Warhol was one of the artists working in this style.

'Op' art (Britain, 1960s)

Op art is short for 'optical art'. The artists working in this movement were interested in deceiving the eye of the viewer in different ways, creating optical illusions. Work was often in black and white and very sharp and well defined. The British artist Bridget Riley was a major exponent of op art, but she also worked in dazzling colours that contrasted and created strong after-images in complementary colours. Her research was highly mathematical and exact, and the illusions she created were not there by chance.

Naïve and Primitive artists

This is not an art movement but a style or type of art. It is often used to describe the work of artists who have received no formal training in art, who have come to painting relatively late in life, or who use aspects of folk art extensively or have a childlike quality. Rousseau and Lowry could be described as having Naïve qualities.

Jack Davies, Year 1

Enhancing children's responses to and understanding of works of art

What do children gain from looking at art?

Children gain two huge advantages from looking at art. The first is that they learn about their heritage as artists – whether that heritage is national or worldwide. For this, they need to see as wide a variety of paintings as possible, so that their working definitions are flexible and generous.

The second gain is to children's own artwork and working methods. Children who have examined other art forms will work with greater technique (provided they have been led to consider how the work was done) and a greater openness about what their painting materials can do. Hopefully, they will also have been inspired by the passion and interest communicated by the teacher. With careful choice of artworks and skilful questioning, children can be led, open-eyed and open-hearted, into the world of the visual arts.

How to access works of art

If the teacher has access to an interactive whiteboard, and most classrooms do have them now, it is relatively easy to download large-scale images of works of art so that children may look at the image at the same time and share their responses. The easiest way is to use the Google search engine (www.google.co.uk) and click on 'Images'. In the search box, enter the image or artist you want and this will bring up a selection of images to choose from.

If an interactive whiteboard is not an option (perhaps work is taking place in an art room where there is no board, or a board is not available for whatever reason), then the school will need to build up a collection of reproductions of works of art, from postcard-sized reproductions to large posters. If the school has contact with a local artist who is able to lend or come and show some of their work, then this opportunity should be exploited. To hear an artist talk about their work is a powerful experience, as is hearing background information about art from an art expert.

In the absence of artists, however, there are many different ways to encourage children to respond to a work of art, to draw them in and to involve them. The teacher can talk about the painting and the children can also talk about it.

What to say and what to ask

Questions the teacher might ask break down into four areas:

* Description: what do you see?
* Analysis: how are things put together?
* Interpretation: what is the artist trying to say?
* Judgement: what do you think of it?

It is probably best to ask children what they see, know and think before we tell them what we see, know and think, although it is tempting to talk first when we are sharing a picture we know and to which we have a strong response ourselves. Between the whole class, they may spot more than we think they will. If we have some information and questions ready, we can fill in the gaps and extend their understanding.

Possible questions might include:

Opening questions
* What do you see?
* Do you like the painting?
* Why?
* What is going on in the picture?
* Do you think there is a story behind it?
* What time of year, day and season do you think it is?
* Do you think it was painted long ago, a while ago, or quite recently?
* Is it realistic (lifelike)?

Colour
* Is the painting bright and colourful?
* Are the colours mostly pale/all in one colour/dark?
* Is there one colour that stands out?
* Why is this?
* Does that colour help the feeling of the painting?
* Has the artist used hot or cold colours?
* How does this fit in with the subject?
* What (kinds of) colours have been used?
* Are the colours 'real life' colours?
* Why is the sky that colour?

Portraits
* Do you know, or have you heard of, the person in the painting?

* Do you think they would have liked it?
* How many people are in the picture?
* What do you think this or that person is thinking/feeling?
* What might they say if they could speak to you?
* Can you see any groups of people within the picture?
* What are they doing?
* Why do you think the artist has put them in?
* How would you describe the clothes they are wearing?
* Which one would you like/not like to be?

General

* What is the weather like?
* Where do you think the light is coming from?
* What might have happened before/after this moment?
* Can you see the artist's brush strokes?
* Why do you think they chose this subject?
* What shapes can you find?
* Would you buy this picture?
* Would you hang it on your wall?
* Why do you think this picture was painted?

* How does this picture make you feel?
* What do you think of it?
* If you had painted it, is there anything you would have changed?
* What do you think the artist was feeling when they painted this?
* Do you think they enjoyed painting it?
* Why do you think that?
* Have you seen the painting before? Where?

Once the first few questions start and children make different responses, it is quite easy to extend this by asking children if they agree or disagree with what someone else has said.

It is important, when the children are discussing their own responses to a work of art, that they understand that they are entitled to have an opinion that is different from those of others. They should know that the artist may well have wanted people to look at their work and have very different responses. Children must feel free to make comment without fear of censure from other children.

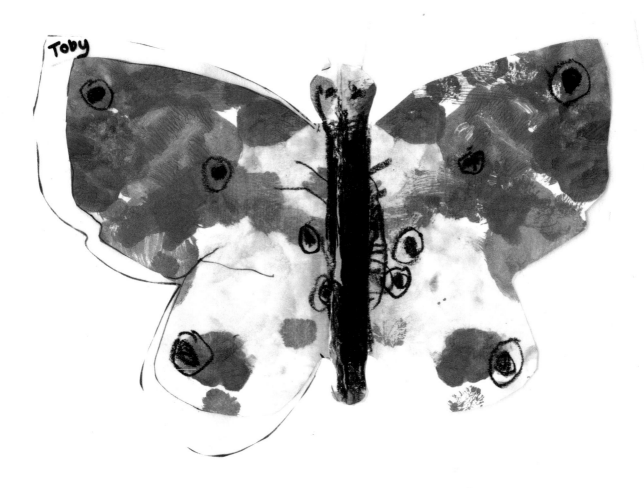

Toby Short, Year 1

Using the work of Hundertwasser (seaside pier pictures)

ACTIVITY

Time
2 hours

Resources
Newspaper for tables

Per group of children:
Pots of made-up 'Brusho®' (see pages 13 and 67) in a selection of bright colours
2–3 boxes of oil pastels
2–3 pots of water

For each child:
A3 cartridge paper
1 medium long-handled brush

For the teacher:
Access to the work of Hundertwasser:
'If you go across the fields you arrive at Grossweissenbach' and others similar
Pictures of seaside piers
Information about Hundertwasser on page 84

National Curriculum
1a,c, 2a,b,c, 4a, 5a

Alanah Stenning, Year 2

Note
You can buy postcard sets of Hundertwasser's work, which are very useful as they can be handed out for children to look at. Books published by Taschen are also available; once you have seen his work, you will want to use it again and again.

Introduction
The Austrian architect and painter Hundertwasser hated straight lines. He felt that straight lines were hard and ugly, so he rounded all the edges on his buildings. You are going to draw some seaside piers in oil pastels as if they had been designed by Hundertwasser. You will then paint over the lines with clear bright colours. Hundertwasser loved bright colours, as you can see from his paintings.

Practical activity
✳ Show the children pictures of Hundertwasser's buildings and designs and drawings and ask them what they think of his work.
✳ Draw their attention to the onion-shaped domes and the lines he drew on them, and ask them to look at the bright lines and colours that he used.
✳ Ask the children what they think of his work.
✳ Now show the pictures of seaside piers with fancy-shaped roofs like the domes on

Russian churches, and iron legs that go into the sea.
✳ Tell them that they are going to draw some piers, but in his style, with lots of lines and bright colours.
✳ They should start by drawing two horizontal lines about 10–12 cm apart across the middle of the paper in a light-coloured oil pastel. This will be the middle of the pier, the walkway and the shops, etc.
✳ Next, in a different colour, children could draw some onion-shaped roofs on the top of the pier and draw coloured lines on them following the curve of the dome.
✳ Now tell them to look at the pictures of piers again and note the patterns of the iron legs that support them. Then they should draw in their own pier supports. These should run down into the sea.
✳ Next they should decorate the middle area of the pier to represent the entertainments, cafes, kiosks and shops. They could draw squares with rounded corners and concentric shapes inside in different colours.
✳ The children could also draw lines in the sky and wave patterns in the sea.
✳ Now they can paint over their picture in Brusho® in different bright colours, using whatever sized brushes are appropriate. The sea should go right over the legs of the pier to emphasize the fact that the pier stands out in the sea.

Using the work of Georgia O'Keeffe (painting flowers)

ACTIVITY

Time
2 hours

Link
Science
Parts of flowers

Resources
Newspaper to cover tables

Per pair of children:
Powder paint or ready-mixed colours:
• crimson + vermilion red
• cyan + brilliant blue
• lemon + brilliant yellow
1 water pot
1 palette

For each child:
1 medium long-handled brush
1 fine long-handled brush
A3 cartridge paper
Test paper

For the teacher:
Access to Georgia O'Keeffe's flower paintings
If possible, some flowers – if not, pictures of flowers
Information about O'Keeffe on page 83

National Curriculum
2a, 4a, 5a,d

Spike Hutchings, Year 2

Note
This work can be done with poppies and makes a lovely Remembrance Day display.

Introduction
Georgia O'Keeffe was an American artist who loved to paint huge paintings of flowers that filled the page, often all in one colour (all red like poppies, or white like lilies). She had loved painting and drawing flowers ever since her art teacher asked her to draw a wild flower called 'Jack in the Pulpit'. She loved painting wild flowers as well as garden or hothouse flowers. She painted big petals in lovely colours, dark middles with markings on, and details like stamens. Sometimes her flowers could even look a bit scary, as if they were going to eat you up! You are going to paint some lovely big flowers and include some dark markings and details too.

Practical activity
❋ Show children Georgia O'Keeffe flower pictures and ask them to tell you what they notice (the size, colour and shapes, etc).

❋ Children should now look at the flowers they will be painting and note the shape of the petals, the colours, the centre and the stamens. They could draw them if they have time.

❋ Quickly revise handling and mixing powder paint, if necessary.

❋ Remind children to test colours on their test papers before they use a colour.

❋ Emphasize that they will be working on a large flower and that it should fill the page just as the artist's work did.

❋ Tell the children to paint the outline shape of the flower in a pale, watered-down version of the flower colour.

❋ Looking carefully at the shape of the petals, they should over-paint the shape of these in a slightly deeper shade of the same colour.

❋ Next, they could paint in the petals, making the colours go deeper or lighter as they go into the centre.

❋ The dark middle can be added last, plus any markings or stamens.

❋ The background could be painted a very dark colour to make the flowers stand out, or they can be cut out and laminated. This really brings the colours out.

Using the work of Gustav Klimt (mixed media: oil pastels, Brusho® and collage)

ACTIVITY

Time
An afternoon

Link
RE

Resources
Newspapers for the tables
Oil pastels
Variety of sizes and coloured sequins
Glue sticks

For three or four children:
Black, yellow and purple Brusho®,
mixed in pots.

For each child:
A3 sized photocopy of Klimt's 'Tree
of Life'
A3 white cartridge paper or, if tracing
tree, A3 thin (photocopy) paper
1 medium long-handled brush
1 black permanent pen

For the teacher:
Access to 'The tree of life' by Gustav
Klimt
Information about Klimt on page 84

National Curriculum
2a,b, 4a, 5a

Lucy Clements, Year 2 (in the style of Gustav Klimt)

Introduction
You are going do some beautiful pictures of a big tree, you can draw your own big tree or trace this one.

Practical activity
✳ Show children the painting of 'The tree of life' and explain to them that the artist Klimt took his inspiration from the Old Testament of the Bible, which mentions the tree of life. The tree of life, as a symbol, pops up in many different religions. The tree represents growth and change and the energy of the earth and all the stages of life from baby to old age, from seed to great tree. (The black bird represents death, but you don't need to mention this.)
✳ Point out the flowers around the base of the tree, the patterns on the bark, the curling shapes of the branches and the hidden eyes.
✳ Ask children to draw a big tree with curling branches that fills the page right from top to bottom on the paper. Younger, or less able, children could paperclip the photocopy

behind thin white paper and trace it through. This is possible with photocopier paper.
✳ When the tree is drawn, they should use colourful oil pastels and draw circles of colours to represent the flowers around the base of the tree and patterns along the trunk and branches.
✳ Next, tell the children to colour in the trunk and branches in any way they like with oil pastels. They could add leaves in pen if they like, or outline the tree and branches in a different colour pastel.
✳ Children should now choose a colour for the background and paint right over the tree and the background. A different colour or the same colour could be used for the foreground.
✳ When the picture is dry they could:
  • scrape off some of the pastels to reveal the colours below with an opened paper clip;
  • over-colour the background behind the tree in white oil pastel so that it stands out;
  • stick on sequins to represent flowers.

Using the work of Monet (water lily paintings)

Time
2 hours

Resources
Newspaper to cover tables

Per pair of children:
Blue, green pink and purple pearlescent paint
Green, white, yellow and crimson ready-mixed colours
1 water pot
1 palette

For each child:
1 large long-handled brush
1 medium long-handled brush
A3 cartridge paper
Test paper

For the teacher:
Access to Monet's water lily paintings
Information about Monet on page 83

National Curriculum
2a, 4a, 5a

James Latham, Year 1

Note
The contrast between pearlescent paint and the flat colour of ready-mixed paint is attractive and helps to differentiate between the plants and the water.

Introduction
Monet was a French artist who loved painting outside. He would often paint the same scene over and over again to capture the light, the time of year and the mood. He had a beautiful garden and he spent years and years painting different views of it. In this garden he had a water lily pond that he loved to paint. You are going to paint a picture a bit like his. You will paint the water and then the lily pads and the lily flowers floating on it.

Practical activity
❋ Show the children some of Monet's water lily paintings and discuss the differences between the different versions, the colours, the scale of the picture (some of Monet's paintings are huge) and the composition.

❋ Point out that you can see his brush strokes, and say that in their paintings their brush strokes will show too.

❋ Tell the children to paint the whole of the background in streaks of blue and green

pearlescent paint. The blues and greens should vary a little.

❋ Explain that it is important that the brush strokes go from side to side, horizontally, across the page, as this will help to create the illusion of water. If the brushstrokes are painted vertically or in different directions, the background will not look quite so much like water. This might seem like a small point, but it makes all the difference.

❋ Next, they should add a few horizontal streaks of lavender blue (made by mixing the blue and purple pearlescent paint).

❋ Tell children to switch now to the ready-mixed paint and mix the green and white, with a little yellow, to make a pale green. They should use variations of this colour to paint broad strokes dotted about the paper, to be the lily pads.

❋ Now they should use the medium brush to mix the pearlescent pink and ready-mixed white together to make a range of pinks, from deep pink to palest pink.

❋ Now they should paint, using a series of short brush strokes, the petals of the lilies.

❋ Lastly, they could add a dot or two of yellow in the centre of the flowers.

Other techniques and media

Paul and Nicky, Year 1 (mixed media, page 98)

Other methods of applying paint

It is important to point out that brushes are not the only method of applying paint to a surface. Most children enjoy inventing and making their own painting implements. Children should have the opportunity to experiment with such things as fingers, rags, strips of card, rollers and sponges.

Sponges, for example, offer endless opportunities for painting experiments. Rough textures and special effects can be achieved when paints of different consistencies are applied with natural or synthetic sponges of various degrees of coarseness.

Cotton buds are useful as they are easy to hold and are absorbent, and they keep their shape well. They are especially useful for painting small, precise areas, such as petals and stamens of flowers, or for painting in the style of the Pointillists or Aborigine dot pictures.

Fur fabric can be used to apply paint, for example to create a grassy effect.

Single prints can be made from paintings while the paint is still wet by placing a sheet of paper on the top of the painting and peeling it off.

Marbles can be rolled in paint and then rolled across the paper.

Paint can also be:
* Dropped or dripped onto the paper
* Thrown on as in action painting (if you are very brave, have a large space to work in and are prepared for the ensuing mess)
* Splattered on by pulling back the bristle of a stiff brush such as a toothbrush or a washing-up brush
* Sprayed on with a diffuser or an aerosol can
* Blown in different directions along the page through a straw (thin paint or ink)
* Sprinkled onto a wet surface as dry powder
* Scraped with a variety of implements

Texture

Fabric can be pressed into wet paint to create a texture in a painting.

Thick paint can be applied with a plastic or palette knife to create a rough, uneven texture which is called 'impasto'.

Substances can be added to paint to make it thicker or textured, including PVA, sawdust, salt, starch, flour, icing sugar, crushed eggshells, sand or Polyfilla®.

Paint applied thickly can be scraped with twigs or the ends of brushes to make lines and marks in the paint.

Bits and pieces can be dropped onto thick wet paint such as dry grass, sand, sawdust, tissue paper, foil, thin fabric, netting or glitter.

Max Wild, Year 1

Pearlescent paint: peacock feathers

ACTIVITY

Time
45 min

Resources
Newspaper to cover tables

Per pair of children:
Pearlescent paint in green, blue and gold
Metallic gold pen
1 palette
1 peacock feather

For each child:
A5 black paper
1 medium paintbrush
Protective clothing
Sketchbook
Pencil

For the teacher:
Some peacock feathers
Paper to demonstrate

National Curriculum
2a,b, 4a, 5a

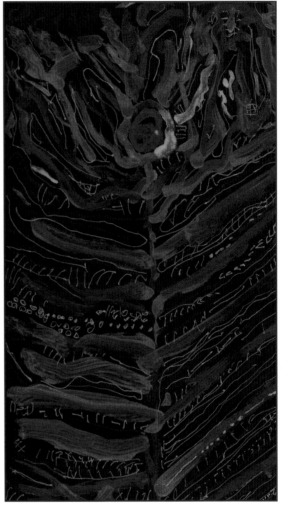

Briony Steele, Year 2

Note
There is information about pearlescent paint on page 12.

Introduction
You are going to use a special kind of paint today, it is called pearlescent paint and it has a lovely shimmery shine. You can mix the colours together just as you would with other paints, so you could mix the blue and green and get a lovely pearly greeny-blue which we could call 'peacock blue'. Pearlescent paint is thinner than usual ready-mixed paint, so the paper might show through it a little. Today you are going to try it on black paper.

Practical activity
❉ Demonstrate the colours and show the children the pearly effect.
❉ Show them a peacock feather and discuss the colours and markings.
❉ Point out that the feather has a shimmer to it as well.

❉ Ask the children to look closely at the feathers and draw one in their sketchbooks.
❉ Draw their attention to the way the feather grows.
❉ Tell the children to draw, in pencil, a line right down the middle of the paper for the centre of the feather (this might be a curved line, depending on the feather).
❉ Now ask them to draw in the fronds of the feather and the eye in the top area.
❉ Now they have the shape, they could paint in the eye blue, with gold and green circles round it, and then the fronds.
❉ They could add the tiny fronds that grow out of each main frond with gold metallic pen.
❉ These could be cut out and displayed in an open fan shape and a peacock's body placed over the middle, to look like a peacock displaying its tail feathers.

Pearlescent paint: butterflies

ACTIVITY

Time
45 min

Links
Maths
Symmetry
Science
Minibeasts

Resources
Newspaper to cover tables

Per pair of children:
Pearlescent paint in full range of colours
1 palette
Tissue paper circles in two sizes

For each child:
A4 paper
1 large long-handled brush
Black oil pastel or permanent pen
Protective clothing

For the teacher:
Some pictures of butterflies
Paper to demonstrate

National Curriculum
1a, 2a,b, 4a, 5a

Giles Gellay, Year 1

Note
There is information about pearlescent paint on page 12.

Introduction
You are going to use a special kind of paint today. It is called pearlescent paint and it has a lovely shimmery shine. You can mix the colours together just as you would with other paints. Today, though, you are going to let the colours mix themselves. You are going to make some butterflies. Butterflies' wings are often beautiful shimmery colours, so the pearlescent paint is ideal to use.

Practical activity
* Show the children pictures of butterflies and discuss their wings' colours and patterns.
* Demonstrate printing a butterfly by:
  1. Folding the paper in half and opening it again.
  2. Placing some big blobs of different colours of pearlescent paint on one side.
  3. Folding the paper and pressing down, pushing the paint away from the fold.
  4. Opening it up.
  5. Adding more colours in other places.
  6. Folding the paper again and pressing down on it.
* Children can now have a go themselves. They should try several different colour combinations.
* Talk to the children about symmetry and tell them to place the tissue paper circles in exactly the same position on either side of the wings. They could place a smaller circle of a different colour inside the first.
* When the pictures are dry, they could add a body, head, feelers and markings with a black oil pastel or pen.
* These can be cut out and then laminated with a sheet of coloured tissue paper behind them, and cut to make a tissue paper coloured border around the edge of the butterfly.
* If the wings are folded back on either side of the body and pinned to a board with a pin through the body, they make a lovely 3-D display, particularly if they are displayed pinned around some paintings of flowers. (See the lesson: Using the work of Georgia O'Keeffe (painting flowers) on page 91.)

Mixed media: oil pastels, Brusho®, collage, rubbings and drawing

ACTIVITY

Time
An afternoon

Links
D&T
Materials
Houses and homes

Resources
Newspapers for the tables
Oil pastels
Scissors
Glue sticks

For three or four children:
Brick red, pink and slate grey
Brusho®, mixed in pots

For each child:
A4 sized photocopy of roof tiles (see note below)
1 medium long-handled brush
1 black permanent pen
Thick black crayon
Thin white paper for rubbings

For the teacher:
Access to pictures of houses, if not going out to look at them

National Curriculum
2a,b, 4a, 5a

Andrew Loat, Year 1

Note
Tile, stone and brick patterned paper, which is used for papering dolls' houses, is ideal for this. It can be obtained from craft shops.

Introduction
You are going do be looking closely at houses and homes, the shape of doors and windows and roofs, and thinking about what materials have been used and the textures of the materials. Then you will be making a picture of a house. You will do some rubbings, some painting, some drawing and some cutting and sticking.

Practical activity
* Show the children some pictures of houses or go for a walk to look at them. The children could do some quick sketches in their sketchbooks. Discuss the shapes, patterns, textures and materials they can see.
* Children should take a big black crayon and lay a piece of paper on a textured surface (eg a chair seat, a wall, carpet, floor or the playground surface) and make rubbings.
* Explain the key points in achieving a good rubbing:
  * Don't let the paper move
  * Use the side of the crayon
  * Rub the crayon to and fro firmly, pressing down well.
* Now children should draw a large rectangle, on their best rubbing, to be the house.
* Tell them to cut a piece of tile paper in a roof shape and stick it on the top of the rectangle.
* Next, the children should think about window and door shapes and how many they want. They should cut these out of the other rubbings, stick them down and draw on frames and panes of glass in permanent pen.
* Details can be added in pen: guttering, drainpipes doorknobs, etc.
* Climbing roses could be drawn up the front of the house in oil pastels.
* Lastly, the children should over-paint the roof and walls in Brusho®.

ACTIVITY Aborigine dreamtime painting

Time
1 hour

Links
Other cultures
Journeys

Resources
Newspaper to cover tables

Per pair of children:
Black, white and one other colour
ready-mixed paint (see note below)
Pot of water

For each child:
1 medium long-handled brush
A3 coloured sugar paper
Pencil

For the teacher:
Access to some dreamtime Aborigine
pictures showing pathways

National Curriculum
2b, 4a,c, 5a

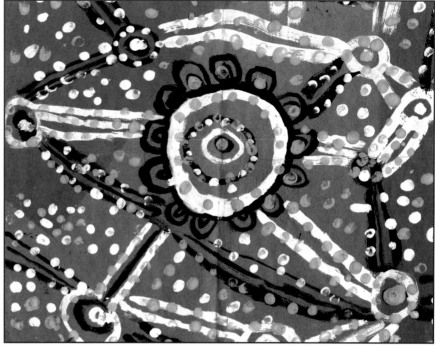

Chloe Gregory, Year 1

Note
If brown or cream sugar paper is used as the background, and an earth colour – yellow, orange or a brown – is used as the third colour, this will give the artwork a more authentic Aborigine look.

Introduction
The Aborigine people of Australia use many different symbols in their artwork. Circles inside other circles mean campsites, water holes or resting places. Several lines in a row mean people travelling or pathways. Wavy lines mean running water or smoke. Dots mean lots of different things like rain, eggs, ants and other things. Sometimes they create whole pictures out of dots of different colours. They use natural materials that they find in the areas where they live to make their colours. You are going to use ready-mixed paint as it is nice and thick. You will paint lines with brushes and print dots with your fingers.

Practical activity
* Show the children the Aborigine artwork and point out the lines, concentric circles, dots and other symbols.

* The children should then draw, in pencil, some concentric circles in the middle of the paper.
* Next, they should draw some smaller circles in other places on the paper.
* Tell the children to join up the small circles to the central circle and to each other with double lines. Now all the circles should be joined. They could make some double lines that go off the page from the small circles.
* Explain that these lines represent journeys of people between campsites, water holes and resting places.
* Now tell the children to paint over the lines, using white or black paint, or first black then white.
* Lastly, they should print dots, in the third colour, with their fingers on top of the black and white lines.

SKILL # Line and wash

Time
45 min

Links
Literacy/History/Transport

Resources
Newspaper to cover tables
Scissors
Glue sticks

For the background:
A3 white/beige sugar paper
A3 blue sugar paper
Chalky pastels

For the ship:
1 pot of pale brown Brusho® (to share with small group)
A4 paper
1 small short-handled brush
1 black fine-line pen
Protective clothing
Sketchbook

For the teacher:
If wanted: A copy of *The Mousehole Cat* to read (or pirate stories)
Some pictures of pirate boats, galleons, etc

National Curriculum
1a, 2a,b, 4a, 5a

Madeleine Nichols, Year 2

Introduction

You are going to create a sea scene and then do some drawings of ships in black pen to go on the sea, but we will be painting over the pen drawing with brown Brusho® to make the ship look as if it is made of wood. Most felt-tip pens are water-based, and if you wet them after you have drawn with them, the colour runs a little and it can make some nice effects. You can paint over a felt-tip drawing and make your drawing look soft and blurry. This is what artists call 'line and wash', and it is a very old technique that artists have used for a very long time. Even thousands of years ago, they were doing it – not with felt-tip pens, of course, because they were not invented then, but with pens made from feathers and ink and some paint or water.

Composition note

If the children draw or paint boats bang on the horizon, they never look very believable. If the boat is well down on the sea, it gives more interest in the foreground and brings the eye down the page.

Practical activity

To make the background

※ Tell the children to fold and cut the blue paper in half and stick it down onto the white/beige background to create the sea.
※ Next, they should draw stormy wave patterns on the sea and storm clouds in the sky, perhaps adding some seagulls and some dark hills on the horizon.
※ Children can now smudge the sea and clouds to create a sombre atmosphere.

To make the boat

※ Show the children pictures of old boats, fishing boats, galleons or whatever is appropriate to the subject, in this case it was *The Mousehole Cat*, but it would work equally well for pirates or for a topic on the history of water transport.
※ Children should practise drawing boats in their sketchbooks; encourage them to add detail, such as nail marks on the wood, masts, riggings, flags, sails, etc.
※ Now they should draw their favourite or most suitable boat in black fine-line pen on white paper. They could draw the cat and the fisherman on board the boat if they want.
※ Next, children should dip their brushes in the weak solution of brown Brusho® and paint over the hull, cabin and sails of the boat. This gives it an 'olde worlde' look.
※ Lastly, they should cut the boat out and glue it on the picture, below the horizon.

Creating a batik effect

SKILL

Time
45 min

Resources
Newspapers for the tables

For a group of three or four children:
Black Brusho®, mixed in a pot, with
three or four brushes in each pot
Selection of coloured crayons

For each child:
1 piece of A5 thin white paper

For the teacher:
Some batik fabric
Paper to demonstrate
An old iron and a pile of newspaper
or paper towels

National Curriculum
2a, 4a,c, 5a

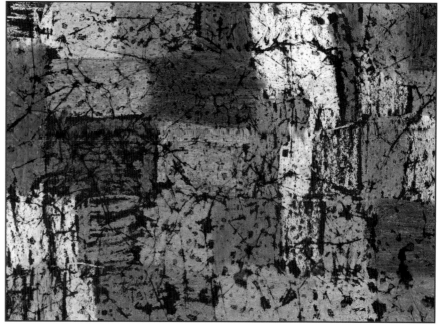

Richard Grasske, Year 1

Introduction

There is a technique of printing on fabric called 'batik'. To do batik you need hot wax and special tools, but today you are going to create a similar look to batik but just using crayons and Brusho®. Batik works by painting hot wax onto cloth and then dyeing the cloth with a colour. Where the wax is, the dye won't take. If the wax has been cracked by crumpling the fabric, the colour will get in the cracks and it makes an interesting effect. It is that effect that we are going to try to create today.

Practical activity

✳ Show the children the fabric and point out the places where the cracks are. If the fabric has several colours, explain that the fabric will have been re-painted with wax and new colours added several times to get a multicoloured effect.

✳ Tell them to cover their piece of paper with patches of thickly applied crayon in different bright colours. Demonstrate (see 'Potential pitfall' below).

✳ Now tell the children to screw up their drawings. They seem to love doing this, especially if you say, 'What a load of old rubbish, this is going in the bin' and screw up your own paper. It is a hoary old joke, but they always seem to like it!

✳ When they have screwed up their papers, tell

them to straighten and smooth them out very carefully. You can say 'Nah, I've changed my mind – we'll keep them.'

✳ Then tell them to screw them up again, saying they will be dumped after all.

✳ Then seem to change your mind again and tell them to straighten them again. Warn them that the paper may have become fragile and they need to open them out very, very carefully or the paper will rip.

✳ The crumpling up and smoothing out should be repeated about three or four times, until the wax crayon colouring is creased and cracked all over.

✳ Now the children should paint over their smoothed paper with black Brusho®. They should paint over once quickly and not do more than one coat, or the crayon colours may go dark and start to disappear.

✳ Finally, when the papers are dry, place each one between two layers of newspaper or paper towels and iron them until they are smooth.

Potential pitfall

In order for the cracked effect to work well, children will need to colour very strongly so that there is a good layer of crayon on every part of the paper.

USING SKILL · Painting 2-D and 3-D in ready-mixed paints (Session 1: 2-D)

Time
1 hour

Links
Maths
Shape

Resources
Newspapers for the tables

For a pair of children:
Black, white, yellow, orange, brown,
pink and light blue ready-mixed paint
1 palette
1 water pot

For each child:
1 piece of A3 cartridge paper
1 medium long-handled brush
Protective clothing

For the teacher:
Box of liquorice allsorts
Paper to demonstrate

National Curriculum
2a, 4a, 5a

Jade Tanton, Year 2

Note
This activity is the first of two linked sessions. It works well with ready-mixed paint, as the focus is on the shape and appearance of the sweets and not the colour mixing. The thickness of the paint is ideal and the colours can be saved by putting cling film over the pots. This can be used for painting the clay sweets another day.

Introduction
You are going to try to paint pictures of these sweets so that people can recognize which sweets they are. To do this, you will need to look at the shapes of the sweets carefully and notice what colours they all are. You will be making sweets out of clay and painting them another day.

Practical activity
* Show the children the sweets and discuss their shapes. They should notice which ones have round faces and which have square faces. (The 3-D shapes can be covered when they make the sweets out of clay.)
* Point out that some sweets have a black circle of liquorice in the middle and some have a stripe of liquorice.
* Children could start by painting some black

circles and stripes dotted around the page.
* They may well need to change the water before going on to the lighter colours; remind them that they must wash their brushes well.
* Now the children should paint pink and yellow circles around the black circles to be the coconut sweets.
* They could paint some pink and some pale blue circles to be the speckled jelly sweets. Darker dots can be added later when they are dry.
* Next, the children could paint some brown, orange or white stripes either side of the black stripes to make the liquorice sandwich sweets.
* Older or more able children could make the many-layered liquorice sandwich sweets in black, white and yellow.
* The background could be left white or painted a contrasting colour.

Potential pitfall
Do use good quality art paper. I didn't, and if you look at the art work illustrated you will see that the paper has wrinkled.

Painting 2-D and 3-D in ready-mixed paints (Session 2: 3-D)

USING SKILL

Time
1 hour

Links
Maths
3-D shape

Resources
Newspapers for the tables
Clay

For each child:
Lump of clay wrapped in a wet paper towel to stop it from drying out
1 clay board
Named piece of card to put clay sweets on
Protective clothing
Ready-mixed paints (see page 102)

For the teacher:
Box of Liquorice Allsorts
Clay to demonstrate

National Curriculum
1a, 2a,b, 4a, 5a

Connor Norden, Year 2

Note
This is the second of two linked sessions. The sweets will have to be left overnight to be dry enough to paint. The colours from the previous session should be used.

Introduction
You are going make sweets out of clay and you are going to think carefully about the shape of each one and try to make it, as near as possible, the same shape as the real sweet. It is not as difficult as it looks and I will show you how to make each one. You will paint them when they are dry.

Practical activity
* Give each child a small lump of clay and allow them ten minutes or less to play around with it and make it into whatever they like. This is so that they won't feel quite so restricted when they have to focus on just making 3-D shapes.
* Start by making a sphere. Tell the children to break off a little lump of clay about the size of a marble and roll it between their palms or on the board until is as close to being spherical as they can manage. Some younger children will need support throughout this activity.

* Now tell them to flatten their ball slightly between their palms to make a cylinder of a similar shape to the coconut sweet or the speckled jelly sweet.
* They could make about six of these and set them aside on their piece of named card.
* Next, the children should make a slightly larger sphere, rolling it as before and then flattening it slightly to make the same shape as before. If they gently squeeze either side of the cylinder (not the circular faces) with a finger and thumb, the cylinder will gradually get straight edges. They will not be able to get sharp corners, but that doesn't matter.
* They should again make about six of these and put them on the card. These will be the liquorice sandwiches.
* Children should now take a piece of clay about the size of a marble and roll it in their palms until it makes a longer cylinder. This will be the liquorice black and white tube.
* To make the two end faces circular, they should just tap each face down on the board. They should make two or three of these.
* If they have any bits left, they could try making a little 'Bertie Bassett' figure.
* When they are dry, the clay sweets can be painted the same colours as the real Allsorts, using the same colours that the children used in the previous lesson. They will look surprisingly realistic.
* The sweets, along with the paintings, make a lovely art/maths display.

SKILL   Scraped painting (two versions)

Time
10 min per child

Resources
Newspaper to cover tables
Thick card cut at one end to make
a jagged comb (or lolly sticks, twigs,
glue spreaders, etc)
Any colour of ready-mixed paint,
Thick brushes or pieces of stiff card
to spread paint
Paint can be thickened (see page 18)

For each child:
A3 or A4 paper (see note below)
Protective clothing

National Curriculum
2a,b, 4a

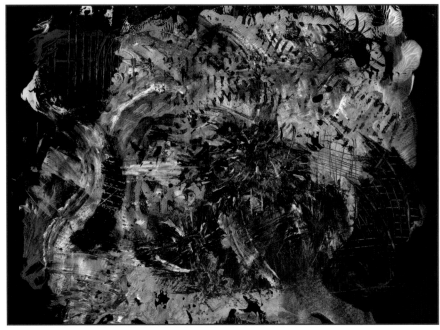

Diane Stubbs, Year 1

Note
If a dark colour is used for the background, then use a light-coloured paint, and vice versa. The painting can look good done in black on a multi-coloured background, which perhaps the children have prepared, eg by rollering paint over or printing with scrunched-up fabric. This makes the end results more visually exciting and more interesting to display.

Introduction
Painting with thick paint and scraping it off to make a picture is easy and good fun to do. It is actually a way of making a picture or changing parts of a picture that artists have used for a long time. Sometimes they might scrape away the paint in just one part of a picture to make that part of it interesting, but you are going to do the whole picture that way.

Practical activity 1
Children should:
* Spread thick paint onto the paper, thickly and right across the surface evenly, using the flat edge of a piece of stiff card or a decorator's brush.
* Scrape a pattern or picture into the wet paint with a lolly stick, a pre-cut jagged-ended

card or whatever implements you have. The colour of the paper beneath will show through where the paint has been scraped away.
* Some children could scrape some finer detail, using the end of an opened paper clip, or remove the paint around the image to leave a painted border.
* A print could be taken from this while the paint is still wet.

Practical activity 2
The children could also try:
* Pouring thick paints in different colours onto a plate or printing tray.
* Dipping the flat edge of stiff card into the paint and scraping it along the paper.
* They could try changing direction with the card without lifting it from the paper, and turning the end of the card so the paint makes arcs of colour.

Finger painting and mono printing

SKILL

Time
5 min per child
Links
Maths
Symmetry
Resources
Newspaper to cover tables
A flat surface to work on
Any colour of ready-mixed paint
(pearlescent works well)
Paper towel or damp cloth
For each child:
Several sheets of coloured paper (see
note below)
Protective clothing
National Curriculum
2a,b, 4a

Linda Dixon, Year 1

Note
If a dark colour is used for the background, then use a light-coloured paint, and vice versa. The prints can look good on a multi-coloured background, which perhaps the children have prepared, eg by rollering paint over or printing with scrunched-up fabric. This makes the end results more visually exciting and more interesting to display.

Introduction
This doesn't really need an introduction, but you could tell the children that they are going to try some printing. Explain that printing is when you press paper down on a freshly inked or painted surface and then peel it away, and that the picture you get is called a print. Sometimes you can make lots of prints, but the sort you will do today will give you just one print.

Practical activity
* Tell the children to spread a quantity of paint onto a flat surface; this could be more than one colour so that the colours mix in the process.
* While the paint is still wet, ask them to draw a picture or a pattern in it with the tip of their finger.

* They should then wipe their finger quickly on a paper towel or damp cloth.
* Ask the children to put their name on the back of their paper and place it directly over the picture.
* Next, they should smooth it down with their hands, not pressing too hard.
* Now tell them to pull the paper away carefully.
* A print could be taken of this print by pressing it down again on another piece of paper. This is nice to do when the children have written words or numbers, as they will come out the same way again.

The two prints can be exhibited side by side as part of a display on symmetry.

Potential pitfall
Children will need to work quickly, as marks can only be drawn and prints taken while the paint is still wet.

SKILL

Stencilling with torn paper

Time
45 min for individual work

Resources
Newspaper to cover tables
Newspaper to tear up
Several different colours of ready-mixed paint
1 medium paintbrush
Oil pastels

For each child:
A3 or A4 paper (see note below)
Protective clothing

National Curriculum
2a,b, 4a

Years 1 and 2 group project (other examples of this activity can be seen on pages 13, 16 and 20)

Note
If a dark colour is used for the background, then use a lighter-coloured paint, and vice versa. The painting can look good done on a background which the children have already prepared, eg by drawing or writing over with oil pastels. The example illustrated was built up in layers over more than one session. It was a large-scale group activity, using A1-sized paper, but the activity can be done individually.

Introduction
You can cover some areas of a picture with pieces of paper and paint over or around them. When the pieces of paper are lifted off, the shape of the paper is left behind. This is called stencilling. It is quite easy; the only tricky bit is stopping the paper moving while you are painting over it.

Practical activity
Children should:
1. Lay scraps of torn newspaper randomly over the background.

2. Hold each piece down with a finger.
3. Paint outwards from their finger over the newspaper and onto the surrounding area of background.
4. Lift off the newspaper before the paint is quite dry.

Children could:
1. Outline those areas left unpainted in oil pastels and draw on the painted areas.
2. Lay more scraps of newspaper and repeat steps 1–4 in a different contrasting colour or type of paint. Pearlescent paint looks good painted over other paints, as it is semi-translucent.
3. When that layer is dry, the children could add more drawings and so on, to create a many-layered picture. This works well when children work on a larger scale and in a group.

Drip and blow paintings

SKILL

Time
1 hour

Resources
Newspaper to cover tables

Per pair of children:
Black Brusho® in a pot
2–3 bright colours of Brusho® in pots
1 water pot

For each child:
A4 white paper
A plastic straw
1 fine paintbrush
Protective clothing

For the teacher:
Paper and a straw to demonstrate

National Curriculum
2a,b, 4a, 5a

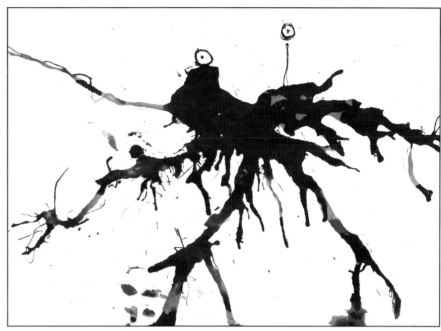

Max Hardwick, Year 1 (a goggly creature)

Note
If children blow too hard and for too long at a time, they may feel dizzy.

Introduction
You are going to try creating some pictures by dripping and blowing thin paint along the paper with a straw. You cannot ever be quite sure which way the paint will go, so the end results may not be what you planned. You have to make the best of what happens!

Practical activity
* Demonstrate the technique to children by showing the children how to:
  * drip a little Brusho® onto the paper
  * place the straw directly above the Brusho®
  * blow hard down on it
  * chase paint outwards to make spiky lines.
* Explain that they can drop a little more Brusho® on if they want to, and continue blowing.
* Tell the children to have a go at this.

* Explain that they can also crouch down, level with the paper, and blow horizontally along the surface.
* Also tell them that they can chase one Brusho® droplet along in any direction, and if they blow from above, the paint will spread outwards.
* Remind them that the Brusho® seems to have a mind of its own.
* These drippings and blowings will create abstract patterns, and the children could paint different colours in some or all of the spaces when the black paint is dry. It will look a little like stained glass.

Potential pitfall
Children must not suck instead of blow. This might seem obvious, but someone in the class will be bound to try it! Warn them that spitting down the straw will make their ink thin and pale. It will not look good. (They will do it anyway!)

SKILL

Painting with felt tips or watercolour pencils

Time
45 min or less

Resources
Per group of children:
2–3 water pots
1 fine paintbrush
Coloured water-soluble felt tips in
fine, medium and broad points, or
watercolour pencils (see note below)

For each child:
A4 cartridge paper

National Curriculum
2a,b, 4a

Daniel Rodgers, Year 2

Note
Watercolour pencils are water-soluble colouring
pencils, and the 'lead' is made of compacted
watercolour paint. They are wonderful to use with
young children, as they really enjoy seeing the colours
change when the pencil marks are wetted. The
colours obtained are surprisingly vivid, but subtle
effects can also be achieved.

Introduction
*You are going to do some drawings of (whatever the subject
is. It could be topic led, but this activity is particularly good
for drawing flowers, seaside scenes or landscapes). After you
have finished the drawings, you are going to turn them into
paintings, but not by painting them!*

Practical activity
* The children should draw whatever the
  subject is, using felt tips or watercolour
  pencils.
* Then, using the tip of the paintbrush, they
  should wet one colour at a time.
* Warn them that if they move the brush
  across several colours one after another, the
  colours will just go muddy as they will all mix
  together.
* Tell them also to try not to use too much
  water on their brushes, as they will flood the

picture and the colours will run where they do
not want them to.
* They might want to leave some areas not
  wetted to make a contrast.
* When the paintings are dry, more drawings
  could be added over the areas that were
  wetted. In this way, detail could be added
  to help create an illusion of distance. For
  example, they could draw fields and hills and
  a sky, and after those parts of the picture
  have dried they could draw trees, buildings,
  animals or people. These would seem nearer
  as the colours would be brighter.
* They also might want to add texture such as
  grass, or put back any parts of their drawings
  that have disappeared when the paper was
  wetted.

Potential pitfall
If the children are using watercolour pencils, they
might need to have a little try at drawing a few
lines and objects and then wetting them before
they embark on the main drawing. That way, they
will discover for themselves that if they colour in
very heavily, the colour is very bright when it is
wetted, while light colouring-in might disappear
altogether with too much water.

SKILL Action painting

Time
2 hours

Resources
Newspapers to cover tables
2–3 squeezy bottles of ready-mixed paint in very bright colours and also black and white (see note below)
Wellington boots with patterned soles
Toy cars, motorbikes, trucks, etc with different tyre patterns
A2 paper or larger (could be a bright colour, eg yellow)
Decorators' brushes

For each child:
Protective clothing

For the teacher:
Protective clothing, definitely!
Lots of patience!!
Information about Jackson Pollock from page 85
Information about Action painting on page 87

National Curriculum
2a,b,c, 4a, 5a,b

Katy Sparks, Year 1

Note
The paint will need to be thinned down with a little water so that it will squirt and dribble satisfactorily. If the squeezy bottles are not full, water could be added directly into the bottles. If this is not possible, some paint could be transferred to old washing-up liquid bottles.

Introduction
There was an American artist called Jackson Pollock who did paintings that were called action paintings, and you are going to do some paintings a bit like his.

Practical activity
※ Tell the children about Jackson Pollock; show his paintings, and explain how he did them.
※ Working with just one child at a time on a very large piece of paper, tell the children to take it in turns to:
  • Squeeze and dribble and splat different colours on the paper
  • Run toy cars, motorbikes, etc to and fro across the paper (or even ride a real bike across if you're brave enough!).

  • Run a roller over one or two small places where paint has fallen to create flat areas of blended paint
  • Make handprints on the paper
  • Scrape and comb the paint to and fro so that the colours blend in one or two areas
  • Flick brushes loaded with paint over the paper
  • Print some finger dots here and there
  • Walk over the painting in Wellington boots
  • Walk over the painting in bare feet.
※ This should create a busy, vibrant, multi-coloured picture full of different types of paint marks, giving an impression of movement and activity.
※ Explain to the children this is what Jackson Pollock wanted to do; he wanted the actual movements (action) of making the painting to show.

Potential pitfall
Hold childrens' hands if they do walk or ride across the painting, or they could slip on the wet paint. I didn't, and when I was doing this lesson the child made wonderful skid marks on the paper with his sliding feet. Thank goodness I caught him in time!

Oriental brush and ink paintings

SKILL

Time
45 min or less

Resources
Newspaper to cover tables

Per pair of children:
Black Brusho® in a pot
Pale grey-blue Brusho® in a pot
1 water pot

For each child:
Practice paper
A4 thick white paper
1 medium watercolour brush with a
pointed tip
1 larger brush for the background
picture
Protective clothing

For the teacher:
Paper to demonstrate
Access to Chinese/Japanese
paintings and lettering

National Curriculum
2a,b, 4a,c, 5a

Margaret Gellay, Year 2

Note
You might want to have a little go at making the marks
on your own before demonstrating (although these
marks are really quite easy).

Introduction
*In countries like China and Japan, there is a great tradition of
painting using a soft brush and black ink. Artists would learn
how to paint something in a very exact way. For example, a
bird or a tree would have to be made using particular marks
and young artists would have to learn how to make these
marks. It would be difficult to tell one artist's work from
another because they would all have a very similar look. You
are going to have a go at painting some of these marks, and
then you will paint a picture in a Japanese/Chinese style.*

Practical activity
Using black Brusho®:
* Demonstrate painting quick, fluid, straight
  brush strokes (about 6 cm in length).
* Next, tell the children to try lifting the brush at
  the end of the stroke so that the mark ends in
  a point.
* Emphasize quickness, lightness and
  smoothness in the making of the marks.

* Now ask the children to try some similar
  marks, but to make them curved.
* Now they could try painting a leaf. Tell them
  to press lightly on the brush, then press
  harder, then lightly again as they make a
  short stroke.
* Now tell the children to try using the sides
  of their brushes to make a series of short
  strokes with a space in between. This will
  represent bamboo stems.
* When they have had a little practice with
  these marks, they could try a whole painting
  by:
  * Painting a horizon with water below, in the
    pale blue/grey Brusho®, using the larger
    brush
  * Adding mountains a few centimetres
    above the horizon so that they look as if
    they are floating on the clouds
  * Using the smaller brushes to paint tall
    bamboo and shooting leaves in black right
    across the background.
* If they want, they could also try doing some
  Japanese-style lettering down one side of the
  picture.

Assessment

Simone Charles, Year 2

Assessment of painting

I am tempted to start this section with the subtitle 'If you really must'!

However, if you must, for whatever reason, here are a few pointers.

* You could keep one good example of some work at the end of a unit (say, colour mixing) and put it in a child's record of achievement with comments by both you and the child.
* You could make a note of aspects of painting where a child has excelled or struggled.
* You could make a note about attitude and confidence in relation to painting.
* You could set each child some simple targets at the end of the first term, for example:
  * Work more independently
  * Use the space on the paper better
  * Mix more of your own colours
  * Don't rush to finish
  * Stop now and then and have a think how things are going

Kyle Hettmann, Year 2

* Don't give up too easily
* Use less watery paint (ie mix it up more thickly)
* Remember to use a brush that is right for the job.

The children could add a target of their own and you could check the targets periodically to see if any of them have been met.

* You could photocopy the 'Progression of skills and experiences' list for the appropriate year group, from pages 9–10, and highlight in green the ones the children have covered or achieved and in red the ones they have struggled with. That would give you an idea of their weaknesses and strengths, and also what aspects you have covered and what they will need to do before the end of the year or in their next class.
* You could do this for the whole class or make three copies: one for each of a higher, middle and lower ability group. Or, if you are feeling very keen, you could do one for each child.
* These might be helpful when you come to write reports or on parents' evenings when you can't even think what the child looks like, let alone what they can or can't do in painting.
* You can always use lovely phrases like 'Seems to really enjoy painting' or 'Is beginning to develop an understanding of colour mixing'.
* Both phrases, of course mean nothing, but they sound positive and they don't pin you down. So, when the parent says, 'Actually he hates art,' you can reply, 'Well, perhaps that's because I'm such an old crab. But he seems to enjoy actually doing it!' Alternatively, if they say, 'She knows diddlysquat about painting,' you can reply, 'I only said she was beginning to develop an understanding … '

If the bird of Ofsted is due to land on your roof, don't worry. If you have used a range of painting media in different scales and genres, you will have done well and they will be happy. Just make sure that you display a few examples in a prominent place. Remember, if they can't find evidence of it, they may assume it is not happening. If the children have 'done well' then show it off!

Pupils' self-assessment

You should encourage self-assessment. This should really be happening during the lessons on a regular basis so that the children start to do it for themselves as they are working, without any prompting from you.

Suggest that the children look at their own work and think:

✳ Am I pleased with it? Why?

✳ Which bits work the best? Why?

✳ What would I change if I did it again/worked on it later?

✳ What is good about the colours I have used? What is not so good?

✳ How does it look from a distance?

✳ Have I done what I was asked, eg mixed up lots of browns?

✳ Do I need to do anything else to it?

✳ What about the background? Am I going to leave it like that?

Allow time for reflection at the end of a session (if that is possible with the mountains of dirty palettes in teetering piles on the draining board).

Children could be asked if they have any comments to make on what they have done, or what others have done. If they are commenting on the work of their peers, encourage a climate of 'being a critical friend' so that their comments are kindly and constructive. You could start the ball rolling by asking one child to select a painting done by another child, hold it up (if it is not dripping wet) and say if they like it and why they think it is good. Then invite that child to choose the work of someone else to comment on. This will give you opportunities to bring out teaching points and reinforce the skills covered in that session.

Leanne Stevens, Year 1

Bibliography

Allen, Janet. *Exciting Things to Do with Colour*. Marks & Spencer Ltd

Barnes, Rob. *Art & Design and Topic Work*. Routledge

Clement, Robert and Page, Shirley. *Investigating and Making in Art*. Oliver Boyd

Cummings, Robert. *Just Imagine. Ideas in Painting*. Kestrel Books (Penguin)

Cummings, Robert. *Just Look. A Book about Paintings*. Viking (Penguin)

Fitzsimmons, Su. *Start with Art*. Stanley Thornes

Gombrich, E.H. *The Story of Art*. Phaidon Press

Hart, Tony. *Small Hands Big Ideas*. Guild Publishing, London

Hay, Penny. *Introducing Painting*. NES Arnold

Hayes, Colin. *The Complete Guide to Painting and Drawing, Techniques and Materials*. Phaidon.

Heslewood, Juliet. *The History of Western Painting*. Belitha Press.

King, Penny and Roundhill, Claire. *Portraits. Artists' Workshop*. A&C Black

King, Penny and Roundhill, Claire. *Animals. Artists' Workshop*. A&C Black

Kluge, Gisela. *Drawing, Painting, Printing*. Lutterworth Press

Meager, Nigel and Ashfield, Julie. *Teaching Art at Key Stage 2*. N.S.E.A.D.

Meager, Nigel. *Teaching Art at Key Stage 1*. N.S.E.A.D.

Pluckrose, Henry. *Paints*. Franklin Watts

Pluckrose, Henry. *The Art & Craft Book*. Evans Brothers Ltd, London

Powell, Gillian. *Painting and Sculpture*. Wayland

Richardson, Wendy and Jack. *Cities through the Eyes of Artists*. Heinemann

Solga, Kim. *Paint!* F&W Publications

Stocks, Sue. *Painting*. Wayland

Walters, Elizabeth and Harris, Anne. *Painting: A Young Artist's Guide*. Dorling Kindersley

Wenham, Martin. *Understanding Art: A Guide for Teachers*. Paul Chapman Publishing

Withey, David, Grosz, Jane and Fulton, Maggie. *Art: A Primary Teacher's Handbook*. Folens

Ellena Meadows, Year 2

Glossary

Abstract art
Pictures or sculptures which create an effect using line, tone, form, shape or colour but do not represent anything recognizable.

Acrylic paint
A water-based paint with a plastic binder.

Background
Anything which is behind the main image or which serves as a setting for an image. It can also mean the surface on which a painting is created.

Block paint
Paint that comes in compacted tablets, water-based and generally in basic bright colours.

Brusho®
Powdered watercolour paint that can be made up into a liquid.

Charcoal
Drawing stick made from charred wood.

Chiaroscuro
Italian for light/dark, meaning the use of light and shade in a painting.

Classical
Usually art that is either Greek or Roman or influenced by those styles.

Collage
A French term for describing artwork which includes items stuck onto a surface.

Complementary colours
Pairs of colours that are opposite on the colour wheel and contrast strongly: blue/orange, yellow/purple, red/green.

Composition
The arrangement of colour, shape, line and so on in a picture.

Contrast
To stand out against something else.

Cubism
A movement in painting that abandoned traditional methods of modelling and perspective and portrayed a subject from several viewpoints at the same time and in simplified planes and shapes.

Elements (of art)
Line, tone, texture, colour, form, shape and composition.

Earth colours
Pigments made from minerals such as ochre, sienna and umber – usually a mixture of browns, greens, blacks and greys.

Egg tempera
Paint using egg as the binder – usually the yolk, but sometimes the whole egg.

Expressionism
A style of art which exaggerates or distorts shape, line and colour to portray feelings.

Fauvism
Painting that uses colour to express emotion rather than reality. The Fauvists worked in the early 20th century to free painting from pictorial representation. Fauves means wild animals.

Ferrule
The metal holder of a brush, where the hair joins the handle.

Figurative
Art that depicts recognizable people, animals or objects; the opposite of abstract art.

Filbert
A conical-shaped brush.

Folk art
Decoration or objects made by people without formal training, who use traditional techniques, patterns, colours and forms.

Foreground
The lower area of a picture, or part of a scene which seems nearer to the viewer.

Form
A 3-D shape, or its representation in 2-D.

Fresco
A method of painting on a plaster wall while the plaster is still wet. The painting becomes part of the wall.

Futurism
Italian movement at its height from 1909–1914, which attempted to capture the beauty of speed and the machine.

Glaze
A thin layer of transparent or translucent paint applied over a picture to create subtle effects. Acrylic paint can be used in this way.

Gouache
A watercolour paint with white pigment added, making the colours more opaque.

Graffito
A method in which a line is produced by scratching through one painted surface to reveal another.

Ground
A substance applied to a support (canvas, board, paper) before the painting begins.

Hue (tint)
A colour or variety of a colour created by adding another colour.

Impasto
The thick application of paint.

Impressionism
A style of painting begun by a group of French artists at the end of the 19th century. They used bright colours, applied freely, to capture the effects of light.

Indian ink
A dense, black ink made from carbon.

Landscape
1. A scene which generally includes some of these elements: fields, hills, trees, grass, rivers, lakes, animals, skies, clouds and rural buildings.
2. In terms of paper or canvas, when the vertical sides are shorter than the horizontal sides.

Lapis lazuli
A blue stone from which the natural ultramarine pigment was once ground.

Media (medium, singular)
In painting, the material the artist uses to make the work of art. A set of materials.

Monochrome
Painted in one colour.

Mono print
A single print taken from a wet image, usually because only one 'take' is possible.

Mural
Painting on walls – implies on a large scale to fill the wall.

Ochre
Natural earths used to make pigments.

Op art
Developed in the 1960s, paintings that used colour and pattern to create optical illusions.

Palette
1. Slab for mixing colours; can be plastic, china, wood, hardboard or paper.
2. A range of colours at an artist's disposal.

Patron
Someone who supports the arts by commissioning artists to work for him or her.

Perspective
A method of creating a sense of space and distance in a picture.

Pigment
Coloured material which gives the paint its colour, usually ground to a fine powder and mixed with a binder which holds it together and makes it stick to the support (paper, canvas, etc).

Pointillism
A painting technique using separate small dots which merge in the eye when viewed from a distance.

Polyptych
An altarpiece which is made up of several panels that are hinged and can close together.

Pop art
An art movement that was at its peak in the 1960s. The artists took images from the consumer society and popular culture such as television, packaging and advertising. They also used commercial methods of production such as printing.

Poster paint
Water-based, slightly opaque paint, similar to gouache.

Realism
The name given to paintings that try to show the world exactly as it is, even if that means painting unpleasant things.

Sable
An animal whose hair is used for fine soft brushes.

Scumble
To apply a thin, often broken layer of paint over a darker paint.

Sfumato
An Italian word meaning the gradual merging of colours with no sudden changes.

Shade
A colour, especially with regard to its depth or having been made darker by adding black.

Still life
A group of objects arranged together so that they can be drawn or painted. At one time, the objects depicted often had a deep significance.

Stipple
Brush marks made by using the vertical end of the brush, usually consisting of flattened dots.

Surrealism
An art movement which stressed the importance of the irrational and the subconscious. Surrealist paintings usually look strange or disturbing.

Technique
The process or practice that is used to obtain a particular effect.

Tempera
A paint that was originally made up from water, egg and colour. Chemical versions of it are still used.

Texture
Representation in a work of different surfaces, or actual variation in surface caused by the application of thick paint.

Tint
A change in a colour when a small amount of a different colour is added.

Tone
The lightness or darkness of a colour. Also used to describe the shades of grey between black and white.

Under-drawing
The drawing beneath a painting.

Under-painting
Layers of paint beneath the top layer of a painting, particularly those which show through glazes or semi-transparent top layers.

Value
In a colour, this means the strength of one colour from its lightest version to its deepest.

Vanishing point
The point or points at which parallel lines appear to meet on the horizon line.

Wash
A thin, diluted coat of paint applied over a broad area of the surface of a painting, often used as a base for painting.

Buddy Morris, Year 2

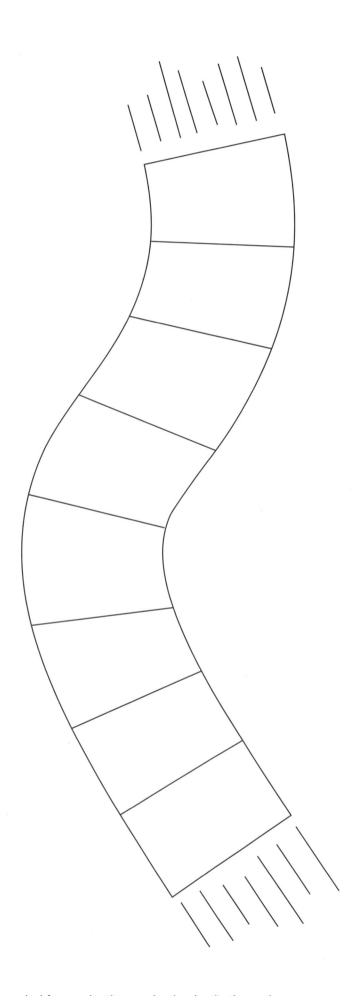

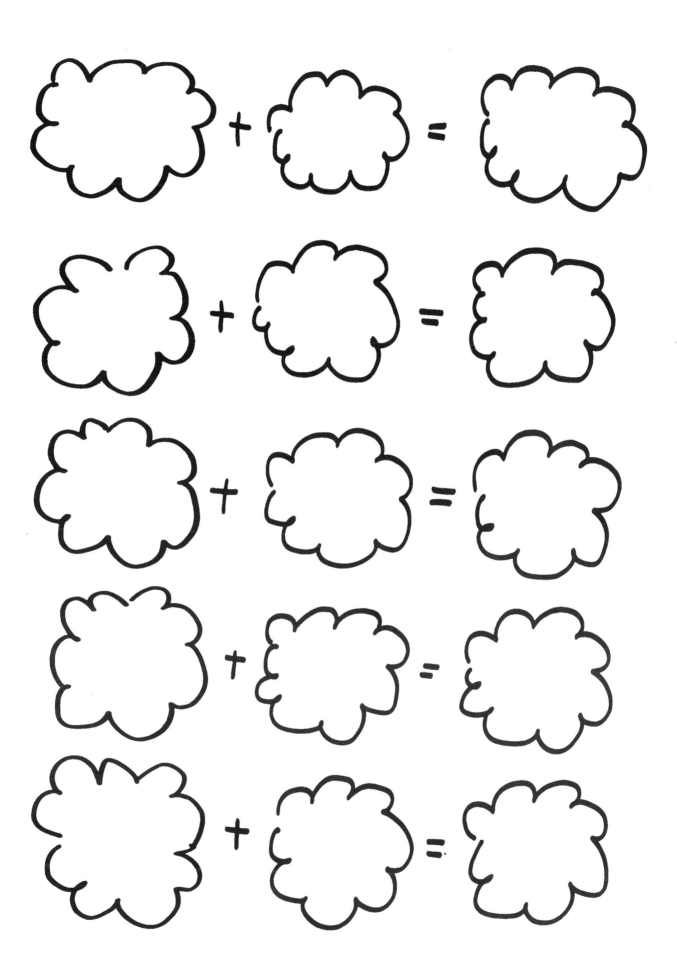

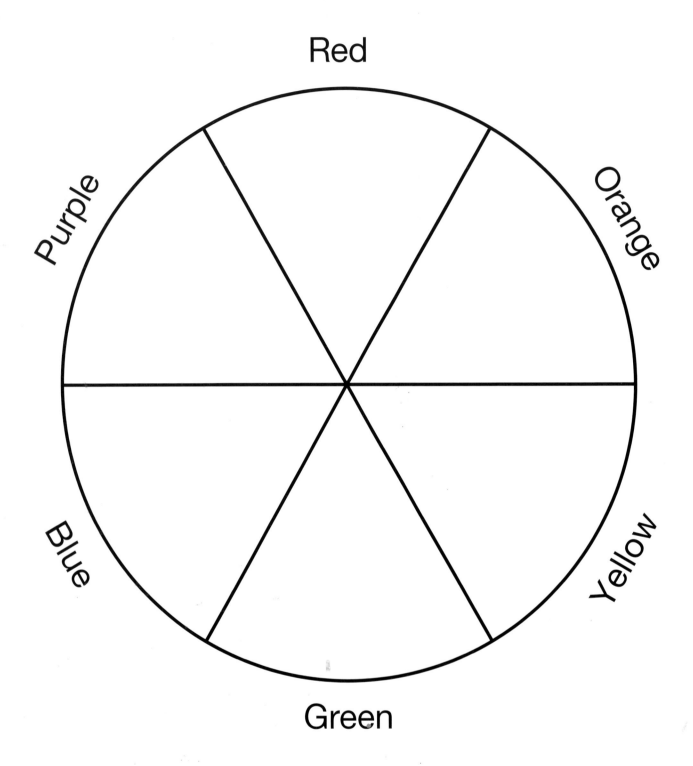

Nico Schuster

Abbildung dynamischer Managementsysteme durch Wiki-Technologie

GRIN Verlag

Bibliografische Information der Deutschen Nationalbibliothek:

Die Deutsche Bibliothek verzeichnet diese Publikation in der Deutschen National-
bibliografie; detaillierte bibliografische Daten sind im Internet über http://dnb.d-
nb.de/ abrufbar.

Impressum:

Copyright © 2008 GRIN Verlag GmbH
Druck und Bindung: Books on Demand GmbH, Norderstedt Germany
ISBN: 978-3-640-19810-8

Dieses Buch bei GRIN:

http://www.grin.com/de/e-book/115437/abbildung-dynamischer-managementsys-
teme-durch-wiki-technologie

GRIN - Your knowledge has value

Der GRIN Verlag publiziert seit 1998 wissenschaftliche Arbeiten von Studenten, Hochschullehrern und anderen Akademikern als eBook und gedrucktes Buch. Die Verlagswebsite www.grin.com ist die ideale Plattform zur Veröffentlichung von Hausarbeiten, Abschlussarbeiten, wissenschaftlichen Aufsätzen, Dissertationen und Fachbüchern.

Besuchen Sie uns im Internet:

http://www.grin.com/

http://www.facebook.com/grincom

http://www.twitter.com/grin_com

Abbildung dynamischer Managementsysteme durch Wiki-Technologie

Diplomarbeit

Studiengang Informationsmanagement

und Unternehmenskommunikation

der

Fachhochschule Neu-Ulm

Nico Schuster

Bearbeitungszeitraum: 08. Mai 2008 - 11. September 2008

Neu-Ulm, September 2008

Inhaltsverzeichnis

1 Einleitung

Web 2.0, Wiki, Blog und Social Software sind nur einige Schlagworte, die es mittlerweile aus dem Bereich der "Nerds" und "Freaks" bis hin zu den höchsten Management-ebenen großer Unternehmungen geschafft haben. Während Technologien wie das Dokumentenmanagement für viele Firmen zur lästigen Pflicht geworden sind, entdecken gleichzeitig immer mehr Führungskräfte das Potential von Social Networking, Collaborative Knowledge und User Generated Content.

Allen Technologien gemein ist die Öffnung des Systems "Unternehmen" nach innen oder außen oder gar in beide Richtungen und damit die Übertragung von Verantwortung auf die Mitarbeiter und das Teilen und Verteilen von Informationen.

Ein Paradebeispiel an geteiltem Wissen und Mass Collaboration ist die Wikipedia. Die Online-Enzyklopedia, die mittlerweile selbst ehrwürdigen Nachschlagewerken wie der Brockhaus-Enzyklopädie das Fürchten gelehrt hat.[1] Nicht zuletzt die enorme Verbreitung der Wikipedia führte auch im Steinbeis Transferzentrum Qualität im Unternehmen (TQU) zu der Erkenntnis "In today's world yesterday's methods just don't work"[2] wie David Allen bereits 2001 konstatierte.

Nicht nur die Zeiten in denen etwas getan wird, sondern auch die Methoden wie etwas getan wird, ändern sich. Der Wandel zur Informationsgesellschaft stellt eine Revolution dar und wird sämtliche Aspekte menschlichen Lebens beeinflussen.[3]

Diesem Wandel auch aus der organisatorischen Sicht einer Unternehmung Rechnung zu tragen, wird eine der größten Herausforderungen und Chancen für aktuelle Managementgenerationen und setzt den Einsatz innovativer und zukunftsweisender Tools und Techniken voraus.

---

[1] Vgl. [Wikipedia – Brockhaus Enzyklopädie]

[2] Vgl. [Allen 2001]

[3] Vgl. [Bühl 2000], S.14

1.1 Zielsetzung

Die vorliegende Arbeit befasst sich intensiv mit den Möglichkeiten, "Wiki- Technologie" auf Managementsysteme anzuwenden und zu übertragen. Zielsetzung ist es, die Möglichkeiten eines auf Wiki-Technologie basierenden Systems und damit verbundene Synergieeffekte mit anderen Web 2.0-Tools aufzuzeigen und anhand praktischer Einsatzszenarien vorzustellen.

Im Fokus liegen dabei die Möglichkeiten der Wiki-Software "Confluence" der Firma Atlassian, die sich zum größten Teil auf andere Wiki-Derivate übertragen lassen.

Gestützt auf aktuell verfügbare Literatur, Internetquellen und die Erfahrungen aus der Projektumsetzung soll diese Arbeit einen objektiven Überblick über die Möglichkeiten, aber auch die Grenzen von Wikis im Bereich der Managementsysteme bieten.

1.2 Vorgehensweise

Die Arbeit gliedert sich thematisch in drei Teile. Im ersten Teil werden grundlegende Begriffe und Techniken aus den Bereichen Managementsysteme und Web 2.0. erläutert. Im zweiten Teil soll der Begriff "Managementsystem 2.0" genauer betrachtet und erklärt, sowie die Akzeptanz durch eine Erhebung belegt werden. Der dritte Teil schildert praktische Umsetzungen eines wikibasierten Managementsystem 2.0 anhand von unterschiedlichen Beispielen. Die Arbeit schließt mit einem Fazit und einem Ausblick.

Neben der wissenschaftlichen Be- und Aufarbeitung des Themas im ersten Kapitel sind die beiden Folgekapitel sehr praktisch geprägt. Die aufgezeigten Methoden und Einsatzbereiche sind dabei im Rahmen des Arbeitskreis "Managementsystem 2.0" der TQU International GmbH projektbegleitend bei mittelständischen Unternehmen erarbeitet und umgesetzt worden und wurden durch verfügbare Literatur verifiziert.

2 Theoretische Grundlagen

Im folgenden Kapitel soll der Grundstein zum einfacheren Verständnis der Kapitel zwei und drei gelegt werden. Im Fokus des Kapitels liegt daher die Definition und Erklärung von Begrifflichkeiten aus den Bereichen Managementsysteme, Web 2.0 und Social Software. Die einzelnen Begriffe werden gegenseitig abgegrenzt und in der Erläuterung mit Beispielen belegt.

2.1 Managementsysteme

Unter einem Managementsystem wird in dieser Arbeit ein System als Instrument[4] der Führung, Planung, Organisation und Kontrolle angesehen.[5] Als System selbst wird eine Gesamtheit von Elementen verstanden, die sich in einer gegenseitigen Wechselwirkung befinden[6] aber durch klare Grenzen von der Umwelt unterscheidbar sind.[7]

Um solche Systeme greifbarer zu machen, werden sie meist durch Modelle grafisch dargestellt. In dieser Arbeit wird unter dem Begriff des Modells die Abbildung bestimmter Merkmale und Elemente verstanden, die in graphischer Darstellung Wirkzusammenhänge aufzeigt, Wichtiges von weniger Wichtigem trennt und der raschen Orientierung dient.[8] Das im Folgenden abgebildete neue St. Galler Management-Modell gehört zu den verbreitetsten Managementmodellen und hat, wie später folgt, auch die Entwicklung des "Managementsystem 2.0-Modells" stark beeinflusst.

---

[4] Vgl. [Schwerdtle 1999], S.13
[5] Vgl. [Staehle 1994], S.68
[6] Vgl. [Macharzina, Wolf 2008], S.71
[7] Vgl. [Remer 2002], S.2ff
[8] Vgl. [Rüegg-Stürm 2002], S.13

Die sechs Grundkategorien des neuen St. Galler Management-Modells

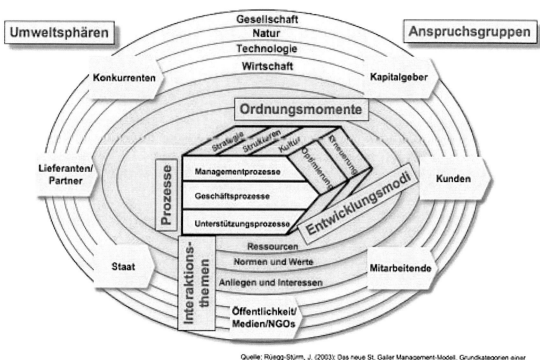

Quelle: Rüegg-Stürm, J. (2003): Das neue St. Galler Management-Modell. Grundkategorien einer integrierten Managementlehre: Der HSG-Ansatz. 2. Auflage, Bern/Stuttgart/Wien: Haupt, S. 22

Abbildung 1. Das St. Galler Management-Modell

2.1.1 Integrierte Managementsysteme

Wird heute von Managementsystemen gesprochen, ist meist ein integriertes Managementsystem oder der Teil eines integrierten Managementsystems damit gemeint. Ein integriertes Managementsystem umfasst die Teilmanagementsysteme eines Unternehmens und ist durch eine vereinheitlichte Gliederung der Strukturen und Prinzipien gekennzeichnet.[9] Es ist daher als ein übergeordnetes System zu sehen, das den Unternehmenserfolg bereichsübergreifend in den Mittelpunkt stellt und[10] die Unternehmensprozesse unterschiedlicher Bereiche integriert.[11] Im Idealfall kann ein noch nicht vorhandenes (Teil)Managementsystem, durch die sich ähnelnden beziehungsweise verwandten Regelungen[12] in den industrieüblichen Normen wie beispielsweise der DIN EN ISO 9001 für Qualitätsmanagement oder DIN EN ISO 14001 für Umweltmanagement, in ein bereits vorhandenes System integriert werden.[13] Durch den integrativen Ansatz lassen sich Synergieeffekte nutzen und Redundanzen vermeiden.[14]

---

[9] Vgl. [Zollondz 2001], S.1237

[10] Vgl. [Bayerisches Staatsministerium für Wirtschaft – Integriertes Managementsystem]

[11] Vgl. [Paeger – Integrierte Managementsysteme]

[12] Vgl. [Zollondz 2001], S.1237

[13] Vgl. [Schwerdtle 1999]

[14] Vgl. [Wikipedia – Integriertes Managementsystem]

Breite Verbreitung fanden integrierte Managementsysteme vor allem in den 1990er Jahren in Folge der "ISO 9001" Zertifizierungen für Qualitätsmanagement und den damit verbindlich vorgeschriebenen Regelwerken in denen eine kontinuierliche Verbesserung der Prozesse wesentlicher Bestandteil sind. Diese Verbesserungen lassen sich auf lange Sicht nur durch eine Integration von einzelnen Managementsystemen erreichen.[15]

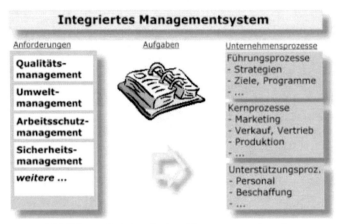

Abbildung 2. Integriertes Managementsystem

2.1.2 Dynamische Managementsysteme

Ein "dynamisches Managementsystem" ist in der einschlägigen Literatur nicht als Art eines Managementsystems definiert. Dennoch sind in diversen Veröffentlichungen die Wörter "dynamisch" und "Managementsystem" in Kombination anzutreffen. Das Lexikon definiert den Begriff Dynamik schlicht als "Bewegung eines Dinges". Allgemein wird auch eine zeitliche Entwicklung mit Dynamik in Verbindung gebracht. In der Informatik hingegen wird als dynamisch bezeichnet, was sich an veränderte Bedingungen anpassen kann[16]. Rüegg-Stürm spricht auch bei komplexen Systemen von dynamischen, sich in ständiger Re-Konstruktion befindenden Systemen, wenn diese Elemente besitzen, die in gegenseitiger Wechselbeziehung stehen, diese Elemente ein gewisses Eigenverhalten in ihrer Interaktion aufweisen und daraus resultierend emergente, d.h. nicht auf ein einzelnes Element zurückzuführende Ergebnisse liefern.[17] Oliver Hebold definiert in seiner Arbeit wie folgt: "Unter einem dynamischen Managementsystem verstehen wir zum einen ein Managementsystem, das den kontinuierlichen Verbesserungsprozess beinhaltet und andererseits möglichst „unempfindlich" gegen Organisationsänderungen ist, beziehungsweise sich diesen zeitnah anpassen kann. Damit erhält das Management ein Managementsystem, mit dem es Organisationsänderungen schnell operationalisieren kann. Dies stellt dann ein zeitnahes Funktionieren der Ablauforganisation nach Organisationsänderungen sicher."[18]

---

[15] Vgl. [Zollondz 2001], S.1238
[16] Vgl. [Wikipedia – Dynamik]
[17] Vgl. [Rüegg-Stürm 2002], S.18
[18] Vgl. [Hebold 2003]

Diese Arbeit schließt sich dem Verständnis nach dieser Definiton an und erweitert es noch um eine partizipative Komponente, die sich aus dem Einsatz der Technologie Wiki ergibt, welche auf dem Gedanken der "massenweisen Zusammenarbeit" beruht.[19] Im folgenden Kapitel wird der partizipative Ansatz für Wikis ausführlich erläutert.

---

[19] Vgl. [Tapscott, Williams 2006], S.10

2.2 Wiki

Der folgende Abschnitt soll einen Überblick über den Begriff Wiki ermöglichen. Beginnend von der reinen Begriffsklärung und der historischen Entstehung erster Wikis werden auch typische Charakteristika, die jeder Wiki-Implementation zuzuschreiben sind, aufgegriffen und erläutert. Vorab ist festzustellen, dass der Begriff Wiki zwar prinzipiell bereits in den vorangegangenen Abschnitten in Kurzform erklärt wurde allerdings zum besseren Verständnis dieser Arbeit einer ausführlichen Erklärung bedarf.

2.2.1 Definition und Historie

„Wikis sind verbreitete, leicht zu bedienende Systeme, die es ermöglichen, Inhalte im Internet zu veröffentlichen, die von einer großen Anzahl von Nutzern bearbeitet werden können."[20] Der Ausdruck „wiki" selbst stammt aus dem Hawaiianischen und bedeutet schnell. Der Namen „WikiWikiWeb" ist den WikiWiki-Shuttlebussen, die in Honolulu, Hawaii, zwischen den Terminals des Flughafens verkehren, entlehnt.[21]

Eine allgemeingültige Definition läßt sich selbst nach einschlägiger Recherche in aktueller Literatur nicht finden. Wikipedia definiert ein Wiki wie folgt:

Ein Wiki, seltener auch WikiWiki oder WikiWeb genannt, ist eine Software und Sammlung von Webseiten, die von den Benutzern nicht nur gelesen, sondern meist auch direkt online geändert werden kann.[22]

Leuf/Cunningham hingegen erweitern die Definition um die Operatibilität innerhalb eines Webbrowser und der Verlinkung einzelner Seiten:

"A wiki is a freely expandable collection of interlinked Web "pages", a hypertext system for storing and modifying information - a database, where each page is easily editable by any user with a forms-capable Web browser client."[23]

 "I'm a lazy guy. I don't know how to organize. Let's just let the community organize." (Zitiert aus einem Video-Interview mit Ward Cunningham: „How did you come up with the idea for the Wiki?")[24] So einfach war die Idee, die hinter dem ersten Wiki stand. Entwickelt wurde das erste Wiki durch den Softwareentwickler Ward Cunningham, im Jahre 1994. Er suchte zu der Zeit nach einer möglichst einfachen Möglichkeit, sog. Design Patterns, Entwurfsmuster für die Entwicklung von Anwendungen, bearbeiten und schnell mit anderen Entwicklerkollegen austauschen zu können. Gleichzeitig sollte

---

[20] [E-Teching.org – Wikis]

[21] Vgl. [Ebersbach, Glaser et al. 2008], S.10f

[22] [Wikipedia – Wiki]

[23] [Leuf, Cunningham 2001], S.14

[24] [Microsoft MSDN Channel 9]

dabei eine Versionierung der Änderungen erfolgen, damit die einzelnen Schritte nachvollziehbar bleiben.

Die vielen untereinander verlinkten Seiten eines Wikis können daher heute meist durch einen im Wiki eingebauten Editor direkt bearbeitet, ergänzt oder gar gelöscht werden. Die Formatierung der eingegebenen Inhalte, die sogenannte Wiki-Syntax ist dabei sehr einfach und auch für Laien sehr schnell zu erlernen.[25] Bemerkenswert dabei ist die automatische Versionierung aller Inhalte. Es kann zu jedem beliebigem Stand zurückgesprungen werden, was Wikis vor allem im Firmeneinsatz, wo eine genaue Nachvollziehbarkeit wichtig ist, interessant macht.

Das bekannteste Wiki ist wie bereits im vorhergehenden Abschnitt erwähnt, die Wikipedia. Der Trend geht aber immer mehr zu spezialisierteren Wikis, wie beispielsweise das StadtWiki der Stadt Karlsruhe[26] oder dem Wikipedia-Ableger Wiktionary[27], welches sich als freies Wörterbuch versteht. Auch die Interaktion mit anderen Systemen, wie SAP oder Microsoft Sharepoint wird für viele Anwender gerade im Unternehmensumfeld immer wichtiger und dementsprechend vorangetrieben.

Abbildung 3. Wiki-Wiki Shuttle auf Hawaii

[25] Vgl. [Wikipedia – Wikitext]

[26] http://ka.stadtwiki.net/Hauptseite

[27] http://de.wiktionary.org/wiki/Wiktionary:Hauptseite

2.2.2 Charakteristika

Ein Wiki verfügt über einige Charakteristika, die sich in fast jeder Implementation wieder finden. Neben den rein technisch greifbaren Funktionen, auf die später noch eingegangen wird, hat Ward Cunningham drei fundamentale Statements veröffentlicht, die seiner Meinung nach die Essenz eines Wikis ausmachen, es also aus Benutzersicht charakterisieren:[28]

- A Wiki invites all users to edit any page or to create new pages within the WIKI Web site, using only a plain-vanilla Web browser without any extra add-ons.

- Wiki promotes meaningful topic associations between different pages by making page link creation almost intuitively easy and showing whether an intended target page exists or not.

- A Wiki is not a carefully-crafted site for casual visitors. Instead, it seeks to involve the visitor in an ongoing process of creation and collaboration that constantly changes the Web site landscape.

Der Internetnutzer wird also vom rein passiven Betrachter zum aktiven Redakteur.[29] Der Aspekt der Massenkollaboration wird hier gezielt aufgegriffen und ist sogar erwünscht. Je mehr Leser sich aktiv an einem Artikel beteiligen und so zum Autor werden, desto wahrscheinlicher ist es, dass der Artikel ein hohes Maß an Richtigkeit erreicht.

Das zweite Statement zeigt auf, wie wichtig für ein funktionierendes Wikisystem die einfache Verlinkung unterschiedlicher Inhalte zueinander ist. Sollte ein Verfasser eines Wiki-Artikels sich zwar bewußt sein, dass ein von ihm aufgezeigter Punkt in seinem Text noch erklärungsbedürftig ist, er dies aber selbst nicht leisten kann, so kann er dennoch einen vorgefertigten Link auf einen weiteren Beitrag anlegen. Sollte im Folgenden ein Leser der Meinung sein, genau dieses fehlende Wissen nachreichen zu können, kann dieser den neuen Beitrag mit nur einem Klick anlegen.

Es geht bei einem Wiki weniger darum, eine bis ins kleinste Detail durchdachte und ausgefeilte Site zu generieren. Ganz zu schweigen von einem Anspruch auf Vollständigkeit und dauerhafter Aktualität.[30] Viel wichtiger ist der andauernde Prozess, der Nutzer dazu einlädt, die Seiten nach eigenem Wissen und Gewissen zu verändern, mit anderen Systemen zu vermischen und letztendlich einen positiven Einfluss auf das Wiki zu nehmen.

---

[28] [Leuf, Cunningham 2001], S.16
[29] Vgl. [Streiff 2005], S.4f
[30] Vgl. [Komus, Wauch 2008], S.4

11

Neben diesen grundlegenden Aussagen zu einem Wiki seien an dieser Stelle auch die üblichen technischen Grundfunktionen eines Wikis beschrieben.

Sie überschneiden sich von ihrer Begrifflichkeit mit den drei Statements von Cunningham, sind aber im Kontext des folgenden Abschnitts als technische Funktion und nicht als soziale Komponente zu verstehen.

Die Grundfunktionen der üblich verfügbaren Wiki-Systeme umfassen:[31]

- Editing / Bearbeiten
- Links
- History / Versionierung
- Recent Changes / Aktuelle Änderungen
- Search / Suche

Desweiteren sind für den jeweiligen Einsatzbereich die folgenden Funktionen nützlich, die sich aber von System zu System unterscheiden können:[32]

- Sandbox
- MultiWebs
- Dateiupload
- Authentifizierung

Um ein Verständnis für die Begriffe zu entwickeln, seien diese im Folgenden erklärt:

Editing / Bearbeiten

Der Editieren- oder Bearbeiten-Link ist eine der Grundfunktionen eines jeden Wikis. Jede Seite kann durch einen simplen Klick in den Bearbeitungsmodus versetzt werden und der Benutzer kann so Fehler ausbessern oder neue Inhalte anfügen. In öffentlichen Wikis wird diese Funktion nur in den seltensten Fällen gesperrt. Im Unternehmensumfeld kann eine Sperrung der Editierbarkeit in bestimmen Bereichen allerdings durchaus sinnvoll und auch gewollt sein.

Links

Eine Grundidee von Wikis ist das einfache Verlinken von Inhalten untereinander. Die Grundeinstellung vieler Wiki-Systeme sieht eine extrem einfache Art der Linkerstellung die sog. WikiWords oder auch CamelCases vor. Ein Link besteht in diesem Fall einfach aus zwei zusammengeschriebenen Wörten. Da es Vielen widerstrebt, Wörter absichtlich falsch zu schreiben und es im Zusammenspiel mit anderen Anwendungen manchmal zu Problemen kommen kann, hat sich auch vielfach die Linkschreibweise

---

[31] Vgl. [Ebersbach, Glaser et al. 2008 – Wiki], S.19f
[32] Vgl. [E-Teching.org – Wiki]

mit den zu verlinkenden Inhalten in eckiger Klammer (engl. Brackets) durchgesetzt. Existiert der verlinkte Inhalt noch nicht, wird beim Klick auf den Link eine neue Wikiseite angelegt und kann direkt durch den Autor mit Inhalt gefüllt werden.

History / Versionierung

Die History-Funktion stellt eine automatische Versionierung jedes Beitrags und eine Dokumentation über jede einzelne Änderung bereit. Sie ermöglicht es zwischen einzelnen Versionen einer Seite zu vergleichen, ohne dafür die gesamten Texte überprüfen zu müssen, da die meisten Wikis über einen Differenzvergleich verfügen und Änderungen zwischen einzelnen Versionen farbig hervorheben. Diese Funktion erlaubt es sehr gut, einzelne Fortschritte zu dokumentieren oder im Falle von Vandalismus eine ursprüngliche Version wiederherzustellen.

Recent Changes / Aktuelle Änderungen

Diese Funktion erlaubt es, sich mit einem Blick die letzten Änderungen im Wiki anzeigen zu lassen. Je nach eingesetztem System kann diese Funktion noch verfeinert eingestellt werden. Manche Wikis ermöglichen das Anlegen sog. Watch Lists, mittels deren Hilfe gezielt die Änderungen von ausgewählten Seiten verfolgt werden können. Vielfach ist auch die Nachverfolgung durch RSS-Feeds möglich, welche bei Änderung einer Seite aktualisiert werden.

Search / Suche

Die Suchfunktion ist für die meisten Nutzer eines Wikis das Wichtigste überhaupt. Fast alle verfügbaren Systeme verfügen über eine Volltextsuche. Weiter entwickelte Wikis erlauben darüber hinaus die Suche in bestimmten Bereichen oder nach Dateianhängen.

Sandbox

In einer Sandbox können Funktionen ausprobiert und der Umgang mit dem Wiki geübt werden. Sie ist weniger eine Funktion, die in das Wiki-System implementiert ist, als eine Seite oder ein Bereich der als "Spielwiese" vom Wiki-Administrator definiert wurde. Sie ist vor allem dann nützlich, wenn ungeübte Nutzer an das Wiki herangeführt werden sollen, ohne Gefahr zu laufen, dass an Produktivinhalten ungewollte Änderungen geschehen.

MultiWebs

Unter MultiWebs wird die Funktion verstanden, mehrere inhaltlich getrennte Wikis unter einem System auszuführen. Je nach eingesetzter Software kann auch der Begriff Spaces, Bereich oder Gruppe verwandt werden. Nützlich ist diese Funktion vor allem im unternehmerischen Einsatz, da so die Administration zentral gehalten werden kann.

Dateiupload

Die meisten Wiki-Systeme erlauben es den Benutzern, Dateien oder Bilder an eine Wiki-Seite zu hängen. Hierbei kann, je nach eingesetzter Software, die automatische

Versionierung auch die Dateianhänge beinhalten. Hochgeladene Bilder können meist direkt auf den Wiki-Seiten eingebunden werden.

Authentifizierung

Je nach Einsatzzweck kann es auch für ein Wiki unabdingbar sein, gegen eine bereits vorhandene oder extra geschaffene Infrastruktur zu authentifizieren. Dies ermöglicht bei komplexen Systemen eine feine Abstufung der einzelnen Benutzerrechte bis hinunter auf Seitenebene. Für die weit verbreiteten Nutzerverwaltungssysteme auf Windows- oder Novellbasis bieten viele Wikisysteme Schnittstellen, so dass ganze Benutzer und Gruppenstrukturen eins zu eins auf das Wiki umgesetzt werden können.

2.2.3 Einteilung verfügbarer Wikilösungen

Wie bei vielen anderen EDV-Anwendungen gibt es nicht „DIE" Wiki-Lösung. Es gibt eine Reihe unterschiedlicher Systeme, die teilweise andere Ziele verfolgen. Laut Meatball, einer der größten Wiki-Communities, gibt es derzeit ca. 200 verschiedene Systeme mit Wikifunktionalität.[33]

Neben den ursprünglichen Open Source Wikis haben sich mit steigenden Anforderungen der Unternehmen sog. Enterprise Wikis herausgebildet. Diese sind bezüglich der Rechtevergabe, Wartbarkeit und Stabilität auf den Betrieb im Unternehmensumfeld optimiert.

Im Folgenden soll ein kurzer Überblick über vier der bekanntesten Systeme gegeben werden. Die Auswahl stützt sich auf eine Vorselektion durch Tecchannel,[34] den Top-Ten Wiki Engines by Ward Cunningham[35] und Koch/Richter.[36]

2.2.3.1   Open Source Wikis

Als Open Source Wikis werden in dieser Arbeit Wikis verstanden, deren Quellcode allgemein verfügbar ist und von einer großen Entwicklergemeinde und nicht einer einzigen Unternehmung entwickelt und veröffentlicht werden. Sie haben häufig einen deutlicheren Fokus auf die Wiki-Grundprinzipien, wohingegen kommerzielle Enterprise Wikis eher auf die problemlose Integration in Firmennetze und die breite Userakzeptanz fokussiert sind.

Es bleibt hierbei allerdings anzumerken, dass es durchaus Open Source Wikis gibt, die sich im Unternehmensumfeld in den Punkten Usability, Rechtevergabe und Erweiterungen nicht vor ihren Klonen aus den kommerziellen Entwicklungsumgebungen verstecken müssen.

---

[33] Vgl. [Ebersbach, Glaser et al. 2008 – Wiki], S.17
[34] Vgl. [Tecchannel]
[35] Vgl. [Ward Cunningham – Top Ten Wiki Engines]
[36] Vgl. [Koch, Richter 2007 – Enterprise 2.0], S.40

MediaWiki

Die MediaWiki[37] Engine ist nicht zuletzt durch ihre Verwendung bei der Wikipedia zu ihrer großen Bekanntheit gelangt.[38] Mittlerweile wird MediaWiki von allen Wikipedia-Schwesterprojekten, wie beispielsweise Wiktionary, WikiCommons etc. und auch vielen anderen Organisationen, Firmen und Institutionen genutzt.

Die Software ist unter GPL (Die GNU General Public License (oft abgekürzt GPL) ist eine von der Free Software Foundation herausgegebene Lizenz mit Copyleft für die Lizenzierung freier Software)[39] lizensiert und in der weit verbreiteten Skriptsprache PHP geschrieben. Als Speicherort für die Seiteninhalte nutzt MediaWiki entweder eine MySQL oder PostgreSQL Datenbank.

Entstanden ist Mediawiki aus den Anforderungen der Wikipedia heraus, die ursprünglich die UseModWiki-Engine einsetzte, welche 2002 allerdings an ihre Grenzen stieß.[40] Es gibt neben den üblichen Grundfunktionen, die bereits ausführlich beschrieben wurden, einige hundert Erweiterungen zum kostenlosen Einsatz.

TWiki

TWiki[41] gehört nach der Einschätzung von Ebersbach et al.[42] zu den am weitesten entwickelten Wiki-Klonen. Es hat einen starken Fokus auf Technologie und kommt daher in vielen Unternehmen als Wissens- und Dokumentenmanagement-System zum Einsatz.[43] Lizenziert ist TWiki durch die GPL.

Das auf der Skriptsprache PERL basierende Wiki besitzt eine große Anzahl an Funktionen und vor allem Erweiterungsmöglichkeiten, sog. PlugIns. Es speichert seine Daten nicht in einer Datenbank, sondern direkt in Dateien, sog. Flatfiles. Es ist daher kein zusätzlicher Datenbankserver notwendig. Erwähnenswert ist die Möglichkeit, das Erscheinungsbild von TWiki durch Vorlagen anzupassen und dadurch nahtlos in bestehende Systeme einzubinden. Daneben existieren für TWiki momentan ca. 200 Erweiterungen.[44]

Im Vergleich zu MediaWiki verfügt es über ein ausgeprägtes System zur Zugangskontrolle und eine einfachere Syntax, um dynamische Inhalte zu generieren.

---

[37] http://www.mediawiki.org/wiki/MediaWiki/de
[38] Vgl. [Koch, Richter 2007 – Enterprise 2.0], S.40
[39] Vgl. [Wikipedia – GNU General Public License]
[40] Vgl. [Wikipedia – MediaWiki]
[41] http://twiki.org
[42] Vgl. [Ebersbach, Glaser et al. 2008 – Wiki], S.18
[43] Vgl. [Wikipedia – TWiki]
[44] Vgl. [TWiki < Plugins]

2.2.3.2   Enterprise Wikis

Für den professionellen Einsatz im Unternehmen reicht der Funktionsumfang vieler der kostenfreien und frei verfügbaren Wikis vielmals nicht aus. Oft muss darauf Rücksicht genommen werden, dass nicht der Nutzer sich an das Wiki, sondern das Wiki sich an den Nutzer anpasst. Auch der Faktor Sicherheit ist im unternehmerischen Umfeld durchaus strenger zu bewerten als im privaten oder semiprofessionellen Umfeld. Hier müssen bisweilen auch Abstriche an der Wiki-Philisophie in Kauf genommen werden. Gerade Punkte wie die Editierbarkeit und Sichtbarkeit aller Inhalte können in einem Unternehmen nicht nur durch interne Vorgaben, sondern auch durch gesetzliche Rahmenbedingungen beschnitten werden.

Dennoch weisen die aufgezeigten Lösungen die grundsätzlichen Funktionen eines jeden Wikis auf. Beispielsweise bereichert um eine feinere Rechtevergabe, WYSIWYG-Editoren (What you see, is what you get) und vor allem professionellen Support durch den Hersteller eignen sich diese Systeme besonders für den Einsatz in Unternehmen.[45]

Social Text

Die Computerwoche führt unter anderem als Enterprise Wiki die Software Socialtext[46] an.[47] Socialtext wird vom gleichnamigen Unternehmen Socialtext Incorporated mit Sitz in Palo Alto produziert.

Es basiert wie TWiki auf der Skriptsprache PERL und speichert seine Daten in einer PostgreSQL Datenbank. Neben der Kaufversion wird es auch als Host-Lösung angeboten. Diese Lösung bietet gerade Firmen, die selbst wenig oder kein Personal aus dem IT-Bereich einsetzen können, die Möglichkeit, auf ein vorkonfiguriertes System auf einem angemieteten Server zuzugreifen.[48]

Socialtext selbst bietet neben der Wiki-Funktionalität, die den Kern des Systems darstellt, weitergehende Funktionen aus dem Social Software Umfeld. Unter anderem bietet es die Integration von E-Mail und Instant Messaging. Es stellt daher eine komplette Social Software Umgebung mit einem Wiki als Kern für Unternehmensarchitekturen dar.[49]

---

[45] Vgl. [Computerwoche – Enterprise-Wiki]

[46] http://www.socialtext.com/

[47] Vgl. [Computerwoche – Enterprise-Wiki]

[48] Vgl. [Tecchannel]

[49] Vgl. [Koch, Richter 2007 – Enterprise 2.0], S.40

Atlassian Confluence

"Confluence - neuer Stern am Wikihimmel?" titelt ein Blogeintrag von Cedric Weber.[50] Laut Computerwoche ist die Wiki-Lösung Confluence[51] der australischen Firma Atlassian mit Sitz in Sydney das derzeit bekannteste Enterprise Wiki. Kunden sind bereits über 1700 Unternehmen wie beispielsweise SAP, IBM und Cisco.

Confluence basiert auf der Programmiersprache JAVA und kann seine Inhalte in einer proprietären Datenbank, einer MySQL Datenbank oder einer PostgreSQL Datenbank speichern.[52] Die Entwicklergemeinde rund um Atlassian ist sehr aktiv und stellt bereits mehrere hundert Plugins, sog. Extensions, für Confluence bereit. Viele der Plugins werden von den Atlassianentwicklern adaptiert und gehören somit zur Grundausstattung des Confluence Systems.

Zu den Besonderheiten von Confluence gehört neben der Möglichkeit, das Wiki in Spaces, also einzelne Bereiche zu unterteilen und diese mit separaten Rechten zu versehen,[53] unter anderem ein Sharepoint Connector, ein Plugin für die weithin eingesetzte Portallösung Microsoft Sharepoint[54]. Seit Anfang 2008 arbeiten Atlassian und Microsoft sogar offiziell als Partner zusammen.[55] Dies ermöglicht eine nahtlose Integration in vorhandene Sharepoint Umgebungen und ein SSO (Single Sign On) Verfahren, das die Anmeldung an nur einer der beiden Anwendungen notwendig macht, um auch die jeweils andere nutzen zu können.

Neben der Kompatibilität zu Microsoft Lösungen erweist sich Confluence auch als sehr kommunikativ mit der weithin eingesetzten ERP-Lösung R/3 von SAP[56]. In beiden Varianten können bereits bestehende Nutzerkonzepte auf das Wiki übertragen werden, was den administrativen Aufwand deutlich schmälert.

Confluence ist unter verschiedenen Lizenzen zu beziehen, die sich in einem Rahmen von ca. 2000 US $ bis 8000 US $ bewegen. Für Privatleute, Bildungseinrichtungen und gemeinnützige Organisationen sind nach entsprechender Prüfung kostenlose oder vergünstigte Lizenzen möglich.

---

[50] Vgl. [Weber – Confluence]

[51] http://www.atlassian.com/software/confluence/

[52] Vgl. [Tecchannel]

[53] Vgl. [Koch, Richter 2007 – Enterprise 2.0], S.41

[54] http://office.microsoft.com/de-de/sharepointserver/default.aspx

[55] Vgl. [Microsoft Blog – Microsoft SharePoint Team Blog]

[56] http://www.sap.com

2.3 Social Software und Web 2.0

Web 2.0 und Social Software sind zwei Schlagworte, die derzeit sehr häufig in den Medien zu finden sind und oft in einem Atemzug genannt werden. Manche gehen gar davon aus, dass die beiden Synonyme sind und verwenden die Begriffe wahllos.[57]

In der deutschsprachigen Wikipedia werden beide Begriffe als Modewort[58] oder Marketing-Schlagwort[59] bezeichnet, wohingegen das englische Wikipedia-Pendant zwar die Kritik, dass beide Wörter gerne von Werbern genutzt werden aufgreift, sie allerdings nicht an erster Stelle der Definition stellt.[60] Es erscheint daher sinnvoll, die beiden Begriffe näher zu erläutern, sie voneinander abzugrenzen und Beispiele aufzuzeigen.

Die untenstehend abgebildete Web Trend Map soll hier als Beispiel für die Vermischung von Technologiebegriffen, Marketingphrasen und Firmennamen dienen.

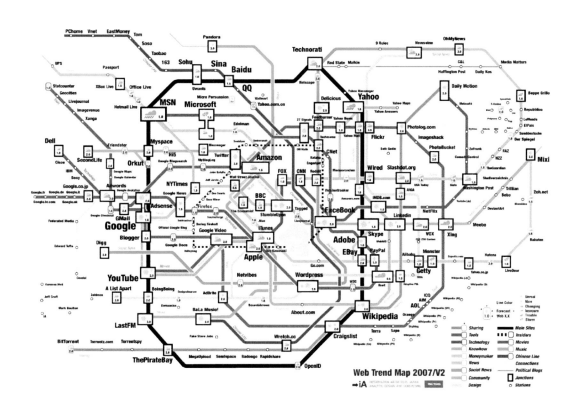

Abbildung 4. Die Web Trend Map

---

[57] Vgl. [Szugat 2007], S.14

[58] Vgl. [Wikipedia – Soziale Software]

[59] Vgl. [Wikipedia – Web 2.0]

[60] Vgl. [Wikipedia – Web 2.0]

2.3.1 Web 2.0

Der Begriff Web 2.0 wurde bekannt, als im Oktober 2004 Dale Dougherty, Vice President von O'Reilly Media und Craig Cline, Editorial Director bei Seybold Publications über eine Konferenz, die den Wandel und Fortschritt des Internet zum Thema hatte, nachdachten und diese kurzerhand "Web 2.0 Conference" nannten. Von den Medien wurde dieser neuartige Begriff dankbar aufgenommen. Auch die Erkenntnis vieler Konferenzteilnehmer, dass das WWW sich gerade im Umbruch befände, half dabei "Web 2.0" in unterschiedlichsten Zusammenhängen zu nutzen und zu verbreiten.

Die Meme Map von O'Reilly gibt einen Überblick in welchen Zusammenhängen „Web 2.0" genutzt wurde und wird.

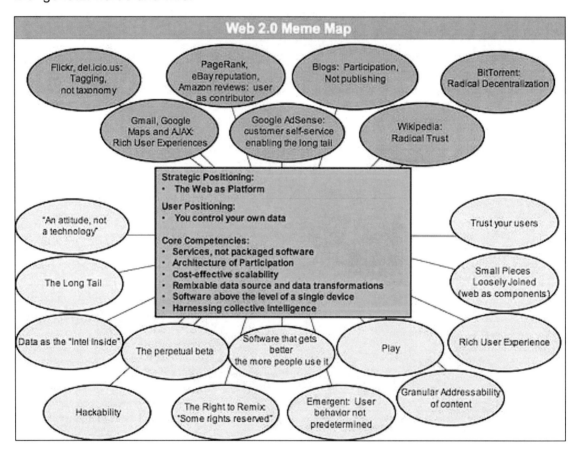

Abbildung 5. Die Web 2.0 Meme Map

Letztendlich führte diese Verbreitung dazu, dass der Begriff für Alles und Nichts stand und immer mehr zu einem Marketing-Schlagwort wurde. Tim O'Reilly, CEO von O'Reilly Media, verfasste daher 2005 seinen bekannten Artikel "What is the Web 2.0"[61], der heute als wichtigste Beschreibung von "Web 2.0" gilt. Für ihn zeichnet sich das Web 2.0 heute vor allem durch folgende Eigenschaften aus:

---

[61] Vgl. [O'Reilly – What is Web 2.0]

- Services statt reiner Software im Paket.

- Web 2.0 Applikationen lassen sich günstig skalieren.

- Einsatz auf unterschiedlichsten Geräten möglich.

- Daten sind wertvoller als Anwendungen. Nicht mehr die Anwendung selbst steht im Vordergrund, sondern die Daten die mit ihnen aggregiert werden können. Daten sollen aus beliebigen Quellen miteinander kombinierbar und einfach zugänglich sein.

- Partizipation. Der Nutzer ist nicht mehr reiner Besucher einer Website, sondern wird aktiv beteiligt.[62]

- Nutzen der kollektiven Intelligenz von Usern durch Verlinkung, Bewertung und Kommentierung oder Empfehlung

Als Beispiel für diesen "Wertewandel" liefert O'Reilly in Form eine Tabelle in der er Techniken, Firmen und Verhaltensweisen des Web 1.0 denen von Web 2.0 gegenüber stellt:

Web 1.0	Web 2.0
DoubleClick	Google AdSense
Ofoto	Flickr
Akamai	BitTorrent
mp3.com	Napster
Britannica Online	Wikipedia
personal websites	Blogging
directories (taxonomy)	tagging ("folksonomy")
content management systems	Wikis
publishing	Participation
stickiness	Syndication
..	..

Tabelle 1. Web1.0 – Web 2.0 in Anlehnung an O'Reilly

---

[62] Vgl. [Szugat 2007], S.15f

Für viele versteckt sich hinter dem Begriff "Web 2.0" auch nur die übliche "Erscheinungsform" diverser Internetangebote, mit den typischen gerundeten, weichen Fonts und den verspielten Logos in knalligen, bunten oder Pastellfarben, wie sie in der Abbildung auf dieser Seite dargestellt sind.

Eine allgemeingültige Definition für Web 2.0 hat sich allerdings bis heute nicht durchgesetzt. Man sollte daher eher versuchen Web 2.0 mit Entwicklungen zu fassen, die charakterisierend dafür sind.[63]

Abbildung 6. Logos im Web 2.0 Design

2.3.2 Social Software

Wie bereits beim Web 2.0 läßt sich auch "Social Software" nicht bis ins kleinste Detail erläutern. Eine der am häufigsten zitierten Erklärungen stammt von Christopher Allen. 2004 hat er auf seiner Website den Eintrag "Tracing the Evolution of Social Software"[64] veröffentlicht, in welchem er versucht, die Geschichte der sozial ausgelegten Software aufzuzeigen. So führte er sogar den "MEMEX" - "Memory Extender", auf Deutsch etwa "Gedächtnis Erweiterer", einem 1945 vorgestellten fiktiven Modell eines Wissensfindungs- und Verwertungssystems von Vannevar Bush[65], als Urform der Social Software an. Griffiger scheint hier schon der Vergleich zu den Anfängen des Computer Supported Collaborative Work (CSCW). Ellis et al. machen deutlich, dass es nicht nur

---

[63] Vgl. [Lange (Hg.) 2005]

[64] http://www.lifewithalacrity.com/2004/10/tracing_the_evo.html

[65] Vgl. [Wikipedia – Memex]

um Computer, sondern um technologische Unterstützung ganz allgemein geht. Sie schreiben CSCW „looks at how groups work and seeks to discover how technology (especially Computers) can help them work".[66] CSCW ist ein multidisziplinäres Gebiet und es gilt zu beachten, dass dabei die Akteure aus den einzelnen Disziplinen ihre spezifische Perspektive und Methodologie mitbringen.[67]

Eine zentrale Definition stammt von Ellis et al. welche meinen, Groupware bestünde aus "[..] computer-based systems that support groups of people engaged in a common task (or goal) and that provide an interface to a shared environment [..]"[68] Groupware umfasst also Software, Hardware und Services zur Unterstützung von Gruppen.

Social Software Anwendungen sind nach dem heutigen Verständnis "internetbasierte Anwendungen, die Informations- Identitäts- und Beziehungsmanagement in den (Teil)Öffentlichkeiten hypertextueller und sozialer Netzwerke unterstützen".[69] Bekannt wurde der Begriff der Social Software durch Clay Shirky.[70] Er organisierte 2002 den "Social Software Summit", in dem es um neue Technologien wie Wiki und Weblogs ging und bevorzugt heute als kurze Definition "software that supports group interaction".

Social Software zeichnet sich sehr stark durch eine Selbstorganisation der Mitglieder aus. Die Gruppenbildung ist hier ein freiwilliger Prozess[71] und mündet in einem dynamischen Geflecht aus sozialen Beziehungen.[72]

2.3.3 Begriffsabgrenzung und Definition

Die Definition beider Begrifflichkeiten - Web 2.0 und Social Software - ist noch immer einem starken Wandel unterworfen und läßt sich hier im wissenschaftlichen Sinne nicht eindeutig klären.Ob etwas Social Software oder Web 2.0 oder beides zugleich ist, ist eher im Verständnis des jeweiligen Nutzers anzusiedeln als durch eine Definition zu fassen.

Da die Beteiligung der User und deren Interaktion und Partizipation nach der Definition von O'Reilly mit zu den Grundsätzen des Web 2.0 gehören und nach Shirky jegliche Software die Gruppeninteraktion unterstützt als social aufgefasst wird, ist daraus zu folgern, dass Social Software aus heutiger Sicht als Teilmenge des Web 2.0 aufgefasst werden kann. Allerdings bleibt festzuhalten, dass nicht jede Art von sozialer Software gleichbedeutend mit einer Web 2.0 Anwendung ist, was sich bereits aus dem früheren Auftauchen des Social Software Begriffs erklärt.

---

[66] [Ellis et al. 1991 – Groupware: some issues and experiences], S.39
[67] [Gross, Koch 2007], S.4
[68] [Ellis et al. 1991 – Groupware: some issues and experiences], S.40
[69] [Schmidt 2006 – Social Software]
[70] http://www.shirky.com
[71] Vgl. [Hippner 2005 – Social Software]
[72] [Sixtus 2005], S.49

In dieser Arbeit soll daher von Folgendem ausgegangen werden:

Während sich das Verständnis von Social Software von einem techniklastigen Ansatz (vgl. CSCW im vorhergendenen Kapitel) hin zu einem soziologischen Ansatz, bei dem der Mensch mit seinen Beziehungen im Mittelpunkt steht, gewandelt hat, wird Web 2.0 eher durch Trends wie Mashups sowie neuartigen Gestaltungsmerkmalen und Techniken wie RSS[73], AJAX[74] und Podcasts[75] charakterisiert.

2.3.4 Anwendungsbeispiele

Um einen Überblick über gängige Anwendungen im Web 2.0 zu schaffen, sind im Folgenden einige Beispiele dargestellt. Die Einteilung ist aus Sicht des Nutzers dargestellt und gliedert sich in das Netzwerk der User, usergenerierte Inhalte und bestimmte Techniken. Orientierung gab hierbei die Unterteilung von Bert Brückmann.[76]

2.3.4.1　Social Networking Services

Unter Social Networking Services, kurz auch SNS, werden diejenigen Websiten verstanden, deren eindeutiger Fokus auf der Vernetzung ihrer User untereinander abzielt. SNS lassen sich besonders gut durch eine eigentlich für den Oberbegriff Social Software gedachten Definition Koch / Richter beschreiben: „Anwendungssysteme, die unter Ausnutzung von Netzwerk- und Skaleneffekten, indirekte und direkte zwischenmenschliche Interaktion (Koexistenz, Kommunikation, Koordination, Kooperation) auf breiter Basis ermöglichen und die Identitäten und Beziehungen ihrer Nutzer im Internet abbilden und unterstützen.[77] Im Vordergrund von SNS stehen also die Pflege eben dieser Beziehungen und der Aufbau neuer Beziehungen wie es Furnham bereits 1997 darstellt: "Networking is the process of relationships within or between groups".[78] Welche Zwecke damit im Einzelnen verfolgt werden, gibt meist die gewählte Plattform selbst vor.

Im Folgenden werden als Beispiele Xing, eine Plattform für Businessnetworking, und Facebook, eine Privatenetworking Plattform, aufgeführt.

---

[73] RSS - Really Simple Syndication wird von Websites genutzt, um Inhalte weiterzugeben.

[74] Asynchronous Javascript and XML - Elemente von Webseiten werden dynamisch geladen.

[75] Allgemeiner Begriff für Audio- bzw. Video-Inhalte, die über das Internet angeboten werden.

[76] Vgl. [Sciencegarden -]

[77] Vgl. [Koch, Richter 2007], S.14

[78] [Furnham 1997], S.541

Xing

Bereits 1967 erkannte der Psychologe Stanley Milgram durch ein Experiment, das später als "small world phenomenon" bekannt wurde, dass (im Durchschnitt) jeder jeden über sechs Ecken kennt.[79]

Mit diesem Spruch wirbt auch Xing[80], einer der größten Anbieter für Business Networking, für seine Dienste. Neben einer eingeschränkten Gratis-Mitgliedschaft bietet Xing eine "Premium" Mitgliedschaft und ermöglicht es seinen Usern sich ein eigenes Profil (Angefangen von Schulbildung, bis hin zu beruflichen Stationen) einzurichten, welches von anderen Usern gefunden werden kann. Wichtigste Funktion bei Xing sind die "ich suche" und "ich biete" Felder im eigenen beziehungsweise fremden Profil, nach denen gezielt nach "brauchbaren" Kontakten gesucht werden kann. Neben einer Funktion zum Versand und Empfang persönlicher Nachrichten, Kontakte vorstellen und einladen, Terminverwaltung sowie Diskussionsforen zu Themen aller Art, besinnt sich Xing auf die eigentliche Kernfunktion "Kontakte generieren und pflegen" und verzichtet weitestgehend auf Interaktion mit anderen Webseiten.

Verwandte Seiten sind LinkedIn[81] oder Ecademy.[82]

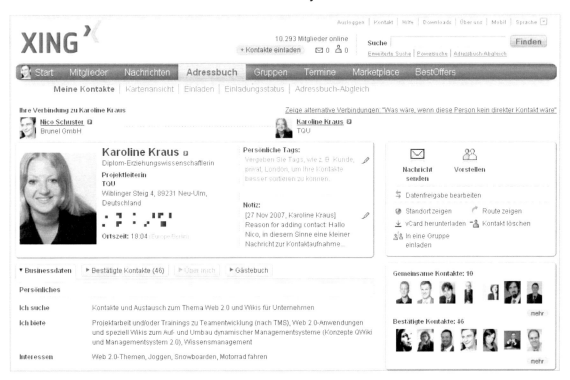

Abbildung 7. Screenshot: Xing-Verbindung Nico Schuster - Karoline Kraus

---

[79] Vgl. [Koch, Richter 2007], S.54

[80] http://www.xing.com

[81] http://www.linkedin.com

[82] http://www.ecademy.com

Facebook

Facebook[83] wurde 2004 für Studenten der Harvard University gegründet und entwickelte sich innerhalb kürzester Zeit zu einer der Networkingsites für Jugendliche in den USA. Anfänglich nur für Harvard-Studenten wurde es nach und nach für einen größeren Kreis zugänglich gemacht und ab 2008 auch auf Deutsch, Spanisch und Französisch übersetzt.[84] Facebook weißt die typischen Merkmale von SNS auf: Kontakte suchen, verwalten, einladen und pflegen. Gleichermaßen gehört es allerdings zu den Vorreitern in der Nutzung von Web 2.0 Technologien. Nicht immer unumstritten ist dabei die Nutzung von an Zielgruppen angepasster Werbung, die anhand der Profildaten ermittelt wird.

Facebook erlaubt neben den Standardfunktionen Nachrichten senden und empfangen, Kontakte pflegen und Foren auch das Hochladen von Fotos in eigene Alben. Personen darauf können verlinkt werden, die Bilder können kommentiert werden und direkt über Schnittstellen an Drittanbieter weitergereicht werden, um beispielsweise Grußkarten davon drucken zu lassen.

Ähnliche Beispiele sind StudiVZ[85] oder Orkut.[86]

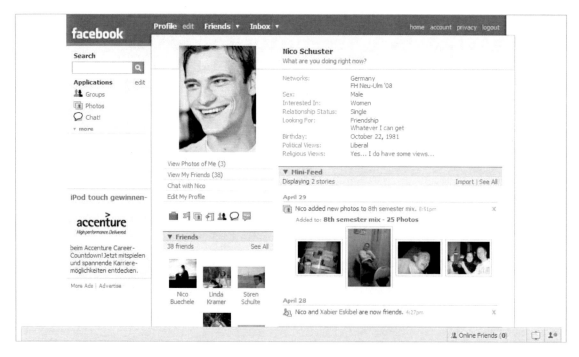

Abbildung 8. Screenshot: Facebook-Profil von Nico Schuster

---

[83] http://www.facebook.com

[84] Vgl. [Wikipedia – Facebook]

[85] http://www.studivz.de

[86] http://www.orkut.com

2.3.4.2   Shared Services

Shared Services, also verteilte Dienste, finden sich als Begriff eher in der Management- oder stark IT-lastigen Literatur. Dennoch scheint die Adaption der vorhandenen Definitionen, wie "Shared Services is a collaborative strategy in which a subset of existing business functions concentrated into a new, semiautonomous bussiness unit that has a management structure"[87] sinnvoll. Unter Shared Services werden also in Anlehnung an diese Definition für diese Arbeit diejenigen Dienste verstanden, die vornehmlich eine definierte Aufgabe erfüllen, allerdings Schnittstellen für weitere Interaktionsmöglichkeiten zur Verfügung stellen. Zeitgleich kommt der soziale Gedanke der Netzwerkbildung hinzu, der weitere Interaktionsmöglichkeiten wie Kommentar- und Bewertungsfunktion bietet.

Flickr

Flickr[88] ist ein klassischer Vertreter der Shared Services. Flickr ist eine Wortschöpfung aus "to flick trough something" was soviel heißt wie "etwas durchblättern"[89] und stellt eine der größten Fotocommunities dar. Hauptaugenmerk liegt daher rein auf der Bildverwaltung. So liest Flickr bereits die in digitalen Fotos enthaltenen IPTC- Kommentare und EXIF-Daten ein (in diesen werden z.B. Belichtung, Blende und Datum gespeichert) oder gar die hinterlegten GPS-Koordinaten aus. Die Bilder können in Alben hinterlegt und mit Beschreibungen sowie einzelnen Tags versehen und von anderen Nutzern kommentiert werden. Durch die offenen Standards ermöglicht es Flickr neben den von Haus aus angebotenen "Badges" (kleinen Animationen ausgewählter Bilder, die auf die eigene Website eingebunden werden können) auch jedem, der programmiertechnisch versiert genug ist, an die Schnittstellen anzudocken und eigene Anwendungen zu schreiben.

Ein ähnliches Beispiel ist Picasa.de[90]

Youtube

Youtube[91] ist entgegen zu Flickr eine Plattform rein für Videos. Innerhalb von nur drei Jahren wurde aus dem kleinen Unternehmen das führende Videoportal. Es wird sogar geschätzt, dass 10% des gesamten Internetverkehrs auf YouTube zurückzuführen sind. Ähnlich wie Flickr konzentriert sich YouTube rein auf Videos und deren einfache Veröffentlichung. So können Videos der Formate MPG, AVI, WMV, MOV hochgeladen werden, welche häufig in Mobiltelefonen eingesetzt werden. Diese werden automatisch

---

[87] [Bergeron 2002], S.2

[88] http://www.flickr.com

[89] [Wikipedia – Flickr]

[90] http://www.picasa.de

[91] http://www.youtube.com

in das Flash-Video-Format konvertiert, was eine weitestgehend problemlose Darstellung auf den meisten internettauglichen Endgeräten gewährleistet. Die Videos können anschließend über einfache HTML-Bausteine direkt auf die eigene Website eingebunden werden. Eine verwandte Website ist unter anderem Myvideo.de.[92]

2.3.4.3 Collaborative Content Management

Der Ursprung des Wortes Kollaboration entstammt dem Lateinischen "co" für zusammen und "labore" für arbeiten.[93] Heute wird unter Kollaboration meist die Zusammenarbeit von mehreren Personen angesehen. Unter Collaborative Content werden demzufolge Inhalte verstanden, die von mehr als einer Person erstellt wurden.[94] Wird eine Zusammenarbeit von mehreren Personen an einem Projekt auf elektronischer Basis angestrebt, so wird zu diesem Zweck meist geeignete Software eingesetzt. Ähnlich den Groupware-Systemen, die es bereits seit einigen Jahren ermöglichen, in Zusammenarbeit Dokumente zu erstellen, geht der Ansatz des Collaborativen Content noch einen Schritt weiter. Collaborative Content Management Software ermöglicht es beispielsweise mehreren Autoren gleichzeitig und nicht wie beim Groupware-Ansatz zeitversetzt an einem Beitrag zu arbeiten.

Wikipedia

Ein klassisches Beispiel der kollaborativen Inhaltserstellung stellt die Online Enzyklopädie Wikipedia dar. Die Wikipedia, ein Kunstwort aus Wiki (hawaiisch für "schnell") und Encyclopedia (eng. für Enzyklopädie), ist ein weltweites Internetprojekt zur Erstellung einer Online Enzyklopädie in mehreren Sprachversionen. Jeder kann nicht nur bereits erstellte Texte bearbeiten, sondern auch neue Inhalte, also Content, einpflegen. Nach eigenen Angaben haben bereits ca. 285.000 Autoren zum Erfolg des Projekts beigetragen. Der oftmals bemängelten Qualität und Richtigkeit der Inhalte wird seit Ende 2007 durch eine Qualitätssicherung Rechnung getragen. Einträge werden nun durch ein Gremium aus erfahrenen Autoren und Redaktionen überprüft und in dieser Version freigegeben. Eine Studie des Wissenschaftsjournal "Nature" fand heraus, dass die Wikipedia pro Artikel vier und dazu im Vergleich die Ecyclopaedia Britannica drei Ungenauigkeiten pro Artikel aufweist.[95] Die deutsche Wikipedia umfasst bis heute (Stand August 2008) ca. 750.000 Artikel und gehört nach Angaben von Alexa.com (Alexa[96] ist ein Serverdienst, welcher Daten über Webseitenzugriffe durch Web-Benutzer sammelt und darstellt) zu den Top 10 der am häufigsten frequentierten Internetseiten der Welt.

---

[92] http://www.myvideo.de
[93] Vgl. [Wikipedia – Kollaboration]
[94] Vgl. [McGovern, Norton et al. 2002]
[95] Vgl. [SPIEGEL ONLINE]
[96] http://www.alexa.com

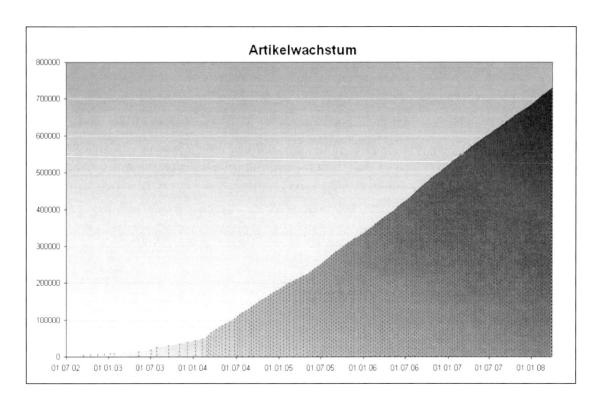

Abbildung 9. Artikelwachstum der deutschsprachigen Wikipedia

2.3.4.4 Supporting Services

Die einfache Übersetzung für Supporting Services aus dem Englischen ins Deutsche ergibt unterstützende Dienstleistungen (leo.org). Allein diese Übersetzung umschreibt die Gruppe an Anwendungen der Kategorie Supporting Services bereits sehr treffend. In Anlehnung an Grönroos werden unter den Supporting Services jene Dienste verstanden, die hauptsächlich dazu eingesetzt werden, die Kernleistung eines Angebots attraktiver zu machen.[97] Die Supporting Services stellen zwar im Kontext dieser Arbeit eigenständige Anwendungen dar, sie kommen aber erst im Zusammenspiel mit übergeordneten Systemen zur vollen Geltung.

Google Maps

Google Maps[98] ist ein webbasierter Kartendienst der Google Incorporated. Google selbst stellt hierbei in erster Linie das Kartenmaterial, entweder als Kartenansicht oder Satellitenbild, zur Verfügung, welches durch das API (Application Programming Interface, eine offenen Schnittstelle, um das System ansprechen zu können) mit weiteren Informationen bereichert wird.[99] Die Karten hat Google anfänglich durch Zukauf von

---

[97] Grönroos in [Zielke 2004], S.43

[98] http://maps.google.com

[99] Vgl. [Wikipedia – Google Maps]

Kartenmaterial entwickelt, weitet diesen Service aber seit geraumer Zeit immer weiter aus und liefert mittlerweile für das Schwesterprogramm Google Earth, das ein eigenständig ablaufendes Programm auf dem Client-Rechner darstellt, auch 3D-Ansichten von Großstädten weltweit.

Während Google Maps zu Beginn meist als reine Landkarte auf der privaten oder firmeneigenen Website genutzt wurde, konnten im Laufe der Zeit nicht nur immer mehr googleeigene Services, wie beispielsweise ein integrierter Routenplaner genutzt werden, sondern die Karten lassen sich zunehmend mit Inhalten aus anderen Anwendungen bereichern. Viele Communities oder Netzwerkseiten nutzen den Dienst mittlerweile, um die Standorte ihrer User zu veranschaulichen. Wichtig dabei bleibt zu betonen, dass die eigentliche Hauptanwendung nicht verlassen wird und die Google Map dieses Angebot lediglich bereichert.

Die Social Networking Plattform Xing bietet die Möglichkeit, die eigenen Kontakte auf einer Karte anzeigen zu lassen. Mit Klick auf einen der Kreise, der einen oder mehrere Kontakte darstellt, werden die jeweiligen Kontaktdaten interaktiv in die Karte eingeblendet.

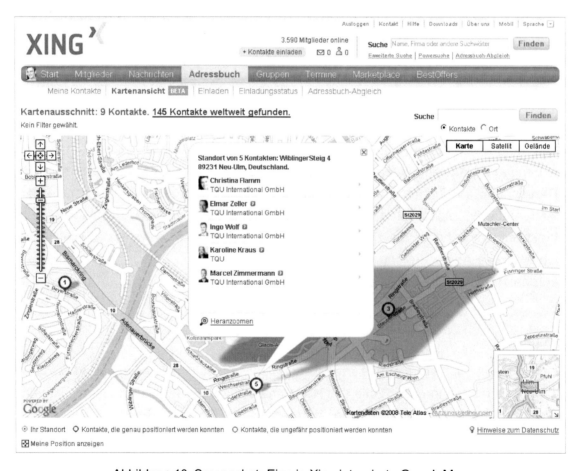

Abbildung 10. Screenshot: Eine in Xing integrierte GoogleMap

Gliffy

Gliffy[100] ist ein noch relativ junges Tool der Gliffy Incorporated. Es läuft im Browser und ermöglicht es, ähnlich dem bekannten Programm Microsoft Visio, Diagramme, Flow-charts, Netzpläne und Ähnliches zu erstellen.

Das Plugin für Confluence erlaubt es, Diagramme auf einzelnen Wikiseiten einzubin-den und diese direkt im Wiki zu bearbeiten. Dabei wird gemäß der Wikitechnik jegliche Version einzeln abgespeichert und versioniert.[101] Es bietet eine für die meisten Anwen-dungsfälle ausreichenden Satz an zur Verfügung stehenden Shapes (Symbolen und Grafiken) die für einzelne Diagrammtypen, wie beispielsweise einem UML-Diagramm aus der Informatik, benötigt werden. Die Diagramme werden vektorbasiert gespeichert und belegen daher nur sehr wenig Speicherplatz im System. Auch ein weiteres Bear-beiten mit Grafik- und Zeichenprogrammen wie Adobe Illustrator ist damit problemlos möglich.

Auch Gliffy ist ursprünglich als eigenständige Anwendung konzipiert. Aber nicht zuletzt die enormen Vorteile durch eine direkte Integration in ein System wie Confluence be-wogen auch Branchengrößen wie IBM, SAP, Cisco und viele weitere dazu, das Tool in ihr Wiki zu integrieren.

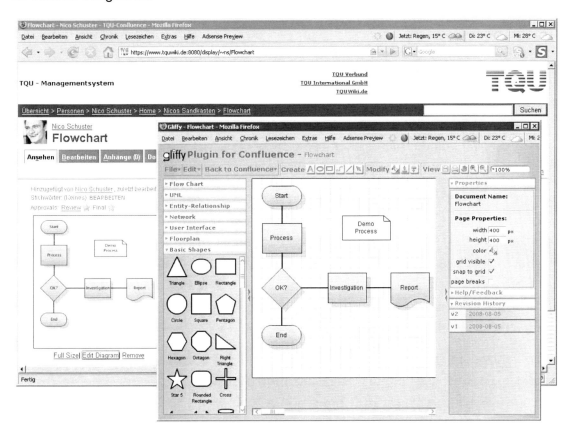

Abbildung 11. Screenshot: Gliffy-Plugin für Confluence

---

[100] http://www.gliffy.com
[101] Vgl. [Gliffy – Confluence Plugin]

3 Managementsystem 2.0

Den Begriff Managementsystem 2.0 als solches gibt es in der einschlägigen Literatur nicht. Er entstammt dem Umfeld dieser Arbeit im Rahmen der Arbeitskreise der TQU International GmbH. Angelehnt ist er an den Begriff Web 2.0. Durch die Versionsnummer soll nicht nur die Verwandtschaft zu neuen Medien und Techniken, eben speziell den bereits genannten aus dem Umfeld von Web 2.0, sondern auch eine Weiterentwicklung im Bereich der Managementsysteme impliziert werden. Als Vergleich seien hier Veröffentlichungen von Algesheimer / Leitl mit dem Titel „Unternehmen 2.0"[102] und und Richter / Koch mit „Enterprise 2.0"[103] angeführt.

Der folgende Abschnitt soll aufzeigen, was unter klassischen Managementansätzen verstanden und gelehrt wird und inwiefern es zum Managementsystem 2.0 Überschneidungen und Neuerungen gibt. Daraus abgeleitet wird eine Definition für Managementsystem 2.0. Desweiteren werden Best Practices für ein Einführungsszenario aufgezeigt und die Überprüfbarkeit anhand von Kennzahlen dargestellt. Eine nicht-repräsentative Umfrage dient dabei als Indikator für die Akzeptanz eines solchen Systems.

3.1 Ansätze der Organisationslehre

Die Entstehung der ersten Organisationstheorien läßt sich im Wesentlichen auf die frühen Jahrzehnte des 20. Jahrhunderts eingrenzen. Namen wie Taylor, Weber und später Ulrich sind aus der Managementlehre nicht mehr wegzudenken. Sie alle haben Ansätze und Theorien aufgestellt, die noch heute ihre Gültigkeit haben.

Alle Organisationsansätze aufzuschlüsseln und deren Inhalte an dieser Stelle wiederzugeben, würde den Rahmen dieser Arbeit sprengen. Vielmehr werden einige der bekanntesten Ansätze analysiert und ihre Übertragbarkeit auf ein wikibasiertes System untersucht. Als weiterführende Literatur sei an dieser Stelle Schreyögg empfohlen.[104] Es wird daher ein Vergleich zum Bürokratieansatz nach Weber und nachfolgend dem dem St. Galler Systemansatz vorgenommen. Auf weitere Ansätze wird innerhalb der Ausführung Bezug genommen.

Die Auswahl der Theorien begründet nicht zuletzt die Reihenfolge ihrer Entstehung und ihrer allgemeinen Verbreitung und Relevanz für die heutige Gestaltung von Organisationen und ist stark beeinflusst von Komus und Wauch.

---

[102] Vgl. [Algesheimer, Leitl 2007]

[103] Vgl. [Koch, Richter 2007],

[104] [Schreyögg 2003]

31

3.1.1 Bürokratieansatz nach Weber

Max Webers (1864-1920) Bürokratieansatz, der in seinem Werk "Wirtschaft und Gesellschaft" 1921 erstmalig veröffentlicht wurde, gilt als der erste wissenschaftliche Ansatz der Organisationstheorie.[105]

Bei der Betrachtung der Ausführungen Webers muss berücksichtigt werden, dass zur damaligen Zeit unter dem Begriff "Bürokratie" ein anderes Verständnis herrschte, als heute. Webers Ansichten waren daher stark geprägt vom "preußischen Bild des staatlichen Beamten".[106]

Die augenfälligen Merkmale der Bürokratie sind nach Weber "Präzision, Schnelligkeit, Eindeutigkeit, Aktenkundigkeit, Kontinuierlichkeit, Diskretion, Einheitlichkeit, straffe Unterordnung, Ersparnisse an Reibungen sowie sachlichen und persönlichen Kosten."[107] Nach Schulte-Zurhausen ergeben sich daher vier Merkmale, die eine Organisationsform charakterisieren: [108]

- Arbeitsteilung
  Jedes Organisationsmitglied hat einen festen Arbeitsplatz und die notwendige, feste Kompetenz zur Aufgabenerfüllung

- Amtshierarchie
  Weisungs- und Kontrollbefugnisse sollten streng hierarchisch und fest verteilt sein.

- Regeln und Normen
  Die zur Aufgabenerfüllung notwendigen Leistungen und Kommunikationswege müssen klar in einem Regelwerk festgelegt werden.

- Aktenmäßigkeit der Verwaltung
  Nachvollziehbarkeit über Entscheidungen und Geschäftsvorgänge muss gegeben sein.

Anders als Taylor beim sog. Scientific Management (auch Taylorismus genannt)[109] sieht Weber in den Menschen zwar keine Arbeitnehmer, die ähnlichen Gesetzen wie die Teile einer Maschine gehorchen,[110] aber auch er identifiziert die persönlichen Bedürfnisse der Mitarbeiter als Störfaktoren.

Komus und Wauch betrachten Webers Bürokratieansatz im Kontext der Wikipedia und schlussfolgern, dass mehr Widersprüche als Übereinstimmungen zu finden sind.[111]

---

[105] Vgl. [Schreyögg 2003], S.31
[106] Vgl. [Wikipedia – Bürokratieansatz]
[107] [Hanke, Knoll (Hg.) 2005], S.185
[108] Vgl. [Schulte-Zurhausen 2002], S.8
[109] Vgl. [Zollondz 2001], S.1142
[110] Vgl. [Wikipedia – Taylorismus]
[111] Vgl. [Komus, Wauch 2008], S.82

Dem ist entgegenzuhalten, dass die Wikipedia zwar ursprünglich als rein selbstregulierendes System konzipiert war, jedoch im Zuge ihrer Entwicklung ebenfalls bestimmten Forderungen wie zum Beispiel denen nach Qualitätssicherung nachkommen musste und sich daher auch in der Wikipedia Regeln, Hierarchien und Arbeitsteilungen herausgebildet haben.

In einem im Unternehmensumfeld eingesetztem Wiki erscheint die Bewertung der Grundsätze Webers noch einmal differenziert werden zu müssen, da hier firmeninterne (Firmenkodex etc.) und externe Regularien (Gesetze, Verordnungen etc.) einzuhalten sind. Die folgende Auflistung orientiert sich an der Gegenüberstellung von Komus und Wauch,[112] wurde aber auf der „Wiki-Seite" entsprechend den Bedürfnissen in einer Unternehmung angepasst.

Prinzipien der Bürokratietheorie	Unternehmenswiki
Arbeitsteilung	nur für abgegrenzte Bereiche, nicht über das gesamte Wiki möglich/sinnvoll (z.B. Sicherheit von Forschungsdaten)
Amtshierarchie	Siteowner/Prozessowner die über einen geprüften Status eines Artikels entscheiden. (Qualitätssicherung)
Regeln und Normen	Welche Inhalte sind in welcher Form einzupflegen. (Tabellen, Charts, Grafiken, etc.)
Aktenmäßigkeit der Verwaltung	Versionierung und Dokumentation erfolgen automatisch durch das System

Tabelle 2. Gegenüberstellung Bürokratieansatz – Wiki. In Anlehnung an Komus / Wauch

---

[112] Vgl. [Komus, Wauch 2008], S.82f

3.1.2 St. Galler Systemansatz

Der Systemansatz geht ursprünglich auf den Biologen Bertalanffy zurück, der in den 1920er Jahren die Allgemeine Systemtheorie entwickelte.[113] Diese begründet sich in der Erkenntnis, dass in der Natur Phänomene nicht einzeln und isoliert auftreten, sondern immer in einer Relation zu anderen Elementen gesehen werden müssen.

Ein System besteht daher aus einer Menge an Elementen, die miteinander in Beziehung stehen und sich gegenseitig beeinflussen.[114] Später wurde dieser Ansatz von Barnard nochmals aufgefasst und für die Führungslehre aufbereitet. Er kennzeichnete Unternehmen als sozio-technische Systeme mit einem hohen Komplexitätsgrad.[115]

Übertragen auf Unternehmen kann daher festgestellt werden, dass ein Unternehmen ein offenes System darstellt, da es sowohl interne Elemente aufweist, die miteinander in Relation stehen, als auch Kontakte zur Umwelt nach Aussen hat, welche das System Unternehmung beeinflussen.[116]

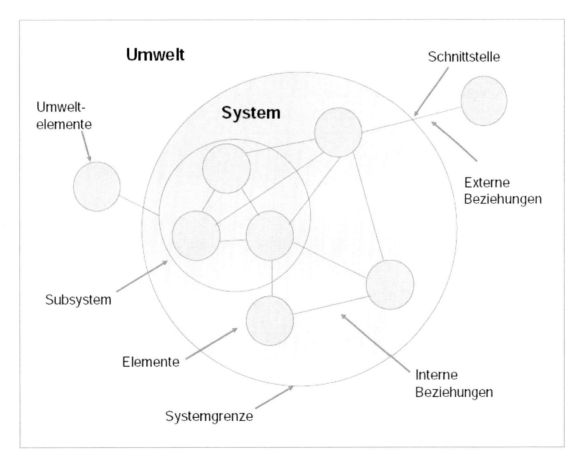

Abbildung 12. Darstellung von System und Umwelt

---

[113] Vgl. [Wikipedia – Systemtheorie]

[114] Vgl. [Rüegg-Stürm 2002], S.18

[115] Vgl. [Macharzina, Wolf 2008], S.71

[116] Vgl. [Ferstl 2006], S.61

Nicht fehlen darf an dieser Stelle ein Vermerk zur Kybernetik. Die Kybernetik als Lehre von der Steuerung technischer Systeme[117] wurde von Norbert Wiener begründet, befasst sich hauptsächlich mit der Regelung und Steuerung von Systemen und ist geprägt von einem eher mechanistischen Denken.[118]

Kybernetische Systeme weisen nach Schweizer folgende Charakteristika auf:[119]

- komplexe / äußerst komplexe Struktur

- dynamisches Verhalten

- zielgerichtetes, selbstregulierendes Verhalten

Gerade die beiden letztgenannten Punkte lassen sich sehr stark im Bereich der Wikis und allgemein im Umfeld von Web 2.0 wiederfinden.

Auf den Grundlagen der Systemtheorie und der Kybernetik wurde unter Federführung von Hans Ulrich das St. Galler Managementmodell begründet. Dabei stehen nach Hill, Fehlbaum und Ulrich vor allem fünf Eigenschaften sozialer Systeme im Mittelpunkt:[120]

- Selbstregelung
  Die Fähigkeit eines Systems, ohne Lenkung einen vorgegebenen Sollwert und eine gewisse Stabilität einzuhalten

- Anpassung
  Die Fähigkeit eines Systems, nicht nur einen Sollwert stabil zu halten, sondern diesen auch an die Umwelt anzupassen.

- Lernfähigkeit
  Die Fähigkeit eines Systems, aus Erfahrungen Konsequenzen für das zukünftige Verhalten zu ziehen

- Selbstorganisation
  Die Fähigkeit eines Systems zur eigenständigen Evolution und Differenzierung

- Automatisierbarkeit
  Die Fähigkeit eines Systems, menschliche Eingriffe zu ersetzen und damit nicht permanent notwendig zu machen.

---

[117] Vgl. [Ellebracht, Gerhard et al. 2003], S.32
[118] Vgl. [Wikipedia – Systemtheorie]
[119] Vgl. [Schweizer 2008], S.48
[120] Vgl. [Hill, Fehlbaum et al. 1998], S.439

Neben diesen Eigenschaften besitzt ein System überdies noch intrinsische Eigenschaften, die sich nach Probst in folgender Weise aufgliedern lassen:[121]

- Komplexität
  Ein System kann weder vollständig beschrieben werden, noch sein Verhalten eindeutig prognostiziert werden

- Selbstreferenz
  Jedes Verhalten eines Systems wirkt wieder auf das System zurück

- Redundanz
  Das Potential zur Selbstorganisation ist mehrfach im System verteilt und fördert dadurch organisationales Lernen

- Autonomie
  Das System ist autonom, wenn Interaktionen und Relationen nur das System selbst und keine anderen Systeme involvieren

Zusammenfassend lässt sich, wiederum angelehnt an Komus / Wauch[122] folgende Tabelle als Vergleich zwischen Systemaspekten und Wiki-Aspekten aufzeigen:

Systemaspekte	Wikiaspekte
Offenheit	Klare Grenzen zwischen Unternehmen und Umwelt (z.B. zwischen Teilbereichen der Unternehmung)
Selbstorganisierend	Bestimmte Regeln müssen vorhanden sein, können aber durch Gruppenprozesse angepasst werden.
Dynamische Entwicklung	Koordination/Anpassung an Wachstum und Komplexität
Flexibilisierung durch Redundanz	Flexible Reaktion nur in Bereichen mit einer Vielzahl an Autoren möglich
Lernfähigkeit für die Zukunft	Durch problemlose Kommunikation und schnellen Austausch können Fehler zukünftig vermieden und Prozesse angepasst werden.
Selbstregelung	Gegenseitige Kontrolle und Korrektur
Automatisierbarkeit	Für wichtige Dokumente ist der Eingriff von höheren Instanzen unabdingbar
Komplexität	Reaktionen sind schwer prognostizierbar

Tabelle 3. Gegenüberstellung von System- und Wikiaspekten. In Anlehnung an Komus / Wauch

---

[121] Vgl. [Probst 1987], S.76ff
[122] Vgl. [Komus, Wauch 2008], S.117

Komus und Wauch haben auch in diesem Fall für ihre Gegenüberstellung die Wikipedia als offene Enzyklopädie zugrunde gelegt. So erklärt sich auch die unterschiedliche Auslegung in den meisten Punkten. Die Wikipedia als eigenständiges System läßt sich zwar sehr gut mit den Systemansätzen in Verbindung bringen, diese Vergleiche können aber nicht eins zu eins auf ein Unternehmenswiki angewandt werden.

Ein Unternehmenswiki als Teil des Systems Unternehmung hat sich in ein bestehendes Geflecht aus Regeln und Grenzen einzugliedern. Es kann diesem System durch seine funktionalen Aspekte dazu verhelfen, einzelne der aufgeführten Systemaspekte zukünftig stärker auszuprägen.

3.1.3 Faktor Mensch

Neben Webers Bürokratieansatz und dem St. Galler Systemansatz sind an dieser Stelle auch Ansätze aus der Motivationstheorie geprägt durch Maslow und Herzberg zu nennen.

Diese Theorien und Ansätze befassen sich weitaus intensiver mit dem Faktor Mensch selbst und sind bei der Analyse eines auf menschlicher Mitarbeit fußenden Systems wie Wiki unabdingbar.

Motivationsmodell nach Maslow

Der US-amerikanische Psychologe Abraham Maslow veröffentlichte 1943 in seinem Werk „Motivation und Persönlichkeit"[123] sein Modell von den Bedürfnissen und Motiven des Menschen, besser bekannt als Maslow'sche Bedürfnispyramide.

Er geht bei seiner Darstellung davon aus, dass der Mensch nur handelt, um gewisse Bedürfnisse zu befriedigen. Einteilen lassen sich diese in fünf Klassen:[124]

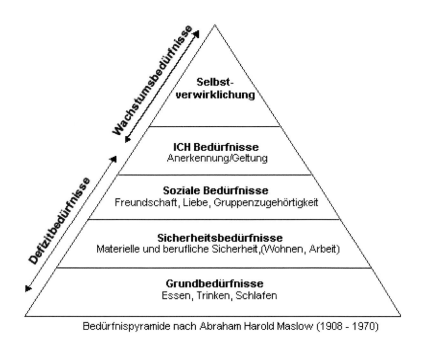

Abbildung 13. Maslow'sche Bedürfnispyramide

Die Stufen eins, zwei und drei und je nach Auslegung des Modells auch die vierte werden als Defizitmotive bezeichnet. Sie werden nur wirksam, wenn ein Defizit besteht. Wer keinen Durst mehr hat, trinkt auch nicht mehr.

---

[123] [Maslow, Kruntorad 2005]

[124] Vgl. [Wikipedia – Maslowsche Bedürfnispyramide]

38

Bedürfnisse auf Stufe vier und fünf, später wurde durch Maslow noch eine sechste Stufe hinzugefügt, die sich mit Transzendenz oder einfacher gesagt der Suche nach Sinngebung befasst, werden als Wachstumsbedürfnisse bezeichnet.

Die bisweilen kritisierte Einteilung von Maslow's aufeinander aufbauenden Stufen wurde 2007 in einer Studie von Communispace[125], einer auf Web 2.0 Community Building spezialisierten Firma mit Sitz in den USA, in einen Kontext zu sozialen Bedürfnissen im Web 2.0 übertragen:[126]

1. Ausdruck der persönlichen Identität. Social Networks ermöglichen es uns Menschen, uns darzustellen und so (immer wieder neu) zu definieren.

2. Status und Selbstvertrauen. Bedürfnisse wie Unabhängigkeit und Anerkennung sind wichtig für unser Selbstwertgefühl. Diese Bedürfnisse können wir mit Communitys, Blogs und anderen sozialen Medien befriedigen, indem wir uns eine digitale Reputation erarbeiten.

3. Helfen und Hilfe bekommen. Menschen haben das Bedürfnis, sowohl anderen zu helfen wie auch selber nach Hilfe zu suchen. Gegenseitige Hilfe (sog. mutual assistance) unter sich völlig fremden Individuen ist ein spezifisch im Internet vorkommendes Phänomen.

4. Anschluss und Zugehörigkeit. Online Communitys sind ein wichtiges Hilfsmittel, um Gleichgesinnte zu finden und sich mit ihnen auszutauschen.

5. Gemeinschaftssinn. Ein Zugehörigkeitsgefühl alleine ist nicht gleichzusetzen mit einem Gemeinschaftssinn. Um letzteren zu erreichen, bedarf es lange andauernder, gegenseitiger Beziehungen und ein gegenseitiges Commitment zu den Zielen der Gemeinschaft.

6. Bestätigung der eigenen Wertvorstellungen und des Selbstwertgefühls. Wir alle wollen uns bestätigt fühlen in unseren Werten und in unserem Wert. Daher suchen wir die Bestätigung, dass das, was wir sagen, schreiben, tun und denken Anderen wichtig ist und auch einen Einfluss auf sie ausübt.

---

[125] Vgl. [Communispace – Move Over Maslow]
[126] Vgl. [Wortgefecht.net – Maslow und das Web 2.0]

Zwei-Faktoren-Theorie nach Herzberg

Während Maslow seine Theorie nur bedingt empirisch nachweisen konnte, gewann Herzberg ab 1959 seine Daten in einer Befragung unter Ingenieuren und Buchhaltern.[127]

Seine Untersuchungen zeigten, dass nicht automatisch ein Grund zur Zufriedenheit bestehe, wenn keine Gründe für Unzufriedenheit vorliegen. Die wichtigste Erkenntnis war daher nach Herzberg die Aufgabe der eindimensionalen Betrachtung der Zufriedenheit.[128]

Er unterschied daher in sog. Motivatoren und Hygienefaktoren. Als Hygienefaktoren werden diejenigen Faktoren verstanden, die zwar Unzufriedenheit verhindern können, was aber nicht gleichzeitig dazu führt, dass Zufriedenheit eintritt. Sie können daher, angelehnt an die medizinische Bedeutung des Wortes Hygiene, Krankheiten verhindern aber keine Gesundheit entwickeln.[129] Motivatoren jedoch tragen aktiv zur Zufriedenheit bei, führen aber bei Nichtvorhandensein nicht zu Unzufriedenheit.

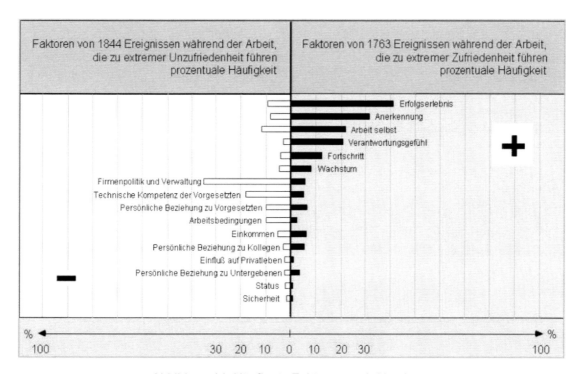

Abbildung 14. Häufigste Faktoren nach Herzberg

[127] Vgl. [Beyer – Inhalts- und Prozeßtheorien der Motivation]
[128] Vgl. [Heinen 1992], S.165
[129] Vgl. [Pelz 2004], S.111

Folgende Abbildung ist einer Abbildung aus Komus / Wauch Wikimanagement entnommen und beruht ursprünglich auf einer Forschungsarbeit der Universität Würzburg.[130] Die Darstellung wurde, wie die bereits angeführten Vergleiche bei Weber's Bürokratieansatz und dem St. Galler Systemansatz auf ihre Anwendbarkeit im Bereich eines Unternehmenswikis angepasst:

Herzberg	Wiki
Motivatoren - Leistung vollbringen - Anerkennung finden - Einen interessanten Arbeitsinhalt haben -Verantwortung übernehmen	Motivatoren - Artikel schreiben, Qualität optimieren - externer Anreize (z.B. Wiki-User-Treffen) - Unterstützung für andere Nutzer bieten - Verantwortung für Seiten / Bereiche
Hygiene-Faktoren - Unternehmenspolitik - Art der Personalführung - Beziehung zu Vorgesetzten und Kollegen - Gehalt - Arbeitsbedingungen	Hygiene-Faktoren - Zu starke Regulierung und Einschräkung könnte demotivierend wirken - Ungenügende Hardware kann Arbeitsbedingungen verschlechtern - Ungenügende Kenntniss vom IT-System kann demotivierend wirken

Tabelle 4. Gegenüberstellung Herzberg und Wiki. In Anlehnung an Komus / Wauch

In Analogie zur Feststellung von Komus / Wauch, dass es der Wikipedia gelungen sei, die Hygiene-Faktoren und Motivatoren entsprechend zu erfüllen[131] lässt sich diese Sichtweise auch auf ein durch Wiki abgebildetes Managementsystem für eine Unternehmung übertragen.

---

[130] http://www.i2.psychologie.uni-wuerzburg.de/ao/research/wikipedia.php
[131] Vgl. [Komus, Wauch 2008], S.100

3.2   Wiki als Managementsystem

Die im vorangegangenen Abschnitt rein faktischen Vergleiche ergaben, dass sich die Theorien der allgemeinbekannten Organisationslehre sehr gut auf ein wikibasiertes Managementsystem übertragen lassen.

Es genügt aber nicht, nur alte Theorien und neue Ideen gegenüber zu stellen. In einem so komplexen System wie einem Wiki gibt es viele verschiedene Faktoren, die nicht immer explizit zu fassen sind. So kommen auch Ebersbach et al zu dem Schluss "Wikis are not automatic success, much less a cure-all"[132].

Es stellt sich an dieser Stelle die Frage, ob ein Wiki sich obgleich seiner bereits aufgezeigten Kompatibilität wirklich für Managementsysteme eignet. Vielmehr stellt sich die Frage, ob es akzeptiert und überhaupt von Seiten der Belegschaft gewünscht wird.

Wer mit auf Sozialität basierender Software arbeitet, muss sich darüber im Klaren sein, dass es eine nicht zu vernachlässigende Menge an Vor- und Nachteilen oder etwas milder formuliert, antreibende und hemmende Faktoren in und um ein Unternehmenswiki geben kann und wird.

Der Frage nach dem Wunsch und der Akzeptanz, ein Wiki einzusetzen, wurde in einer nicht-repräsentativen Onlineumfrage nachgegangen, deren Ergebnisse im Folgenden dargestellt werden. Die wiederkehrenden Phänomene der Wiki-Ablehnung oder Wiki-Befürwortung, welche allgemein auch als Wikipatterns[133] bekannt sind, werden im Anschluss behandelt.

---

[132] [Ebersbach, Glaser et al. 2006], S.26
[133] http://www.wikipatterns.com

3.2.1 Wiki - nur ein Hype?

Das Wikis nicht nur unter Techies und IT-affinen, jungen Menschen ein Trend und nützliches Werkzeug sind, zeigen bestenfalls so renomierte Unternehmen wie Gartner[134], die in ihrem jährlich veröffentlichten „Hype Cycle for Emerging Technologies" und dem „Magic Quadrant for Team Collaboration and Social Software" zum einen aktuelle und frisch aufkommende Technologien und Firmen, die diese Technologien einsetzen, gegenüberstellen und miteinander vergleichen.

Die folgende Abbildung zeigt den zum Erstellungszeitpunkt dieser Arbeit verfügbaren Hype Cycle. „Der Hype-Zyklus stellt dar, welche Phasen der öffentlichen Aufmerksamkeit eine neue Technologie bei deren Einführung durchläuft. Der Begriff des Hype-Zyklus wurde von der Gartner-Beraterin Jackie Fenn geprägt und dient heute Technologieberatern zur Bewertung in der Einführung neuer Technologien."[135] Aus ihm geht hervor, dass Wikis sich gerade in der Phase der Desilusion befinden. Dies bedeutet, dass die Zeit der überzogenen Erwartungen bereits vorüber ist und die Technologie Wiki nun auf dem Weg zum tatsächlich im Unternehmen nutzbaren Werkzeug ist.

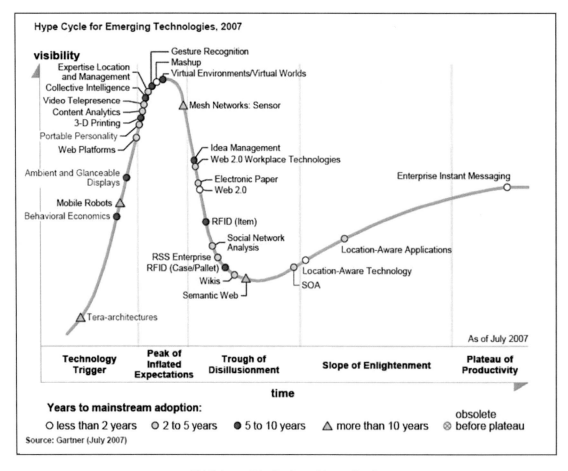

Abbildung 15. Gartner Hype Cycle

---

[134] http://www.gartner.com
[135] [Wikipedia – Hype-Zyklus]

Neben dem Hype Cycle veröffentlicht Gartner jährlich ebenfalls das sog. Magic Quadrant for Team Collaboration and Social Software. „Magic Quadrants stellen dar, wie bestimmte Anbieter sich nach von Gartner definierten Kriterien innerhalb dieses Marktes positionieren. Die Positionierung erfolgt in einem der vier Quadranten: Leader, Visionär, Herausforderer und Nischenakteure."[136]

Auch die beiden in dieser Arbeit vorgestellten Anbieter von Enterprise Wikis finden bei Gartner ihre Würdigung im Magic Quadrant. Wie die nachfolgende Abbildung zeigt, sind sowohl Socialtext als auch Atlassian's Confluence den großen und bekannten Anbietern von Anwendungssoftware wie IBM und Microsoft bereits dicht auf den Fersen und entwickeln sich von Nischenanbietern zunehmend zu Herausforderern.

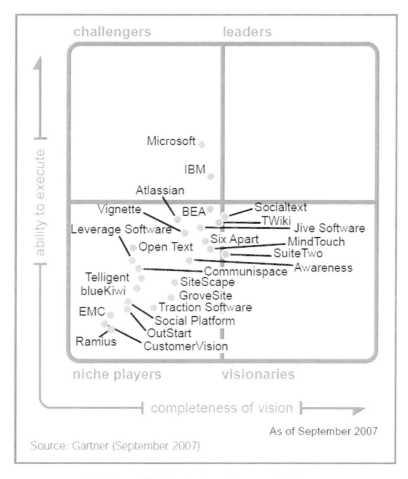

Abbildung 16. Magic Quadrant nach Gartner

---

[136] [Wikipedia – Gartner]

3.2.1.1 Online-Befragung

Gartner zeigt durch seine beiden Darstellungen von Magic Quadrant und Hype Cylce bereits auf, dass Wikis und Socialsoftware einen gewissen Reifegrad und Marktstellung erreicht haben bzw. bald erreichen werden. Für diese Arbeit ergibt sich allerdings aus der Themenstellung eine andere Frage:

- Sind Unternehmen und ihre Mitarbeiter bereit ein Wiki als Managementsystem einzusetzen?

- Wo werden Stärken und Schwächen gesehen?

- Welche Bereiche kommen dafür in Frage?

Bei der Online-Befragung kamen sowohl geschlossene als auch offene Fragen sowie skalierte Fragen zum Einsatz. Auch wurde die Möglichkeit genutzt, voneinander abhängige Fragen zu nutzen und den Teilnehmern wurde durch ein gesondertes Kommentarfeld ermöglicht, weitere Anmerkungen zu machen.

Die 95 Teilnehmer der Befragung (N=95) wurden durch persönliche Einladung und Veröffentlichungen in Internetforen und Webseiten auf die Umfrage aufmerksam gemacht. Es scheint daher bereits vorweggenommen, dass sich der Teilnehmerkreis eher positiv zum Thema der Umfrage äußern wird. Bei der Auswahl der zur Ankündigung genutzten Internetforen wurde daher Wert darauf gelegt, nicht allein durch die Forenwahl reine Web 2.0-Befürworter zu erreichen. Wie die Auswertung ergab, ist eine Streuung der Teilnehmer über mehrere Branchen erreicht worden.

Die beruflichen Positionen der Teilnehmer variieren vom Praktikant bis zum Vorstand. Auch die Unternehmensgröße vom Kleinstbetrieb bis hin zum Großunternehmen konnte erfasst werden. Auffällig ist das Verhältnis von weiblichen Teilnehmern zu männlichen Teilnehmern. So waren zwei Drittel der Teilnehmer männlichen Geschlechts und lediglich ein knappes Drittel weiblich.

Der Fragebogen, dem diese Ergebnisse entnommen wurden, ist im Anhang dieser Arbeit begefügt.

Im Folgenden werden die Teilnehmer der Umfrage charakterisiert, die Vorteile und Nachteile von Wikis analysiert, sowie deren Einsatzfelder herausgearbeitet. Im Anschluss wird der Bezug zu dieser Arbeit hergestellt und eine Schlussfolgerung aufgestellt.

Charakterisierung der Teilnehmer

Alter:

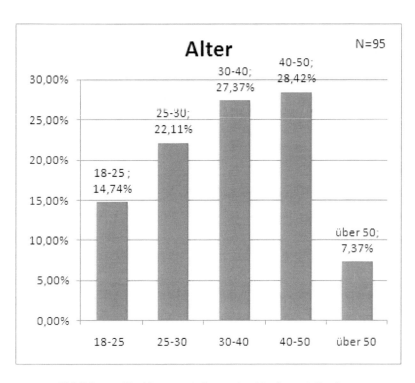

Abbildung 17. Altersverteilung der Umfrageteilnehmer

Von 95 Teilnehmern der Umfrage entfallen mit 27,37% und 28,42% auf die Gruppe der 30 bis 40 Jährigen bzw. 40-50 Jährigen. Sie stellen damit den größten Teil der Teilnehmer. Mit 22,11% liegt die Gruppe der 25-30 Jährigen relativ dicht dahinter. Einen deutlich geringeren Teil machen mit 14,74% die 18-25 Jährigen Teilnehmer aus. Die kleinste Gruppe mit 7,35% stellen die über 50 Jährigen Befragungsteilnehmer dar.

Diese Zahlen sind nicht weiter verwunderlich, wenn sie im Kontext anderer Studien gesehen werden. So ergab eine Erhebung der Forschungsgruppe Wahlen, dass der größte Anteil der Internetnutzer unter 30 Jahren ist und die Zahl der Internetnutzer ab 50 Jahren deutlich sinkt.[137] Unter Berücksichtigung der anvisierten Zielgruppe der Berufstätigen ist auch zu erklären, weshalb entgegen anderer Studien das Teilnehmerfeld der 18-25 Jährigen schwächer ausgeprägt ist.

---

[137] Vgl. [Forschungsgruppe Wahlen – Internet-Strukturdaten]

Geschlecht:

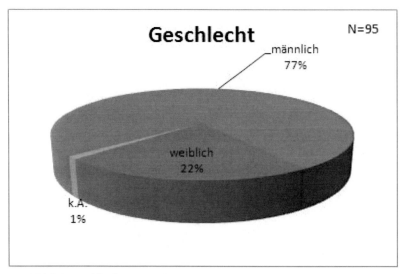

Abbildung 18. Geschlechterverteilung der Umfrageteilnehmer

Von den Befragten gaben 99% ihr Geschlecht an und nur 1% enthielt sich, was ein Indiz für die Offenheit in Social Networking Umgebungen sein kann. Durch die Verteilung von 22% weiblicher Teilnehmer gegenüber 77% männlicher Teilnehmer lässt sich die bereits seit Jahren in anderen Studien festgestellte Lücke zwischen den Geschlechtern im Bereich der Internetnutzung erklären. Die Forschungsgruppe Wahlen hat in ihrer Erhebung zur Internetznutzung für Quartal II 2008 für Männer über 18 Jahren eine Internetnutzung von 74% und für Frauen eine Nutzung von 56% angegeben.

Der Unterschied zu dieser Umfrage liegt wohl in der Tatsache begründet, dass die meisten Zugriffe auf die Online-Umfrage über die Social Networking Site Xing getätigt wurden, welche nach einer Studie von Fittkau & Maaß[138] eine der wenigen Seiten ist, die einen geringeren weiblichen Nutzeranteil aufweist (38,8% Frauen/61,2% Männer).

---

[138] Vgl. [Worldsites Schweiz – Die beliebtesten Social Network Communities]

Position innerhalb des Unternehmens :

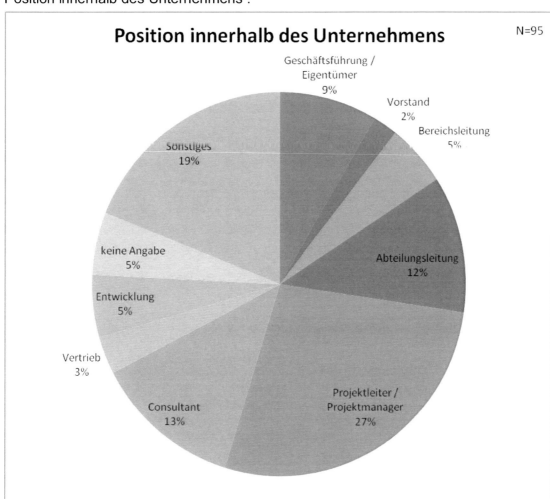

Abbildung 19. Position der Teilnehmer innerhalb des Unternehmens

Wie durch die Art der Bekanntmachung zu erhoffen war, wurde die Befragung von einem gestreuten Benutzerkreis wahrgenommen. Neben den beiden (zusammenge-fassten) großen Gruppen der Leitenden Positionen (ab Abteilungsleitung) und der Projektverantwortlichen mit 28% bzw. 27% gab es noch einen erheblichen Teil „Sonsti-ger" Antworten. Unter diesen waren unter anderem die Nennungen: Praktikant, Büro-kraft, Administrator, Controller oder Dozent. Interessant hierbei ist vor allem der 13%ige Anteil an Beratern, was darauf schließen lässt, dass das Thema „Wiki" auch in der Beratungsbranche zunehmend von Interesse sein wird.

Ebenfalls zu bemerken ist der mit 5% ausgefallene Anteil von Entwicklern. Diese Zahl wird im späteren Bezug auf den Einsatzzweck eines Wikis noch interessant, da gerade für das Feld „Entwicklung" mitunter die meisten Stimmen abgegeben wurden.

Kritisch anzumerken ist an dieser Stelle eine nicht optimal gewählte Einteilung der zur Verfügung stehenden Antwortmöglichkeiten. Dadurch ist auch der hohe Anteil „Sonsti-ger" und die damit verbundenen Nennungen der Position durch eine Kommentarfunkti-on zu erklären.

Unternehmen und Branche:

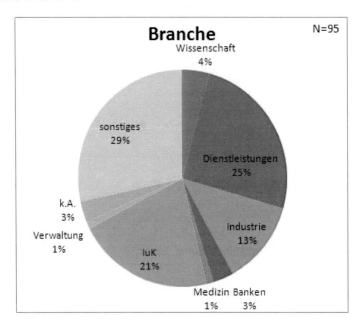

Abbildung 20. Verteilung der Teilnehmer nach Branche

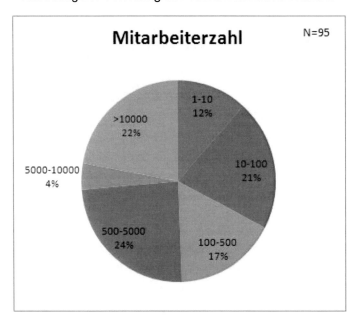

Abbildung 21. Mitarbeiteranzahl der Unternehmen

25% der Befragten ordneten sich der Dienstleistungsbranche zu. Aus Industrie stammen 13% der Teilnehmer. Der Anteil von 21% aus Informations- und Telekommunikationsbranche war bei einer Umfrage mit diesem Hintergrund zu erwarten. Kritisch an der Stelle ist wiederum der Anteil von 29% „Sonstiger". Unter diesen wurde per Kommentar Chemie, Luft- und Raumfahrt, Forschung und Bildung genannt.

Die Unternehmensgröße spiegelt mit 50% kleine (<100 MA) und mittlere (100-500 MA) Betriebe sowie 24% große Betriebe (500-5000 MA) und 26% sehr große (>5000 MA) Betriebe wider. Dem ist zu entnehmen, dass ein Wiki nicht nur für Kleinbetriebe, sondern auch für Konzerne in Frage kommen kann.

Auswertungen:

Bewertung der Eigenschaften eines Wikis:

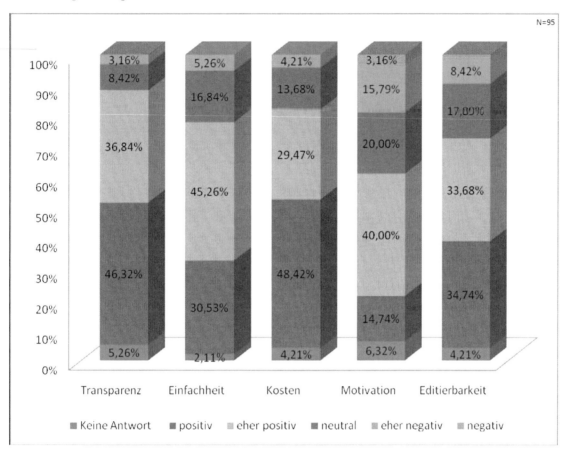

Abbildung 22. Bewertung der Eigenschaften eines Wikis

Die Faktoren Transparenz (über das System), Einfachheit (des Systems), Kosten (der Software), Motivation (bezogen auf Mitarbeiter) und Editierbarkeit (der Inhalte) wurden durch ein Gespräch mit Kollegen für diese Umfrage festgelegt und entstammen den bereits in den ersten Kapiteln dieser Arbeit beschriebenen Eigenschaften die üblicherweise einem Wiki zugeschrieben werden.

Wie sich zeigt, sind vor allem die Punkte Transparenz und Kosten von 46,32% bzw. 48,42% der Teilnehmer positiv bewertet worden. Auch die Punkte Einfachheit und Editierbarkeit sind mit jeweils über 30% ein weiterer Punkt, der dem System Wiki als Vorteil angerechnet wird. Lediglich im Bereich der Motivation sind mit 15,79% eher negative bzw. 3,16% negative Meldungen zu vernehmen.

Trotz der negativen Ausschläge bei Motivation ist in Summe auch diesem Faktor eine positiv gestimmte Grundhaltung von 54,74% zuzuschreiben.

Aktueller Einsatz von Wikis im Unternehmen:

Gegenüberstellung IuK[139] / Nicht-IuK-Unternehmen

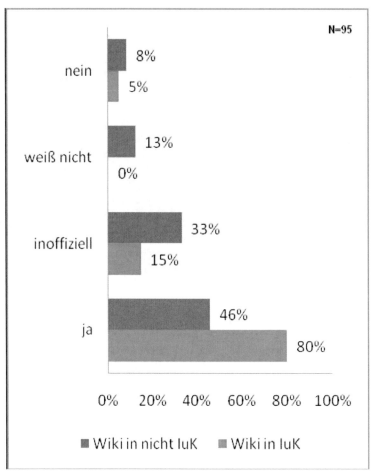

Abbildung 23. Gegenüberstellung Wikieinsatz in IuK und Nicht-IuK-Unternehmen

Entgegen den Erwartungen zeigt die Frage nach bereits im Einsatz befindlichen Wikis in der Gegenüberstellung von IuK-Unternehmen und Nicht-IuK-Unternehmen, dass Wikis nicht nur in der technikaffinen IT-Welt eingesetzt werden.

Bei 80% der befragten Unternehmen aus der IuK-Branche sind bereits offizielle Wikis installiert. In den Nicht-IuK-Unternehmen ist dieser Anteil auf 46% gesunken.

Interessant ist in diesem Zusammenhang der Branchenvergleich bei inoffiziellen Installationen. Diese treten immer dann auf, wenn Mitarbeiter eigenständig ein neues System einsetzen. Hier zeigt sich, dass diese „Entwickler-Wikis", wie sie in der Umfrage genannt wurden, doppelt so häufig (33%) in IuK-fremden Firmen auftreten als in Unternehmen der IuK-Branche (15%).

---

[139] IuK = Informations- und Kommunikationstechnik

51

Einsatzmöglichkeiten für Wikis:

Die folgenden Grafiken zeigen, in welchen Bereichen und für welche Zwecke Wikis von den Umfrageteilnehmern bereits eingesetzt werden. Zusätzlich wurde nach den möglichen bzw. denkbaren Einsatzbereichen und Nutzungsarten gefragt. Hierbei waren Mehrfachnennungen möglich.

Abbildung 24 zeigt sehr deutlich, dass ein Wiki bereits in 60% der Unternehmen als Tool für Wissensmanagement und mit je ca. 40% für das Dokumentenmangement und als Kommunikationsplattform eingesetzt wird. Dicht dahinter mit jeweils knapp über 35% liegt der Einsatz für Projektmanagement und als Intranet. In diesem Zusammenhang ist es interessant zu sehen, dass die denkbaren Einsatzzwecke eines Wikis ebenfalls die bereits genannten Felder Wissensmanagement, Projektmanagement, Kommunikationsplattform und Intranet mit je ca. 40% einen deutlichen Zuspruch erfahren. Auffällig ist neben der Überschneidung in diesen Bereichen der Unterschied zwischen den bereits im Einsatz befindlichen und den denkbaren Wikis für die Bereiche Qualitätsmanagement und Führungsinformationssystem. In diesen Bereichen werden von einem Drittel der Teilnehmer ebenfalls Einsatzmöglichkeiten für ein Wiki gesehen.

Betrachtet man den Einsatz nach Unternehmensbereichen (Abbildung 25), so wurde mit über 50% angegeben, dass ein Einsatz unternehmensweit denkbar sei, wohingegen die bereits im Einsatz befindlichen Wikis nur zu 20% unternehmensweit eingesetzt werden. Ebenfalls gute Einsatzmöglichkeiten werden von den Teilnehmern für die Bereiche Service & Support (intern) mit über 45% und Forschung / Entwicklung sowie IT mit je ca. 40% gesehen. Auffällig ist, dass die IT mit 40% der aktiven Wikis gegenüber denkbaren Wikis annähernd gleichauf liegt, die Bereiche Forschung / Entwicklung und Service & Support (intern) mit je ca. 20% der Wikis im aktiven Einsatz deutlich hinter den denkbaren Möglichkeiten liegen. An dieser Stelle fällt ebenfalls auf, dass knapp 30% der Befragten auch eine Einsatzmöglichkeit im Bereich Marketing / PR sehen und über 35% ein Wiki auch für externen Kundendienst einsetzen würden, was für beide Bereiche bei jeweils nur 10% der bereits existierenden Wikis genutzt wird.

Da rund ein Drittel der Teilnehmer aus der Leitungsebene und ca. zwei Drittel der Teilnehmer aus der Nicht-Leitungsebene stammen, erscheint hier ein Vergleich der Erwartungen beider Fraktionen angebracht.

Vergleicht man nun die denkbaren Möglichkeiten aus Sicht von Leitungsebene und Nicht-Leitungsebene (Abbildung 26) lässt sich im Groben annähernd von einer Normalverteilung sprechen. Die Einschätzungen sind lediglich in den Einsatzfeldern Wissensmanagement, Qualitätsmanagement und Dokumentenmanagement von Leitungsebene deutlich höher bewertet als von Nicht-Leitungsebene. Tendenziell wird das Wiki von Teilnehmern der Leitungsebene besser bewertet. Bezogen auf den Einsatz in unterschiedlichen Unternehmensbereichen (Abbildung 27) ist auch hier die Tendenz der besseren Bewertung durch die Leitungsebene festzustellen. Interessant ist dieser Ausschlag von Erwartungen der Leitungsebene vor allem mit 55% zu ca. 40% im Bereich Service und Support (intern) und 30% zu 10% für den Personalbereich.

Einsatz eines Wikis nach Zweck:

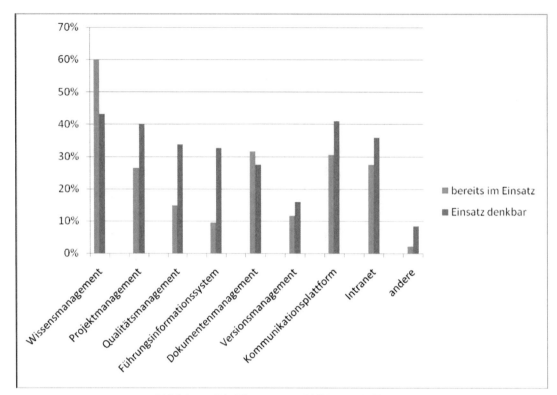

Abbildung 24. Einsatz von Wikis nach Zweck

Einsatz eines Wikis nach Abteilung:

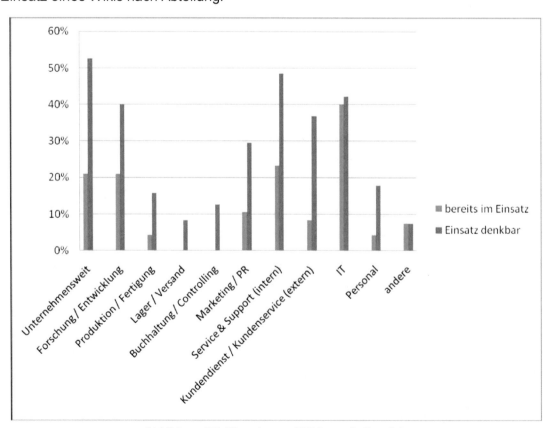

Abbildung 25. Einsatz von Wikis nach Bereich

Einsatz eines Wikis nach Zweck:

Vergleich zwischen Erwartungen der Leitungsebene und der Nicht-Leitungsebene*

*Leitungsebene = Abteilungsleitung und höher

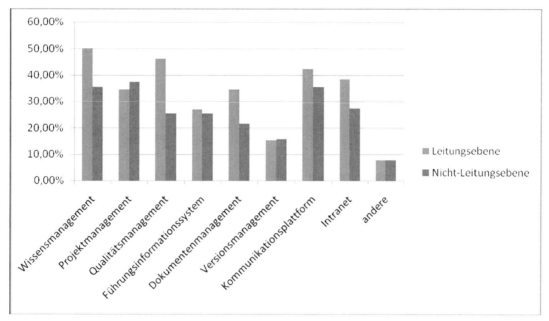

Abbildung 26. Einsatz eines Wikis nach Zweck - Leitungsebene/Nicht-Leitungsebene

Einsatz eines Wikis nach Abteilung:

Vergleich zwischen Erwartungen der Leitungsebene und der Nicht-Leitungsebene*

*Leitungsebene >Abteilungsleitung und höher

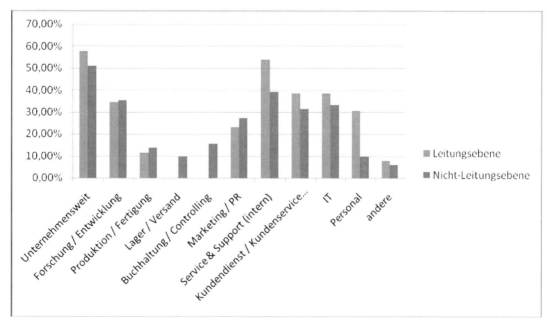

Abbildung 27. Einsatz eines Wikis nach Bereich - Leitungsebene/Nicht-Leitungsebene

Fazit der Umfrage:

- Die unterschiedliche Geschlechterbeteiligung läßt sich durch das gewählte Umfragemedium bzw. die gewählte Plattform zur Publikation erklären.

- Die Streuung über mehrere Altersklassen wurde erreicht und die dementsprechenden Unterschiede in der Beteiligung sind durch andere Studien belegt.

- Die Teilnehmer kamen aus den unterschiedlichsten Bereichen eines Unternehmens. Allenfalls auffallend war der Anteil von 27% in Projektleitungsebene.

- Die Streuung über mehrere Branchen wurde erreicht, wobei durch die Wahl des Umfragemediums ein höherer Anteil aus IuK-Branche abzusehen war. Wikis werden mittlerweile auch in fast der Hälfte aller Nicht-IuK-Unternehmen offiziell eingesetzt. Ein Drittel der Teilnehmer aus diesen Unternehmen gab ebenfalls an, das bereits inoffizielle „Entwicklerwikis" im Einsatz sind.

- Die Faktoren Transparenz, Einfachheit, Kosten, Motivation und Editierbarkeit wurden von jeweils deutlich über der Hälfte der Befragten positiv bzw. eher positiv bewertet. Ein eher negativer bzw. negativer Ausschlag war nur beim Faktor Motivation mit 18% festzustellen.

- Wikis wird die Einsatzmöglichkeit in verschiedenen Anwendungsfeldern zugesprochen, wobei sie von ca. 60% überwiegend im Wissensmanagement und ca. in einem Viertel der Unternehmen im Dokumentenmanagement, Projektmanagement, Versionsmanagement und als Intranet eingesetzt werden. Steigerungspotential scheinen vor allem die Bereiche Projektmanagement, Qualitätsmanagement und Führungsinformationssystem zu haben. Wobei Mitglieder der Leitungsebene vor allem Vorteile für den Einsatz im Bereich Wissensmanagement, Qualitätsmanagement zu sehen scheinen.

- Ein Einsatz in unterschiedlichen Unternehmensbereichen ist für den Großteil der Teilnehmer denkbar. Über die Hälfte können sich einen unternehmensweiten Einsatz vorstellen, was bei knapp 20% der Befragten bereits realisiert ist. Potential wird hier vor allem für die Bereiche Forschung/ Entwicklung, Marketing/PR, Service&Support (intern) sowie dem Kundenservice (extern) gesehen. Mitglieder der Leitungsebene sehen zusätzlich noch einen Einsatzbereich im Personalwesen.

Für diese Arbeit ist daher anzunehmen, dass die Unternehmen und ihre Mitarbeiter durchaus bereit sind, ein Wiki als Managementsystem einzusetzen und von den genannten Faktoren keiner als stark negativ bewertet wird. Ein unternehmensweites System ist zu empfehlen. Die Entscheidung, ob ein Wiki eingesetzt wird, sollte über mehrere Ebenen besprochen und unter einem Konsens getroffen werden.[140]

---

[140] Die Umfrage enthielt eine Frage nach der Entscheidungsbefugnis über neue Softwareinstallationen. Sie wurde wegen einer annähernden Gleichverteilung auf Grund der Streuung über mehrere Branchen, Firmengrößen und Positionen der Befragten nicht weiter berücksichtigt.

3.2.2 Wikipatterns

Der Begriff Pattern beschreibt im Grunde nichts weiter als ein "Entwurfsmuster" für wiederkehrende Probleme und Aufgabenstellungen. Die Idee geht hierbei auf die Architektur und speziell auf den Architekt Christopher Alexander zurück.[141] Wikipatterns stellen daher eine Sammlung von nach unterschiedlichen Kriterien eingeteilten Patterns dar.

Viel bekannter als in der Architektur sind sog. Design Patterns im Bereich der Softwareentwicklung, wo unter anderem auch Ward Cunningham seinen Beitrag in der Entwicklung von Entwurfsmustern für grafische Benutzeroberflächen unter Smalltalk leistete.[142]

Neben den reinen Patterns gibt es danebenen ebenfalls die Anti-Patterns. Sie stellen genau den nicht erwünschten Zustand dar, beschreiben allerdings auch, wie er vermieden werden kann.

Zur weiteren Einteilung wird bei Wikipatterns auf die Besonderheit Rücksicht genommen, dass es grundsätzlich zwei Problemstellungen gibt:

- Problemstellungen, die direkt den Nutzer betreffen

- Problemstellungen, die mit der Struktur und der Einsatzart des Wikis zusammenhängen.

Die Einteilung der Wikipatterns erfolgt daher in:

- People Patterns

- People Anti-Patterns

- Adoption Patterns

- Adoption Anti-Patterns

Im Folgenden soll ein kurzer Abriss über die aus Sicht des Autors erfolgversprechendsten Muster und die Anti-Muster gegeben werden, die mit hoher Wahrscheinlichkeit bei einem Einsatz von Wikis als Managementsystem eintreten können. Es gilt hierbei zu erwähnen, dass auch die Patterns sich noch im Entwicklungsstadium befinden und noch nicht allgemeingültig verifiziert sind.

Als weiterführende Literatur sei an dieser Stelle Wikipatterns von Stewart Mader erwähnt.[143]

---

[141] Vgl. [Wiki Patterns – About]
[142] Vgl. [Wikipedia – Entwurfsmuster]
[143] [Mader 2008 – Wikipatterns]

90-9-1 Theory

Die 90-9-1 Regel geht auf Jacob Nielsen zurück, der in seinem Artikel "Participation Inequality: Encouraging More Users to Contribute"[144] wie folgt beschreibt:

- 90% der Nutzer lesen und schauen nur zu, steuern aber selber nichts bei.

- 9% der Nutzer beteiligen sich von Zeit zu Zeit, aber andere Dinge sind ihnen wichtiger.

- 1% der Nutzer macht häufig mit, von ihnen stammen die meisten Beiträge

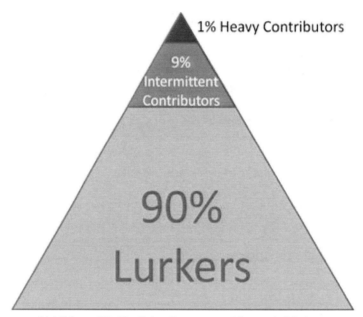

Abbildung 28. Partizipationspyramide nach Nielson

Die 90-9-1 Regel wird häufig im Zusammenhang mit Web 2.0 angeführt, um die vermeintliche Sinnlosigkeit einer solchen Anwendung aufzuzeigen, allerdings zeigt sie gleichermaßen den Lösungsweg auf und dient daher in dieser Arbeit nicht als einzelnes Pattern. Es kann mit Hilfe dieses Phänomens jedes andere Pattern und Anti-Pattern belegt oder gelöst werden, da sich im bei näherer Betrachtung drei Fragen stellen:

- Warum ist 1% die fleissigste Gruppe?

- Warum sind 9 % mehr oder weniger aktiv?

- Warum sind 90 % passiv?

Diese Fragen führen jeweils zu weiteren Fragen, die sich gezielt mit Patterns lösen bzw. vermeiden lassen.

---

[144] Vgl. [Nielson – Participation Inequality]

Beispiel: Wieso lesen 90% der Mitarbeiter nur?

Ist es vielleicht zu schwer neue Inhalte zu erfassen?

è Vorlagen bereitstellen

Ist den Mitarbeitern überhaupt klar, dass sie etwas ändern sollen und dürfen?

è Multiplikatoren unter den Mitarbeitern finden

Es wird dabei nicht gelingen, eine Umkehrung der Prozentanteile zu erreichen, aber eine Verschiebung in Richtung 80-16-4 ist laut Nielsen durchaus zu erreichen.[145]

3.2.2.1   People Patterns

Viral / Invitation

Viral und Invite sind laut Beschreibung zwei eigenständige Muster. Während das Viral Pattern am ehesten dem klassischen Word of Mouth entspricht, ist das Invitation Pattern in Unternehmenswikis eher aus strategischer Sicht anzuwenden. Wer zuerst eine Einladung zur Nutzung des Wikis von der Geschäftsleitung bekommt und im Anschluss durch Wikiaffine-Kollegen lobende Worte über das neue System hört, wird sich gerne ebenfalls beteiligen.

Wiki Charter

Die Wiki Charter ist ein Dokument, in dem die einfachsten Grundregeln der Community im Bezug auf Zusammenarbeit im Wiki festgehalten sind. Sie bilden allerdings lediglich einen flexiblen Rahmen und sollen keinesfalls als ein unerschütterliches Regelwerk sein.

MySpace

MySpace oder persönlicher Bereich sollen den Mitarbeitern die Möglichkeit geben, eigene Profilseiten anzulegen und sich selbst darzustellen und dabei den Umgang mit dem Wiki zu lernen.

---

[145] Vgl. [Nielson – Participation Inequality]

PageMaintainer / Maintainer

Der Maintainer oder PageMaintainer kümmert sich um bestimmte Seiten eines Wikis. Er besitzt neben einem Verständnis für das "Konzept Wiki" auch die technischen Skills, um die Seiten zu pflegen und zu verbessern.

WikiGnome / Wiki ZenMaster / Champion

WikiGnome, oft auch Wiki Gärtner genannt, Wiki ZenMaster oder Champions sind sehr ähnliche Rollen in einem Wiki. Während die Gnome und ZenMaster sich eher auf die Verbesserung von Inhalt und Design stützen, ist der Champion meist in der Anlaufphase eines Wikis wichtiger Multiplikator und Ansprechperson.

Sponsor / Patron

Ein Sponsor oder Patron ist meist ein hierarchisch höhergestellter Mitarbeiter. Ein positives Vorbild aus der Managementhierarchie ermutigt auch andere, aktiv am Wiki mitzuarbeiten.

3.2.2.2 People Anti-Patterns

Bully / Vandal

Bully und Vandal sind zwei Beispiele aus dem Bereich der personellen Anti-Patterns. Ein Bully übertreibt den Einsatz eines Wikis. Er fordert andere ununterbrochen dazu auf, das Wiki zu nutzen, will keine Mails mehr empfangen sondern alles nur im Wiki lesen. Ein Vandale hingegen versucht absichtlich Inhalte zu verfälschen und die Arbeit im Wiki zu stören. In Unternehmenswikis ist Vandalismus allerdings eher selten zu beobachten. Ein Gespräch mit den jeweiligen Personen ist hier das Mittel der Wahl.

WikiNoob

Ein WikiNoob gehört zu den Wikibefürwortern, hat aber das Konzept nicht verstanden. Er arbeitet nach alten Schemata. Er versioniert zum Beispiel einzelne Wikiseiten von Hand, obwohl das System automatisch Versionen der einzelnen Seiten anlegt. Er sollte in seinem Enthusiasmus nicht gebremst werden, aber benötigt erfahrene Unterstützung, zum Beispiel von einem Wiki ZenMaster oder Champion.

Copyright Infringement

Autoren verwenden im Wiki Inhalte, deren Nutzungsrechte sie nicht haben. Darunter fallen beispielsweise auch das Kopieren aus anderen Veröffentlichungen, oder das Veröffentlichen von Inhalten unter eigenem Namen. Besonders gefährlich ist dieses Anti-Pattern bei öffentlichen Wikis, da hier Klagen durch den Rechteinhaber drohen können.

OverOrganizer

Ein Überorganisator ist ständig damit beschäftigt Seiten neu anzuordnen, Überschriften zu verbessern, neue Links und Anhänge hinzuzufügen. So gut gemeint dieses Verhalten sein mag, es stört die anderen Nutzer. Das Wiki verbessert sich von selbst, Stück für Stück. Es muss nicht bei jeder neuen Seite reorganisiert werden.

TransparencyComplaints

Projektverantworliche bemängeln das Fehlen der notwendigen Informationen. Sie kommen sich "im Dunkeln belassen" vor. Dieses Pattern tritt häufig auf, wenn Führungskräfte das Wiki so lange ignorieren, bis die nötigen Informationen sie auch nicht mehr durch andere Wege erreichen. Eine E-Mail an alle Teammitglieder mit dem Link auf die entsprechende Seite im Wiki behebt diese Informationslücke meist wieder.

3.2.2.3 Adoption Patterns

Assess Wiki-Ability

Ob nun im internen Firmeneinsatz oder bei einem Kundenprojekt, wenn der Einsatz eines Wikis geplant ist, sollte zuerst die Möglichkeit einer solchen Lösung geklärt werden. Versteht der Kunde, verstehen die eigenen Mitarbeiter, was das System erreichen soll und wie es funktioniert?

Agenda

Ein einfacher Weg, Mitarbeiter zur aktiven Gestaltung des Wikis zu bewegen ist es, die Agenda für kommende Besprechungen in das Wiki zu stellen. Auf diese Weise ist der gleiche Informationsstand für alle gewährleistet und jeder Teilnehmer hat die Möglichkeit, eigene Änderungen vorzunehmen.

ContentAlert

Durch das Hinterlassen von ContentAlert Nachrichten auf einer Wikiseite kann die Aufmerksamkeit der Nutzer für das Wiki gesteigert werden. Am Anfang einer Seite kann so beispielsweise ein farbig untermalter Infotext "Kapitel 1.2 bedarf einer Korrektur" hinterlegt werden. Das gleiche System macht sich auch Wikipedia zu nutze, wenn für einen Eintrag nicht genügend Quellen oder Referenzen vorhanden sind.

FAQ

Frequently Asked Questions, häufig gestellte Fragen, sollten zu einer Liste zusammengetragen werden. Hier können sich neue Nutzer bei Fragen informieren und andererseits erfahrene Nutzer Antworten verfeinern. Dieses Patterns eignet sich auch für einzelne Projektwikis sehr gut, um neue Teammitglieder rasch mit den Inhalten vertraut zu machen.

Lunch Menu / Magnet

Ein Magnet ist eine exklusiv im Wiki vorhandene Information. So kann zum Beispiel der bisher wöchentlich per E-Mail verschickte Menuplan der Kantine an einer Stelle im Wiki veröffentlicht werden. Das erspart unnötigen Mailverkehr und bringt gleichzeitig die Nutzer näher an das System.

Scaffold

Viele Nutzer würden gerne Inhalte bereitstellen, sind sich aber nicht sicher, wie und in welcher Form sie das am Besten tun sollten. Hier sollte man ihnen ein Gerüst oder Template zur Verfügung stellen. Einige Wikilösungen bieten ein solches System von Haus aus an und erleichtern so den Einstieg.

Seed it with content

Eine leere, weiße Seite hindert neue Wiki-Nutzer oft psychologisch daran, sich am Wiki zu beteiligen. Noch schlimmer, wenn das ganze Wiki nur eine leere Hülle ist. Es ist daher von Anfang an darauf zu achten, dass bereits vor dem Kick-Off ein gewisser Anteil an aktuellem Inhalt im Wiki hinterlegt ist.

3.2.2.4 Adoption Anti-Patterns

Registration Required

Wie soll jemand freiwillig und gerne an etwas mitarbeiten, was ihn durch unsinnige Registrierformulare daran hindert? Die Idee, das Wiki dadurch vor Spam und Vandalismus zu schützen, scheitert ebenfalls. Wer sich die Mühe macht, eine Wikiseite abzuändern, der scheut auch nicht davor zurück, sich mit falschem Namen zu registrieren. Hier ist allerdings anzumerken, dass ein Unternehmenswiki meist bereits durch die Integration in ein bestehendes Authentifizierungssystem oder User Directory (LDAP, Active Directory, SAP) vor solchen Attacken geschützt ist.

All wiki all the time

Einer der größten Fehler beim Einsatz eines Wikis im Unternehmen stellt das All wiki all the time Pattern dar. Ein Wiki benötigt Zeit, um angenommen zu werden. Wird der Nutzer mit ständig neuen Funktionen und Vorschlägen überschüttet, wird das Wiki nicht angenommen. Über die Zeit werden sich die Nutzer mit dem Wiki anfreunden und von selbst Vorschläge machen, welche Funktionen benötigt werden.

Sandbox

Die Sandbox ist ein umstrittenes Pattern. Während sie auf Wikipatterns.com ein Anti-Pattern ist, benutzt das erfolgreichste Wiki der Welt, die Wikipedia genau diese Funktion, um den Nutzern den Einstieg zu erleichtern.[146] Hier gilt es jeweils abzuwägen. In „jungen" Belegschaften kann man eher vom Spieltrieb der Nutzer ausgehen, die sich auch an Inhalte trauen; in „älteren" Belegschaften kann eine Hemmschwelle vorhanden sein, solche Inhalte zu verändern. Hier erscheint eine Sandbox nützlich.

Too much structure

Ein Wiki ist ein selbstregulierendes System. Es besitzt zwar Punkte, an denen steuernd eingegriffen werden kann, aber die exakte Struktur eines Wikis vorab zu planen, wird nicht funktionieren. Die Struktur ergibt sich aus den Anforderungen der Nutzer selbst. Es ist daher besser, am Anfang wenig Struktur vorzugeben und später bei Bedarf nachzurüsten.

---

[146] Vgl. [Wikipedia – Spielwiese]

Wikiphobia

Vielfach wird der Nutzen eines Wikis einfach verkannt und auch die Idee die dahinter steckt ins Lächerliche gezogen. Die Reaktionen reichen hierbei von "Wieso nehmen wir nicht einfach E-Mail dafür" bis zu "Da kann ja jeder Alles löschen". Die auf Wikipatterns.com genannten Tips werden hier allerdings als nicht durchsetzbar und zu aufwendig bewertet. Der beste Weg, einer solchen Haltung entgegen zu wirken ist es wohl, durch positive Beispiele aus verwandten Branchen den Sinn und Mehrwert eines Wikis darzustellen.

3.2.3 Erfolgsfaktoren

Der Erfolg eines Systems hängt nicht nur von einer einzelnen Komponente ab. Er ist von einer Vielzahl unterschiedlicher Wechselwirkungen abhängig. Die genannten Erfolgsfaktoren stehen nicht für eine bestimmte Strategie, oder eingesetzte Technik, sondern sie stehen für ein neues Denken, das zunehmend in den Konzernen aber auch kleinen und mittleren Firmen Einzug findet.

Tapscott und Williams sprechen in diesem Zusammenhang von den Wikinomics Prinzipien, die sich im Wesentlichen auf Offen sein, Gleichrangigkeit, Teilen und globales Handeln stützen.[147] Diese seien im Folgenden näher erläutert und mit dieser Arbeit in Verbindung gebracht.

Offen sein

Unter Offen sein wird in diesem Zusammenhang von Offenheit in mehreren Bedeutungsnuancen gesprochen. Offen gegenüber Veränderungen, offener Umgang mit den Medien, mit Partnern etc. Ob nun im Bereich der Finanzen, als Stichwort diene der Sarbanes-Oxley Act in den Vereinigten Staaten von Amerika oder in der Open Source Software Entwicklung, wo durch das Wissen der Vielen möglichst schnell Fehler in Programmen gefunden werden, der Grundgedanke lässt sich auf ein Managementsystem übertragen und schafft größeres Vertrauen unter den Mitarbeitern, Führungskräften und letztendlich auch Kunden.

Gleichrangigkeit

Oder auch Peering ist ein Schritt vom hierarchischen zum horizontalen Denken und auch Handeln. In der Wirtschaft ist diese Gleichrangigkeit mittlerweile oft anzutreffen im Bereich von Produktion und Entwicklung und wird Peer Production genannt. Tapscott gibt hier als Beispiel die Entwicklung des Linux Betriebssystems an, an dem sich jeder beteiligen kann, wenn er bestimmte Regeln einhält.[148] Viele Menschen auf einer gleichen Ebene arbeiten zu lassen ermöglicht Selbstorganisation und damit verbunden auch eine höhere Innovationskraft.

---

[147] Vgl. [Tapscott, Williams 2006], S.20f
[148] Vgl. [Tapscott, Williams 2006], S.24

Teilen

Der englische Begriff „Sharing" ist über die letzten Jahre vielfach in Verruf geraten. Von Raubkopierern und Piraten wird dabei gesprochen, wenn es um „File Sharing", also das Teilen von Dateien geht. Einige Musiker haben aber den Vorteil dieser „Verteilung" ihrer Musik gesehen und proaktiv gehandelt. Auf MySpace finden sich tausende Musikgruppen, die ihre Songs kostenlos anbieten, um auf diese Weise bekannter zu werden. Übertragen auf eine Unternehmung können durch geteiltes Wissen vielfach schlummernde Potentiale freigesetzt und gewinnbringend genutzt werden.

Globales Handeln

Ist nicht jede Firma, die eine Vertretung in den USA oder in China hat, bereits global? Nein. Unter globalem Handeln wird hier nicht die rein regionale Verteilung von Firmenstandorten gesehen. Auch das Wissen, die Menschen und die Methoden sollen global eingesetzt werden. Was in einzelnen Firmen mit flexiblen Arbeitsplätzen schon praktiziert wird, sollte auch im größeren Maßstab angewandt werden. Die körperliche Präsenz an einem anderen Ort ist im Zeitalter der virtuellen Realitäten und Echtzeit-Konferenzsysteme nicht mehr zwingend erforderlich. Ein System, auf das von allen Teilnehmern, jederzeit, von jedem Ort der Welt zugegriffen werden kann, leistet hier wertvolle Dienste. Für ein Unternehmenswiki einer (momentan) nur in Deuschland agierenden Firma scheint dies auf den ersten Blick keinen Sinn zu machen, es ist aber hier zu unterstellen, dass Globales Handeln schon damit beginnt, über Abteilungsgrenzen hinweg zusammen zu arbeiten.

Aus diesen vier Prinzipien lassen sich weitere Faktoren ableiten, die zum Erfolg beitragen. Unter Ihnen stehen die Partizipation und die Motivation der Mitarbeiter mit an oberster Stelle. Sie tragen, neben einem technisch funktionsfähigen System, einen wesentlichen Teil zum Erfolg eines Wikis bei. Auch die weitaus höhere Transparenz über Prozesse stellt einen zusätzlichen Faktor dar, der Anreize schafft, sich aktiv zu beteiligen.

Die einzelnen Faktoren bedingen sich gegenseitig. Transparenz beschreibt in der Optik die Möglichkeit, ein Objekt zu durchschauen.[149] Es läßt also erkennen, was hinter diesem Objekt liegt. Hinter dem Objekt Unternehmen stehen Mitarbeiter, Zahlen, Produkte etc. Ein Wiki ermöglicht es dieses Wissen transparent zugänglich zu machen. Daraus entsteht nicht nur Partizipation, sondern sie wird auch gefordert. Inhalte sind nur dann nützlich, wenn sie aktuell sind. Die Aktualität wiederum wird durch aktive Mitgestaltung durch die Mitarbeiter erreicht, welche das Detail- und Fachwissen über Prozesse und Abläufe besitzen. Der sichtbare Erfolg, nämlich ein funktionierendes Wiki, ist also eine Wechselwirkung zwischen diesen unterschiedlichen Faktoren.

---

[149] Vgl. [Wikipedia – Transparenz]

Den eigentlichen Erfolg eines solchen Systems kann man im Endeffekt aber nur den damit arbeitenden Menschen zu zuschreiben. Sie sind es, die offen sein müssen, sich mit dem neuen System anzufreunden und über unterschiedliche Hierarchien hinweg gemeinsam am Gesamtsystem Wiki zu arbeiten. Die Kultur im Unternehmen sollte entsprechend gestaltet sein, Wissen nicht in Aktenschränken zu horten, sondern dieses im Unternehmen zugänglich zu machen und bei Bedarf nicht nur im Unternehmen selbst sondern auch mit externen Partnern zu teilen, um eine gemeinsame Win-Win Situation zu schaffen. Das Zusammenspiel der Einzelkomponenten wird dabei entschieden von Führungskräften getragen, die den Wikigedanken unterstützen und auch die Verbesserungen ihrer eigenen Wikeinträge durch Mitarbeiter mit genug Selbstvertrauen akzeptieren.[150]

---

[150] Vgl. [Bergmann 2007]

3.3 Modell des Managementsystem 2.0

Um die Einflussfaktoren und die Stellhebel für ein wikibasiertes Managementsystem anschaulich zu machen, wurde in einem mehrtägigen Workshop mit Führungskräften und Projektleitern der TQU International ein Modell für das Managementsystem 2.0 entwickelt.

Es gründet sich auf den drei Säulen

- Orientierung

- Transparenz

- Partizipation

Diese sind den von Tapscott und Williams aufgeführten Prinzipien für Wikinomics nicht unähnlich. Aufgebaut auf diese Säulen werden die drei Eckpunkte:

- Ergebnisse/Kennzahlen

- Wissen/Definitionen

- Spielregeln/Prozesse

Den Mittelpunkt des Systems stellt der Mensch mit seinen Werten bzw. das Unternehmen mit seiner Unternehmenskultur dar.

Im Folgenden wird der Aufbau und die zugrundeliegenden Überlegungen genauer beschrieben.

Ein System wird nicht um seiner selbst Willen eingeführt es verfolgt einen bestimmten Zweck. Dieser Zweck läßt sich, angewandt auf ein Unternehmen, mit dem übergeordneten Ziel der Gewinnerzielung ausdrücken.[151] Ob dieses Ziel erreicht wird, läßt sich im Voraus anhand von Kennzahlen und im Rückblick durch realisierte Ergebnisse erkennen. Sie stellen daher auch die Spitze des Modells eines Managementsystems 2.0 dar. Gleichzeitig stellt diese Komponente auch die Weichen für die zukünftigen Handlungen und schafft somit Orientierung für Unternehmensführung und Mitarbeiter.

Aus jeglicher Handlung läßt sich Wissen generieren. Ob Erfolg oder Mißerfolg ist für das entstandene Wissen nachrangig. Je mehr Wissen desto besser. Auch das Wissen über gescheiterte Projekte ist in einem Unternehmen von großem Wert, verhindert es doch, dass Fehler wiederholt werden. Die Definition von neuen Zielen und die Formulierung von Ideen fällt ebenfalls in diesen Bereich des Modells. Es fordert und schafft Transparenz zugleich.

---

[151] Vgl. [Wikipedia – Gewinnerzielungsabsicht]

Der dritte Bereich ist die Sicht auf Prozesse und Spielregeln. Ein vollkommen selbstregulierendes System ist für Unternehmen nicht umsetzbar. Die aktive Gestaltung des Systems durch die aktive Beteiligung aller Mitarbeiter hingegen ist wünschenswert. Festgeschriebene Prozesse können durch das immer wieder aktualisierte Wissen permanent optimiert werden und somit in der Umsetzung zu besseren Ergebnissen führen.

Kern des Systems sind die Menschen, die es tragen und permanent weiterentwickeln. Als Voraussetzung dafür gilt es aber im Unternehmen die entsprechenden Werte und eine diesen Werten angepasste Unternehmenskultur zu etablieren.

Die technische Umsetzung mit einer Wikisoftware ist hierbei nicht zwingend notwendig, stellt aber die Basis aller ursprünglichen Überlegungen dar.

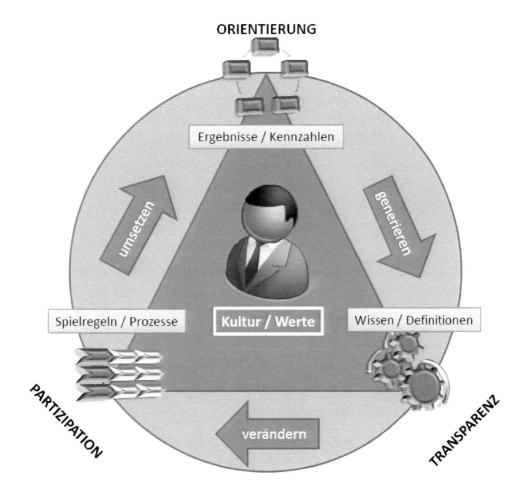

Abbildung 29. Modell Managementsystem 2.0

Für diese Arbeit sei daher ein Managementsystem 2.0 als ein auf aktueller Internettechnologie (z.B. Wiki) beruhendes integriertes System mit den drei Säulen Orientierung, Transparenz und Partizipation, welche es, getragen durch Werte und Kultur, ermöglichen, Wissen zu generieren, Prozesse zu verändern und diese zu Ergebnissen umzusetzen, definiert.

3.4 Wiki Implementierung

Die Implementierung eines Wikis in bestehende Systeme stellt mit die größte Herausforderung dar. Die Fachzeitschrift Computerwoche hat sich in ihrem Onlineableger mit den Erfolgsfaktoren für die Einführung eines Unternehmenswikis befasst.[152] Diese von Computerwoche identifizierten Faktoren werden den Erfahrungen aus der Praxis gegenübergestellt und im Anschluss in die acht Phasen eines Veränderungsprozesses nach Kotter[153] eingeordnet.

Die von Computerwoche identifizierten Faktoren sind demzufolge:

- Unterstützung durch einen Management-Sponsor

- Klare Regeln und Zuständigkeiten

- Nicht mit einem leeren Wiki beginnen

- Champions sollen den Weg ebnen

- Umdenken bei der Informationsaufbereitung

- Keine Auslagerung an professionelle Autoren

- Sparsamer Einsatz von Wiki-Erweiterungen

- Jeder darf (fast) alle Seiten bearbeiten

- Vernetzung des Wikis

- Praktische Informationen mit Nutzwert

Aus der Praxis wurden als wichtigste Lessons Learned festgehalten:

- Eindeutiges Auftragsziel (Was wollen wir?)

- Rückhalt durch die Geschäftsführung

- Klare Rollenverteilung

- Gutes Kernteam aus übergreifenden Bereichen (IT, Management)

- Partizipation der Menschen – Multiplikatoren

- Struktur des Systems (QM, Organisation, persönliche Bereiche)

---

[152] Vgl. [Computerwoche – Erfolgreiches Wissens-Management]
[153] Vgl. [Kotter 1996]

Vergleicht man die beiden Listen, sind klare Überschneidungen ersichtlich, wenngleich auch die Bezeichnungen und die Anzahl variieren, sind die Kernaussagen durchaus miteinander vereinbar.

Der Veränderungsprozess wird nun am Beispiel der Wiki-Einführung bei der Hirschmann Automotive GmbH (s. 4.1) dargestellt.

The eight-step path to success		
1. Increase Urgency	Raising a feeling of urgency so that people start telling each other 'we must do something' about the problems and opportunities. Reducing the complacency[23], fear, and anger that prevent change from starting.	
2. Build the Guiding Team	Helping pull together the right group of people with the right characteristics and sufficient power to drive the change effort. Helping them to behave with trust and emotional commitment to one another.	
3. Get the Vision Right	Facilitating the movement beyond traditional analytical and financial plans and budgets. Creating the right compelling vision to direct the effort. Helping the guiding team to develop bold strategies for making bold visions a reality.	
4. Communicate for Buy-In	Sending clear, credible, and heartful messages about the direction of change. Establishing genuine gut-level buy-in that shows up in how people act. Using words, deeds, and new technologies to unclog[24] communication channels and overcome confusion and distrust.	
5. Empower Action	Removing barriers that block those who have genuinely embraced the vision and strategies. Taking away sufficient obstacles in their organizations and in their hearts so that they behave differently.	
6. Create Short-Term Wins	Generating sufficient wins fast enough to diffuse cynicism, pessimism, and scepticism. Building momentum. Making sure successes are visible, unambiguous, and speak to what people deeply care about.	
7. Don't Let Up	Helping people create wave after wave of change until the vision is a reality. Not allowing urgency to sag[25]. Not ducking the more difficult parts of the transformation, especially the bigger emotional barriers. Eliminating needles work so you don't exhaust yourself along the way.	
8. Make Change Stick	Ensuring that people continue to act in new ways, despite the pull of tradition, by rooting behavior in reshaped organizational culture. Using the employee orientation process, the promotions process, and the power of emotion to enhance new group norms and shared values.	

Tabelle 5. Die acht Phasen des Change Prozesses

1. Increase Urgency
   In der ersten Stufe geht es darum, gemeinsam eine Einigkeit für den Bedarf einer Änderung zu erkennen und daraus eine Handlung abzuleiten.
   Am Beispiel der Hirschmann Automotive GmbH war dieser Auslöser ein nicht mehr praktikables Qualitätsmanagementsystem.

2. Build the Guiding Team
   Wer trägt die Veränderungen, wer führt sie durch? Ein interdisziplinäres Team, das die Änderung durchführt, kommuniziert und bei Bedarf eingreift.
   Bei Hirschmann war der Rückhalt der Geschäftsführung sichergestellt und ein Team aus Management und Fachabteilung wurde gebildet.

3. Get the Vision right

Welches Ziel steht am Ende der Veränderung? Dieses Ziel muss fest definiert und kommuniziert werden, um mögliche „Helping Hands" zu identifizieren.

Bei Hirschmann war das Ziel daher, ein neues Qualitätsmanagementsystem auf Basis eines Wikis.

4. Communicate for Buy-In

Frühzeitige Information aller Beteiligten, um Bedenken und Ängste abzubauen und Anmerkung und Anregungen aufzugreifen.

Das Hirschmann-Wikiteam besprach von Anfang an mit der Belegschaft die geplante Veränderung und identifizierte so hilfreiche Multiplikatoren.

5. Empower Action

Hilfe aufzeigen wo nötig, Mitarbeiter befähigen, Hindernisse der Veränderung vorab aus dem Weg zu räumen.

Die Multiplikatoren wurden bei Hirschmann vorab geschult und können ihren Kollegen hilfreich zur Seite stehen.

6. Create Short-Term Wins

Mit kleinen Erfolgserlebnissen die Mitarbeiter motivieren.

Die QM-Dokumentation bei Hirschmann wurde eins zu eins ins Wiki übertragen und kann wesentlich einfacher abgerufen und auch auf den neuesten Stand gebracht werden.

7. Don't Let Up

Nicht aufhören, die angestoßene Veränderung zu überprüfen und kontinuierlich zu verbessern.

Neben Rankweil in Österreich hat Hirschmann noch weitere Werke, deren Seiten ebenfalls in Arbeit sind. Auch wurden Programme von Drittanbietern in das Wiki integriert.

8. Make Change Stick

Die Veränderung sicherstellen und überprüfen.

Das alte Intranet wurde bei Hirschmann abgeschaltet. Es gibt als zentrale Plattform nur noch das Wiki. Bereits am ersten Tag wurden durch die Mitarbeiter über 150 Seitenänderungen durchgeführt.

Diese acht Stufen lassen sich auf drei Kernpunkte verdichten:

- Einführung

- Entwicklung

- Bewertung

3.4.1 Einführung

Die Einführung eines Wikis beginnt bereits vor dem tatsächlichen Go-Live der Anwendung im Unternehmensnetzwerk. Wie bereits aufgezeigt, ist hierbei vor allem der Rückhalt durch die Geschäftsleitung bzw. ein Management Sponsor notwendig. Entfällt der Rückhalt von Oben, ist das Projekt auch für die restliche Belegschaft unglaubwürdig und damit von Anfang an zum Scheitern verurteilt. Gleichermaßen sollte auch von Vorncherein genau definiert werden, was mit dem Wiki erreicht werden soll. Das „Wie" ist am Anfang noch nicht relevant, sondern ergibt sich bei einem System dieser Technologie im Projektverlauf von selbst.

Besonderes Augenmerk sollte auf das Kernteam gelegt werden. Die Praxis hat gezeigt, dass eine Mischung aus Management und IT-Abteilung und evtl. Vertreter von Fachabteilungen am produktivsten agieren.

Das Projektmarketing sollte gleichzeitig als flankierende Maßnahme auf die Neuerung im Unternehmen hinweisen. Dadurch lassen sich frühzeitig Multiplikatoren unter den Mitarbeitern identifizieren, welche später als Key User ihren Kollegen mit Rat und Tat zur Seite stehen können oder gar durch persönliche Erfahrungen wertvolle Anregungen für die Systemeinführung geben können.

Die Schulung der Multiplikatoren kann gleichermaßen genutzt werden, um das Wiki bereits mit Inhalten zu befüllen. So können Hemmschwellen der anderen Benutzer abgebaut werden, welche sich erfahrungsgemäß nicht an leere Seiten trauen.

3.4.2 Entwicklung

Ist das Wiki erfolgreich eingeführt, werden früher oder später die Rufe nach zusätzlichen Funktionen auftreten. Meistens lassen sich diese durch Plugins oder Extensions relativ einfach in das System nachrüsten. Vom Einsatz zu vieler Plugins wird aber gerade in der ersten Gewöhnungsphase abgeraten. Die Lernfortschritte im Umgang mit dem System werden innerhalb der Belegschaft variieren und permanent neue Funktionen und Plugins wirken daher abschreckend.

Ein Grundstock von nützlichen Funktionen ist daher nach realem Nutzen für das System und den Erfahrungen der Nutzer abzuwägen.

Als Beispiel sei hier die Implementierung von Google Maps genannt, die vielen Nutzern schon aus dem alltäglichen Umgang mit dem Internet vertraut sind. Ebenfalls kann erwogen werden, bereits auf Browsertechnologie basierende Systeme wie ein Fachwörterbuch oder ein Telefonverzeichnis direkt im Wiki abzubilden. Nach und nach können dann in Absprache weitere benötigte und für sinnvoll erachtete Funktionen, wie beispielsweise ein Plugin zur Prozessmodellierung, nachgerüstet werden.

Abbildung 30. Screenshot: Im TQU-Wiki integrierte GoogleMap auf einer Kundenseite

3.4.3 Bewertung

Um den nachhaltigen Erfolg des neuen Systems sicherzustellen, sollten von Anfang an kontinuierlich Kennzahlen erhoben und bewertet werden.

Es gibt in der Literatur noch keine Definition, welche Kennzahlen sich zur Erfolgskontrolle eines Wikisystems mit Managementbezug heranziehen lassen. Auf der Basis von Projekterfahrung und der bereits für Internetauftritte üblichen Kennzahlen, lassen sich dennoch einige Indikatoren herausarbeiten.

Je nach Einsatzzweck können zur Überprüfung und Bewertung des Erfolgs eines Wikis auch bereits vorhandene Kennzahlen zum Einsatz kommen. Auch die Aufwendungen in den unterschiedlichen Lebensphasen des Systems lassen sich durch diese Zahlen abbilden und mit anderen Systemen oder Wettbewerbern vergleichen.

Als Einteilung für ein Wiki bieten sich hier finanzielle Kennzahlen, IT-Produkt- und IT-Serviceprozess-Kennzahlen[154] und schliesslich reine Wiki-Kennzahlen an. In der folgenden Tabelle werden exemplarisch ausgewählte Kennzahlen, die sich im Rahmen dieser Arbeit als nützlich erwiesen haben, aufgeführt. Je nach verfolgtem Ziel können auch weitere Kennzahlen aus der Betriebswirtschaft, die nicht direkt auf ein Wiki zurückzuführen sind, herangezogen werden, um den nachhaltigen Erfolg des Systems zu messen.

---

[154] Vgl. [Tiemeyer 2005], S.136ff

73

Zuordnung	Kennzahl	Erklärung
Finanzen	Lizenzkosten	Lizenzgebühren für die eingesetzte Software
Finanzen	Schulungskosten	Kosten für die Schulung der Mitarbeiter mit dem System umzugehen
IT-Produkte	Auslastungsgrad	Für Systemkomponenten, Netzwerk, Server
IT-Produkte	Verfügbarkeit	Für Systemkomponenten, Netzwerk, Server
IT-Prozesse	Help-Desk-Auslastung	Anzahl der vom Help-Desk bearbeiteten Calls
IT-Prozesse	Dauer der Problem-behebung	Durchschnittliche Dauer pro Call bis zur Lösung des Problems
Wiki	Seitenaufrufe	Gesamtseitenaufrufe - aktivste Bereiche - aktivste Seite
Wiki	Seitenänderungen	Anzahl der Seitenänderungen - Bereiche mit den häufigsten Änderungen -Seiten mit häufigsten Änderungen - aktivste User
Wiki	Kommentare	- Bereiche mit den häufigsten Änderungen, -Seiten mit häufigsten Änderungen - aktivste User
Wiki	Dateianhänge	- Anzahl der Dateianhänge - Anzahl der Versionen von Dateianhängen

Tabelle 6. Kennzahlen für Wikisysteme

4 Praxisbeispiele

Die Praxisbeispiele entstammen dem direkten Umfeld dieser Arbeit. Die Management-systeme auf Wikibasis bei Hirschmann Automotive GmbH[155] und Kräss GlasCon GmbH[156] wurden während eines Arbeitskreises mit mehreren anderen Firmen im Hau-se der TQU International GmbH[157] von Grund auf entworfen und bis zur Einführung begleitet. Besonders von Vorteil war in diesem Zusammenhang vor allem der rege Austausch unter den teilnehmenden Firmen bzw. den jeweiligen Mitarbeitern in den Arbeitskreistreffen. Über vier Monate hinweg fanden diese Treffen regelmäßig statt und trugen mit den daraus gewonnenen Erkenntnissen einen großen Teil für das theoreti-sche Konstrukt dieser Arbeit bei. Das letzte Beispiel stellt das Controlling dar, welches während der Erstellung dieser Arbeit die Kolleginnen und Kollegen auf dem aktuellen Stand hielt.

---

[155] http://www.hirschmann-automotive.com/

[156] http://www.kraess.de/

[157] http://www.tquwiki.de/

4.1   Hirschmann Automotive GmbH

Unternehmen:

Das Unternehmen Hirschmann Automotive GmbH mit Hauptsitz in Rankweil (Österreich) wurde 1959 gegründet und unterhält zwei weiteren Standorte in Tschechien und
in Ungarn. Es ist einer der führenden Automobilzulieferer für Steckverbindungen jeglicher Art. Dazu stellt Hirschmann auch die entsprechenden Werkzeuge zum Guß der
Steckverbindungen her. Hirschmann übernimmt die komplette Prüfung der Teile und
hat ein entsprechendes Labor. Insgesamt beschäftigt die Hirschmann Automotive
GmbH rund 1300 Mitarbeiter.

Startseite

Hinzugefügt von Samuel Neuhauser, zuletzt bearbeitet von Martin Lorünser am 03. Jul. 2008 (Änderung anzeigen)
Stichwörter   EDIT LABELS
einstieg

Herzlich Willkommen im Wiki vom Werk Rankweil!

Unser Wiki ist die Intranetplattform für
die Hirschmann Automotive Gruppe. Wiki
heißt auf Hawaiianisch "schnell" - und
genau so möchten wir diese Plattform
nutzen. Jeder Benutzer soll schnell und
einfach alle Inhalte finden und anwenden.

Außerdem zeichnet sich ein Wiki durch die
einfache und schnelle "Mitarbeit" aus.

Jeder kann in den angebotenen Seiten
direkt Änderungen oder wenigstens
Kommentare anbringen und somit aktiv
und eigenverantwortlich an der
Gestaltung unseres Intranets und
unseres Unternehmens teilhaben.

Also, macht mit und seid dabei !!

Beachtet bitte auch:

• Wiki-Regeln von Hirschmann
• Infos zum Wiki-Prinzip bei Hirschmann

Abbildung 31. Screenshot: Startseite der Hirschmann Intranet Plattform auf Wikibasis

Motive:

„Unser Qualitätsmanagementsystem war so einfach nicht mehr praktikabel" erläutert
der "Wikibeauftragte" Samuel Neuhauser von Hirschmann Automotive. Als er in einer
Fachzeitschrift einen Artikel über das Managementsystem 2.0 las, war die Entscheidung schnell für Wiki gefallen. Vor allem die Chance, sich im Rahmen eines Arbeitskreises näher mit der Thematik „Wiki" auseinander zu setzen, stieß auf großes Interesse. Mehr Dynamik in den Systemen, besser eingebundene Mitarbeiter, ein einfach zu

bedienendes Werkzeug um das alles zu erreichen und nicht zuletzt die im Vergleich zu anderer Software moderaten Kosten, waren letztendlich Faktoren, die auch von der Geschäftsleitung voll getragen wurden und das „go" für ein Wiki bedeuteten.

Durchführung:

Schnell war klar, dass ein Wiki sich nicht nur für die geplante Umsetzung des Qualitätsmanagementsystems eignet, sondern es auch das bestehende Intranet und weitere Anwendungen einfangen kann und als zentrale Plattform genutzt werden soll.

Das interdisziplinäre Team aus IT, Management und Fachabteilungen arbeitete Hand in Hand und entwickelte eine ein neu gestaltetes Qualitätsmanagementsystem, das sich in ein Wiki abbilden läßt. Die Struktur des Wikis wurde auf drei Kernbereiche festgelegt:

- Qualitätsmanagementhandbuch

- Abteilungsseiten

- Persönliche Bereiche

Das Handbuch wurde nach Möglichkeit als Wiki-Seite übernommen und nur bei Bedarf mit Anhängen angelegt. In den Abteilungsseiten spiegelt sich der Aufbau der Organisation durch Organigramme und eine Gliederung nach Aufgabengebieten wieder. Angereichert werden diese Seiten beispielsweise durch Raumpläne, welche es auch neuen Mitarbeitern schnell und einfach ermöglichen sich in den Gebäuden zurecht zu finden. Auf den persönlichen Seiten können die Mitarbeiter nach freier Entscheidung sich und ihr persönliches Umfeld vorstellen, was sich als Träger für eine hohe Identifikation mit dem System darstellt.

Der Einführung des Systems ging ein Schulungskonzept über 50 Multiplikatoren voraus. Diese hatten bereits im Vorfeld ihr Interesse bekundet und wurden nun in mehreren Schulungen mit dem neuen System vertraut gemacht und im Umgang mit den eingesetzten Plugins geschult. So bilden nun ein bis zwei Wikiverantwortliche je Abteilung einen optimalen Anlaufpunkt, sowohl unter den Kollegen als auch von Führungsebene.

Bis zur Einführung wurden Teilbereiche des Wikis mit Inhalten befüllt und Verantwortliche für bestimmte Bereiche benannt. Ein gezieltes und gut aufbereitetes Informations- und Kommunikationskonzept, als Metapher wurde oft Wickie und die starken Männer verwendet, haben die Belegschaft über die Neuerung informiert und Interesse daran geweckt. Für die Einführung in allen drei Werken wurde ein „Wiki-Admin-Day" durchgeführt.

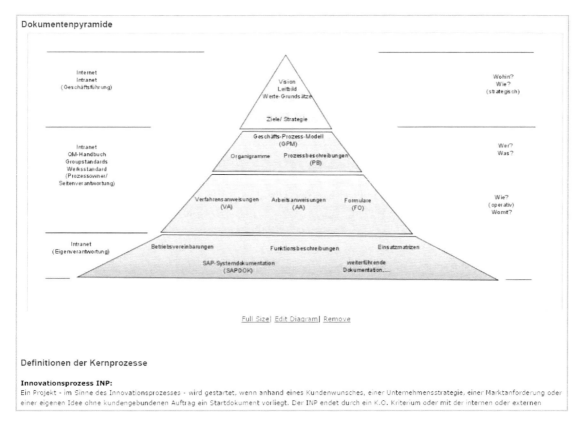

Abbildung 32. Screenshot: Gliffy-Diagramm im Hirschmann Wiki

Einzellösungen:

Grafiken werden im Wiki einheitlich durch das Gliffy Plugin dargestellt. Dies ermöglicht eine unkomplizierte Bearbeitung und nahtlose Integration in das eingesetzte Confluence System. Bilder für Dokumentationen werden direkt im Wiki hinterlegt und sind somit mit dem Inhalt der jeweiligen Wikiseite verbunden. Über Iframes wurde bereits die firmeninterne Fachbuchverwaltung in das Wiki integriert, um einen zentralen Anlaufpunkt zu schaffen. Für den Zugriff von aussen werden VPN-Zugänge eingesetzt.[158]

Erfolge:

Die Mitarbeiter identifizieren sich mit dem System und liefern ständig neue Ideen für das Managementsystem. Die Vernetzung über mehrere Standorte trägt einen großen Teil zum Wir-Gefühl bei. „Es ist jetzt unser System, und nicht mehr das aus Rankweil" zitiert Samuel Neuhauser. Die Multiplikatoren bringen sich engagiert ein und tragen zur weiteren Verbesserung des Systems bei. Das QM-Handbuch ist komplett in das Wiki übertragen und nun deutlich besser bei den Mitarbeitern bekannt, was zu einer wesentlich aktiveren Beteiligung und Umsetzung qualitätsrelevanter Prozesse führte. Die persönlichen Bereiche werden von vielen Mitarbeitern genutzt und helfen eine starke Community zu schaffen.

---

[158] VPN – Virtual Private Network; Eine Technik von Ausserhalb über gesicherte Verbindungen auf das Unternehmens zuzugreifen.

Das Wiki bei Hirschmann lebt und ist in aller Munde. Offene und frühzeitige Kommunikation innerhalb des Unternehmens, ein gut durchdachter Projektablauf und ein interdisziplinäres Team halfen, das neue Managementsystem erfolgreich zu etablieren. Das Wissen über Prozesse und die Motivation, sich in Eigenverantwortung einzubringen, haben spürbar zugenommen und es ist eine starke Gemeinschaft entstanden. Wichtig dabei war vor allem die Regelung, dass das gesamte Wiki für jeden frei editierbar ist, es aber Regeln und Seitenverantwortliche gibt, die für Ordnung sorgen.

Stramme Projektplanung und Anleitung durch die TQU International halfen bei Projektbeginn, die nötige Zeit, die zum Austesten der neuen Technik und des Systems nötig ist, im Rahmen zu halten.

Zukünftig soll noch mehr Wert auf eine zentrale Plattform gelegt werden. Auch die ausländischen Werke werden daher immer mehr eingebunden und es laufen bereits die Übersetzungen in die einzelnen Landessprachen.

Qualitätsrelevante Prüfungen / Quality-related Checks

Prüfung	Art der Prüfung	Ort	Vorgabe	Verantwortung	Intervall
Fertigungs-integrierte Prüfung	kontinuierliche Überprüfung der eigenen Tätigkeit	alle Produktions-bereiche	Prüfplan	Produktions-mitarbeiter	laut Prüfplan
Fertigungs-integrierte Prüfung	kontinuierliche Überprüfung der Produktion	alle Produktions-bereiche	Prüfplan	Vorgesetzter des Produktions-mitarbeiters	laut Prüfplan
Endprüfung	100% Prüfung	alle Produktions-bereiche	Prüfplan	befähigtes Prüfpersonal	laut Prüfplan
AQL-Prüfung	Stichproben-prüfung	alle Produktions-bereiche	Prüfplan	befähigtes Prüfpersonal	laut Prüfplan
Finale Endstückprüfung	Stichproben-prüfung	Spritzerei Kontaktierung	Prüfplan und Spezifikationen (siehe VA-012)	siehe VA-012	laut Prüfplan

Bei allen oben genannten Prüfungen sind die Verantwortungen über die Durchführung und ggf. Kennzeichnung im Detail zu definieren. Weitere Informationen zu Prüfungen:

- Alle Prüfungen sind entsprechend den von der Prozessplanung erstellten Prüfpläne durchzuführen. Prüfungen werden auch mit SPC-Prüfplänen durchgeführt, die im System hinterlegt sind.
- Prüfungen, die bei der elektrischen Prüfung keine Beanstandung aufweisen, erhalten eine Kennzeichnung. Diese wird durch das Prüfgerät in Form einer Markierung oder eines Datumstempels vorgenommen oder erfolgt manuell mittels Etikettierung am Produkt. Ausnahme: Für Auslaufprodukte und Ersatzteile ist diese Regelung nur beschränkt gültig! Fehlerhafte Prüfmittel sind dem Vorgesetzten unverzüglich zu melden. Bei der Entscheidung über das weitere Vorgehen gilt die GS von VA-G-02 "Risikominimierung bei Produktfehlern".
- Durch die Endprüfung freigegebene Produkte werden auf der Verpackung im Bereich des Produktionsetiketts mittels Prüfstempel gekennzeichnet.

Check	Type of Check	Place	Requirement	Responsibility	Interval
checks during the ongoing production	continuous check of everybody's own work	all production divisions	inspection plan	worker	according to inspection plan
checks during the ongoing production	continuous check of the production	all production divisions	inspection plan	superior of a worker	according to inspection plan
End check	100% check	all production divisions	inspection plan	qualified personnel	according to inspection plan
AQL-checks	random check.	all production divisions	inspection plan	qualified personnel	according to inspection plan
Final last piece check	random check	molding, contacting	inspection plan and specifications (see VA-012)	see VA-012	according to inspection plan

For all above mentioned checks it is necessary to clearly define the responsibility regarding their performance and if necessary the labeling. Further information regarding checks:

- All checks have to be performed according to the inspection plan which is created by the process planning department. For some checks the inspection plan in the SPC-System has to be used.
- Electrically ok tested parts get a mark. This mark is either a marking from a testing device, or a date stamp, or a manually fixed label. Exception: Discontinued products and spares! Supervisors have to be informed about malfunctioning testing devices. When deciding about further actions theGS von VA-G-02 "Risikominimierung bei Produktfehlern" is valid.
- The finally released products get a stamp on the packaging near by the production label.

Abbildung 33. Screenshot: Mehrsprachige Anleitungen im Hirschmann Wiki

Dass Hirschmann und TQU mit ihrem Managementsystem 2.0 auf dem richtigen Weg sind, zeigen nicht nur die Zahlen, es wurden bereits am ersten Tag der Wiki-Einführung über 150 Seiten von den Mitarbeitern selbständig geändert, sondern auch die abschließende Aussage von Samuel Neuhauser: „Alles in allem sehen wir uns den Herausforderungen für die Zukunft, sowohl wikitechnisch als auch auf dem Automobilmarkt, gewachsen und sind echt davon überzeugt, das wir mit Wiki eine super Plattform für einen schnellen, direkten und einfachen Infoaustausch geschaffen haben."

4.2 Kräss GlasCon GmbH

Unternehmen:

Die Kräss GlasCon GmbH wurde 1904 im bayerischen Weißenhorn gegründet und ist heute ein international operierendes Unternehmen und ein führender Hersteller kommerzieller Gewächshäuser und Gartencenter in Europa. Heute unterhält Kräss eine eigene Tochter in Moskau, Russland, und beschäftigt rund 60 Mitarbeiter.

Motive:

Die Grundidee für ein Wiki war der Aufbau einer Wissensbibliothek, um Mitarbeitern in Russland und Deutschland ein einheitliches Werkzeug an die Hand zu geben sich aktiv an der Gestaltung des Managementsystems zu beteiligen. Das bestehende Qualitäts-managementsystem sollte durch Wiki abgebildet und damit dynamischer werden.

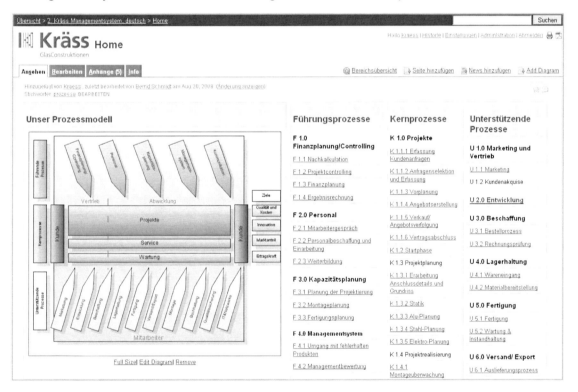

Abbildung 34. Screenshot: In Wiki abgebildetes Prozessmodell

Durchführung:

In enger Zusammenarbeit mit Bernd Schmidt, Managementbeauftragter der Kräss GlasCon GmbH, wurden die notwendigen Strukturen für die Wissensbibliotheken ge-schaffen. Die Inhalte wurden durch Praktikanten in das System eingegeben und mit den entsprechenden Dokumenten hinterlegt. Der Zugriff auf Konstruktionszeichnungen wird durch im Wiki abgebildete Links auf Netzwerklaufwerke zur Verfügung gestellt. Einzelne Prozesse werden durch das Gliffy Plugin direkt im Wiki abgebildet. Es wurde ebenfalls die Möglichkeit geschaffen, per VPN auf das Confluence Wiki zuzugreifen.

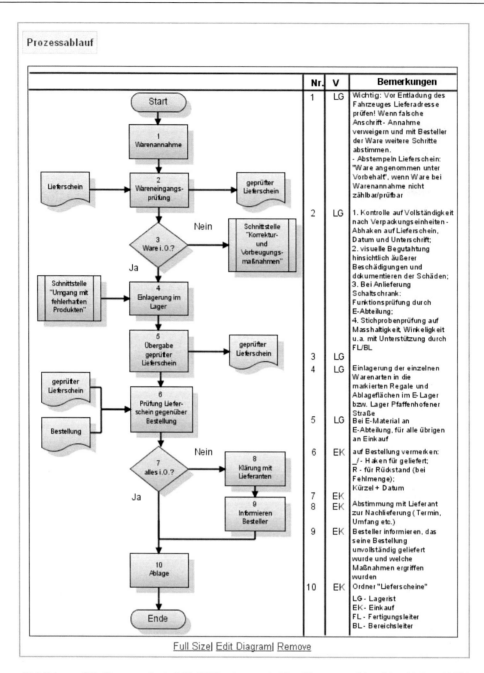

Abbildung 35. Screenshot: Mit Gliffy dargestellter Prozessablauf im Kräss Wiki

Erfolge:

Durch abgestufte Benutzerrechte wurde es möglich, einzelne Bereiche unterschiedlichen Nutzergruppen zugänglich zu machen. Die Projektleiter in Deutschland und Russland haben nun eine gemeinsame Plattform und zugleich für einzelne Projekte abgetrennte Bereiche. Das System ist transparent geworden und vor allem die jüngeren Mitarbeiter bringen sich mit Ideen und Vorschlägen ein. Auch werden Unternehmensmitteilungen über einen zentralen Bereich im Wiki kommuniziert und allen Mitarbeitern gleichermaßen zur Verfügung gestellt.

4.3 TQU International GmbH - Controlling Diplomarbeit

Unternehmen:

TQU International GmbH mit Sitz in Neu-Ulm ist eine Tochtergesellschaft der Steinbeis-Stiftung Baden-Württemberg und seit vielen Jahren spezialisiert auf Beratung, Projektarbeit, Coaching und Training in den Themen Ausrichtung von Unternehmen, Business Excellence, Weiterentwicklung und Umsetzung von Managementsystemen, sowie methodische Optimierung von Organisations- und Produktrealisierungsprozessen. Ständig auf der Suche nach Innovation wurde 2006 die Idee geboren, Managementsysteme auf Basis von Web 2.0 Technologien abzubilden.

Motive:

Im Rahmen dieser Arbeit wurde das eingesetzte Confluence System nicht nur bei Kunden und in Projekten, sondern auch als Controllingtool für diese Arbeit eingesetzt. Unkomplizierter, zeit- und ortsunabhängiger über Zugriff auf relevante Daten und zugleich ein zentraler Speicherplatz für alle Daten, die im Zusammenhang mit dieser Arbeit genutzt wurden. Auch die Versionierung und somit automatische Sicherung der einzelnen Versionsstände waren hierbei von großem Nutzen. Für die Mitarbeiter des TQU war es wichtig zu sehen, wie der aktuelle Stand der Diplomanden ist.

Durchführung:

Um eine gemeinsame Plattform zu schaffen, wurde ein Bereich für Diplomarbeiten innerhalb des Wikis abgegrenzt. Dieser wurde mit einem Cockpit bzw. Dashboard für die wichtigsten Einzelschritte einer wissenschaftlichen Arbeit versehen.

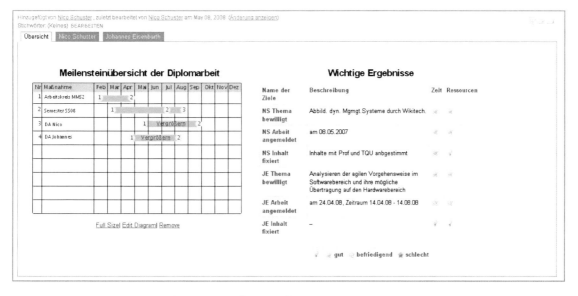

Abbildung 36. Dashboard für das Controlling der Diplomarbeit im Wiki

Die Cockpitansicht kann durch Karteireiter verfeinert werden und somit auf einen Blick Informationen über weitere Inhalte oder den genauen Plan der Einzelschritte liefern. Auf diese Weise wurde ein per Gliffy visualisierter Projektplan für jede einzelne Diplomarbeit realisiert. Durch die Möglichkeit, aus den Diagrammen heraus auf andere Wikiseiten zu verlinken kann direkt aus dem Projektplan zum entsprechenden Abschnitt der Arbeit gesprungen werden.

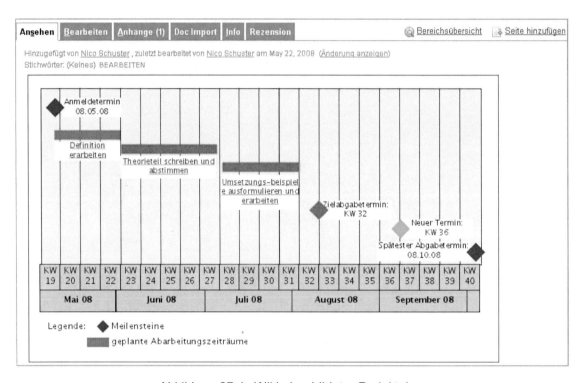

Abbildung 37. In Wiki abgebildeter Projektplan

Die Teilabschnitte wurden jeweils in Form einer Checkliste dargestellt, die es ermöglichte, einzelne Punkte als erledigt zu kennzeichnen. Durch die Visualisierung mit Fortschrittsanzeige war auf den ersten Blick ersichtlich, bei welchem Abschnitt sich die Arbeit gerade befand.

Dateianhänge wie Präsentationen und PDF-Dokumente oder Abbildungen wurden ebenfalls im Wiki verwaltet und konnten bei Bedarf von allen anderen kommentiert werden.

Die Möglichkeit, einzelne Seiten zu beobachten oder sich wöchentlich (wenn gewünscht auch täglich) per E-Mail oder RSS-Feed über Änderungen informieren zu lassen, ermöglichte einen Informationsaustausch auch ohne reguläre Meetings.

Erfolge:

Die Arbeit wurde für alle Mitarbeiter transparent geschrieben und konnte bei Bedarf kommentiert und verbessert werden. Das erworbene Wissen wird im Unternehmen weiterhin zugänglich sein und kann gewinnbringend genutzt werden. Durch den Einsatz eines dynamischen Systems konnten Fehler und Irrtümer frühzeitig erkannt und Korrekturen vorgenommen werden. Das permanente Feedback durch Kollegen und Führungskräfte motiviert und verbindet mit dem Thema.

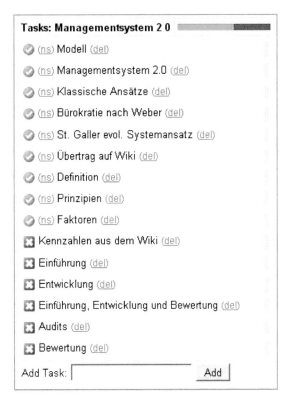

Abbildung 38. Checkliste im Wiki

5   Fazit

Die Arbeit mit einem Wiki ist eigentümlich und anfangs befremdlich. Man erstellt eine Seite nach bestem Wissen und Gewissen und beim nächsten Blick ist der Inhalt verändert. Jemand hat, ebenfalls nach bestem Wissen und Gewissen, die Seite überarbeitet und mit seinen Inhalten erweitert. Zusammengenommen ergibt sich daraus ein Inhalt, der von Änderung zu Änderung an Qualität gewinnt, ganz ohne umständliche und hierarchische Qualitätssicherungsprozesse durchlaufen zu müssen. So ähnlich sollte der Idealfall eines Wikis aussehen. Und tatsächlich, sind die ersten technischen Hürden genommen und hat man sich mit der Tatsache arrangiert, dass in einem Wiki alles einerseits vergänglich, dafür aber die Inhalte auf dem aktuellsten Stand sind, beginnt es Spaß zu machen. Auch die Möglichkeit, sich über andere Dinge, die im Unternehmen vor sich gehen, informieren zu können macht die Arbeit mit einem Wiki interessant. Hinzu kommt, dass Software zunehmend ineinander greift, seien es eingebundene GoogleMaps, um den Standort des Kunden darzustellen oder Videos, um interaktive Anleitungen für Mitarbeiter zu erstellen.

Gerade die Einfachheit und Schlichtheit, die ein Wiki in seiner ursprünglichen Form bietet, ziehen Nutzer an, da sie nicht wie so oft, umständliche und lange Schulungen über sich ergehen lassen müssen, sondern sofort loslegen können. Selbst wenn ein Fehler auftreten sollte, ist das kein Problem, denn die automatische Versionierung ermöglicht das Wiederherstellen einer älteren Version. Auch die Bedenken, ein offenes System könne zu Mißbrauch führen, konnten durch gezielte Rechtevergabe und die Nutzung des Wikis unter Realnamen zerstreut werden.

Sich ein solches System für das Speichern von Unternehmenswissen und -Prozessen zu Nutze zu machen scheint daher der logische Schluss. Werden doch die Bedürfnisse aller Seiten, sei es das Bedürfnis nach Anerkennung der eigenen Arbeit durch positive Kommentare der Kollegen, oder das Bedürfnis der Firmenlenker nach mehr Transparenz über Vorgänge oder mehr Nähe zur Belegschaft, befriedigt.

Für ein Managementsystem eignet sich ein Wiki über mehrere Bereiche hinweg aus den vorgenannten Gründen sehr gut. Viel wichtiger als die technische Komponente und eine durchdachte, sich selbst aktualisierende Struktur des Wikis sind aber die Menschen, die es nutzen. Sie müssen ihr Denken und Handeln auf ein offenes, partizipatives System umstellen und manchmal aus alten Hierarchien ausbrechen. Dies erfordert von allen Beteiligten einen offenen Umgang mit- und untereinander. Es wird Aufgabe und Herausforderung für Unternehmen sein, die Grenzen und Entwicklungsmöglichkeiten von Wikis gerade in Einsatzfeldern abseits des üblichen Wissensmanagements weiter zu erproben.

Es ist mehr als nur eine neue Technologie, es ist vor allem auch ein Umbruch alter Denkmuster. Man kann also auf die Zukunft von Wiki und Co. gespannt sein.

Abbildungsverzeichnis

Abbildung 1. Das St. Galler Management-Modell. Online verfügbar unter http://upload.wikimedia.org/wikipedia/de/thumb/b/bf/SGMM2.jpg/500px- SGMM2.jpg, zuletzt geprüft am 27.03.2008

Abbildung 2. Integriertes Managementsystem . Online verfügbar unter http://www.paeger-consulting.de/assets/images/ims.gif, zuletzt geprüft am 05.09.2008

Abbildung 3. Wiki-Wiki Shuttle auf Hawaii. Online verfügbar unter http://upload.wikimedia.org/wikipedia/commons/4/42/HNL_Wiki_Wiki_Bus.jpg, zuletzt geprüft am 06.08.2008

Abbildung 4. Die Web Trend Map. Online verfügbar unterhttp://www.informationarchitects.jp/slash/iA_WebTrends_2007_2_1600x1024.gif, zuletzt geprüft am 27.03.2008

Abbildung 5. Die Web 2.0 Meme Map. Online verfügbar unter http://www.oreillynet.com/oreilly/tim/news/2005/09/30/graphics/figure1.jpg, zuletzt geprüft am 09.05.2008

Abbildung 6. Logos im Web 2.0 Design. Online verfügbar unter http://farm2.static.flickr.com/1180/1169522415_32eb2765d3.jpg?v=0, zuletzt geprüft am 09.05.2008

Abbildung 7. Screenshot: Xing-Verbindung von Nico Schuster - Karoline Kraus. Quelle: Autor

Abbildung 8. Screenshot: Facebook-Profil von Nico Schuster. Quelle: Autor

Abbildung 9. Artikelwachstum der deutschsprachigen Wikipedia. Online verfügbar unter http://de.wikipedia.org/wiki/Bild:Meilensteine.png, zuletzt geprüft am 05.08.2008

Abbildung 10. Screenshot: Eine in Xing integrierten GoogleMap. Quelle: Autor

Abbildung 11. Screenshot: Gliffy-Plugin für Confluence. Quelle: Autor

Abbildung 12. Darstellung von System und Umwelt. Quelle: [Schulte-Zurhausen 2002], S. 34

Abbildung 13. Maslow'sche Bedürfnispyramide. Online verfügbar unter http://www.wortgefecht.net/img/maslow.gif, zuletzt geprüft am 01.09.2008

Abbildung 14. Häufigste Faktoren nach Herzberg. Online verfügbar unter http://de.wikipedia.org/wiki/Bild:Herzbergs_Faktoren.jpg, zuletzt geprüft am 13.08.2008

Abbildung 15. Gartner Hype Cycle. Online verfügbar unter
http://infoaccess.wiki.zoho.com/Gartner-Hype-Cycle-2007.html,
zuletzt geprüft am 07.08.2008

Abbildung 16. Magic Quadrant nach Gartner. Online verfügbar unter
http://www.socialtext.com /resources/resourcefiles/Socialtext_2513_GartnerM.pdf,
zuletzt geprüft am 07.08.2008

Abbildung 17. Altersverteilung der Umfrageteilnehmer. Quelle: Autor

Abbildung 18. Geschlechterverteilung der Umfrageteilnehmer. Quelle: Autor

Abbildung 19. Position der Teilnehmer innerhalb des Unternehmens. Quelle: Autor

Abbildung 20. Verteilung der Teilnehmer nach Branche. Quelle: Autor

Abbildung 21. Mitarbeiteranzahl der Unternehmen. Quelle: Autor

Abbildung 22. Bewertung der Eigenschaften eines Wikis. Quelle: Autor

Abbildung 23. Gegenüberstellung Wikieinsatz in IuK und Nicht-IuK-Unternehmen.
Quelle: Autor

Abbildung 24. Einsatz von Wikis nach Zweck. Quelle: Autor

Abbildung 25. Einsatz von Wikis nach Bereich. Quelle: Autor

Abbildung 26. Einsatz eines Wikis nach Zweck - Leitungsebene/Nicht-Leitungsebene.
Quelle: Autor

Abbildung 27. Einsatz eines Wikis nach Bereich - Leitungsebene/Nicht-
Leitungsebene. Quelle: Autor

Abbildung 28. Partizipationspyramide nach Nielson. Online verfügbar unter
http://www.useit.com/alertbox/community-participation-pyramid.gif,
zuletzt geprüft am 25.08.2008

Abbildung 29. Modell Managementsystem 2.0. Quelle: Autor

Abbildung 30. Screenshot: Im TQU-Wiki integrierte GoogleMap auf einer
Kundenseite. Quelle: TQU International GmbH

Abbildung 31. Screenshot: Startseite der Hirschmann Intranet Plattform auf Wikibasis.
Quelle: Hirschmann Automotive GmbH

Abbildung 32. Screenshot: Gliffy-Diagramm im Hirschmann Wiki.
Quelle: Hirschmann Automotive GmbH

Abbildung 33. Screenshot: Mehrsprachige Anleitungen im Hirschmann Wiki. Quelle:
Hirschmann Automotive GmbH

Abbildung 34. Screenshot: In Wiki abgebildetes Prozessmodell.
Quelle: Kräss GlasCon GmbH

Abbildung 35. Screenshot: Mit Gliffy dargestellter Prozessablauf im Kräss Wiki.
Quelle: Kräss GlasCon GmbH

Tabellenverzeichnis

Tabelle 1. Web1.0 – Web 2.0 in Anlehnung an O'Reilly, Online verfügbar unter http://www.oreillynet.com/pub/a/oreilly/tim/news/2005/09/30/what-is-web-20.html, zuletzt geprüft am 08.09.2008

Tabelle 2. Gegenüberstellung Bürokratieansatz – Wiki.
In Anlehnung an [Komus- Wauch 2002], S.82f

Tabelle 3. Gegenüberstellung von System- und Wikiaspekten.
In Anlehnung an [Komus-Wauch, 2008], S.117

Tabelle 4. Gegenüberstellung Herzberg und Wiki.
In Anlehnung an [Komus-Wauch], S. 100

Tabelle 5. Die acht Phasen des Change Prozesses. [Siebert 2006], S.140

Tabelle 6. Kennzahlen für Wikisysteme. Quelle: Autor

Literaturverzeichnis

Algesheimer, René; Leitl, Michael (2007): Unternehmen 2.0. In: Harvard Business Manager, Jg. 29, H. 06, S. 88ff.

Allen, David (2001): Getting Things Done. The Art of Stress-Free Productivity: Penguin Books Australia Ltd.

Bayerisches Staatsministerium für Wirtschaft, Infrastruktur Verkehr und Technologie: Integriertes Managementsystem. Ein Leitfaden für kleine und mittlere Unternehmen. Online verfügbar unter http://www.stmwivt.bayern.de/pdf/wirtschaft/Integriertes_Managementsystem.pdf, zuletzt geprüft am 31.08.2008.

Bergeron, Bryan P. (2002): Essentials of Shared Services: John Wiley & Sons.

Bergmann, Jens (2007): Die gläserne Firma. In: Brand Eins, H. 03, S. 109–155.

Beyer, Horst-Tilo: Inhalts- und Prozeßtheorien der Motivation. Online verfügbar unter http://www.economics.phil.uni-erlangen.de/bwl/lehrbuch/gst_kap4/mottheo/, zuletzt geprüft am 13.08.2008.

Bühl, Achim (2000): Die virtuelle Gesellschaft des 21. Jahrhunderts. Sozialer Wandel im digitalen Zeitalter. 2. Aufl. Wiesbaden: Westdt. Verl.

Communispace: Move Over Maslow. Online verfügbar unter http://www.communispace.com/assets/pdf/R_All_Communispace_Gaining_Business_Value_Release_11_29_07.pdf, zuletzt geprüft am 13.08.2008.

Computerwoche: Erfolgreiches Wissens-Management: Zehn Tipps für die Einführung von Enterprise-Wikis - computerwoche.de. Online verfügbar unter http://www.computerwoche.de/knowledge_center/it_strategie/1871031/, zuletzt geprüft am 05.09.2008.

Computerwoche: Enterprise-Wiki [Computerwoche Wiki]. Online verfügbar unter http://wiki.computerwoche.de/doku.php/web_2.0/enterprise-wikis, zuletzt geprüft am 07.08.2008.

Ebersbach, Anja; Glaser, Markus; Heigl, Richard (2006): Wiki. Web collaboration ; with 47 tables. Berlin: Springer.

Ebersbach, Anja; Glaser, Markus; Heigl, Richard; Warta, Alexander (2008): Wiki. Web Collaboration. 2. Aufl. Berlin, Heidelberg: Springer-Verlag

Ellebracht, Heiner; Gerhard, Lenz; Osterhold, Gisela; Schäfer, Helmut (2003): Systemische Organisations- und Unternehmensberatung. Praxishandbuch für Berater und Führungskräfte. 2., überarb. Aufl. Wiesbaden: Gabler.

Ellis et al. (1991): Groupware: some issues and experiences. Communications of the Acm January 1991: Association for Computing Machinery.

E-Teching.org: Wikis. Online verfügbar unter http://www.e-teaching.org/technik/kommunikation/wikis/, zuletzt geprüft am 01.09.2008.

E-Teching.org: Wiki. Online verfügbar unter http://www.e-teaching.org/didaktik/kommunikation/wikis, zuletzt geprüft am 06.08.2008.

Ferstl, Otto K. (2006): Grundlagen der Wirtschaftsinformatik. 5., überarb. u. erw. Aufl. München, Wien: Oldenbourg.

Forschungsgruppe Wahlen: Internet-Strukturdaten. Repräsentative Umfrage - II. Quartal 2008. Online verfügbar unter http://www.forschungsgruppe.de/Studien/Internet-Strukturdaten/web_II_08.pdf, zuletzt geprüft am 02.09.2008.

Furnham, Adrian (1997): The Psychology of Behaviour at Work. The Individual in the Organisation: Taylor & Francis Ltd.

Gliffy: Confluence Plugin - Diagram in Confluence. Online verfügbar unter http://www.gliffy.com/confluencePlugin/, zuletzt geprüft am 05.08.2008.

Gross, Tom; Koch, Michael (2007): Computer-Supported Cooperative Work. München: Oldenbourg (Interaktive Medien).

Hanke, Edith; Knoll, Thomas (Hg.) (2005): Wirtschaft und Gesellschaft. Die Wirtschaft und die gesellschaftlichen Ordnungen und Mächte. Nachlass. Herrschaft: Mohr Siebeck.

Hebold, Oliver (2003): Weiterentwicklung von Managementsystemen. Online verfügbar unter http://dok.bib.fh-giessen.de/opus/volltexte/2003/647/pdf/Weiterentwicklung_von_Managementsystemen.pdf, zuletzt geprüft am 03.05.2008.

Heinen, Edmund (1992): Betriebswirtschaftliche Führungslehre. Grundlagen - Strategien - Modelle; ein entscheidungsorientierter Ansatz. 2., verb. und erw. Aufl., Nachdr. Wiesbaden: Gabler.

Hill, Wilhelm; Fehlbaum, Raymond; Ulrich, Peter (1998): Organisationslehre 2. Theoretische Ansätze und praktische Methoden der Organisation sozialer Systeme

Hippner, H. /. Wilde T. (2005): Social Software. In: Wirtschaftsinformatik, Jg. 47, H. 6, S. 441–444.

Koch, Michael; Richter, Alexander (2007): Enterprise 2.0. Planung, Einführung und erfolgreicher Einsatz von Social Software in Unternehmen. München: Oldenbourg.

Komus, Ayelt; Wauch, Franziska (2008): Wikimanagement. Was Unternehmen von Social Software und Web 2.0 lernen können: Oldenbourg, R.

Kotter, John P. (1996): Leading Change: Harvard Business School Press.

Lange, Christoph (Hg.) (2005): Wiki. Planen - Einrichten - Verwalten: C & L Computer- und. Literaturverlag.

91

Leuf, Bo; Cunningham, Ward (2001): The Wiki way. Quick collaboration on the Web. Boston: Addison-Wesley.

Macharzina, Klaus; Wolf, Joachim (2008): Unternehmensführung. Das internationale Managementwissen - Konzepte - Methoden - Praxis: Betriebswirtschaftlicher Verlag Gabler.

Mader, Stewart (2008): Wikipatterns. [a practical guide to improving productivity and collaboration in your organization]. Indianapolis, Ind.: Wiley.

Maslow, Abraham H.; Kruntorad, Paul (2005): Motivation und Persönlichkeit. 10. Aufl. Reinbek bei Hamburg: Rowohlt (rororo rororo-Sachbuch, 17395).

McGovern, Gerry; Norton, Rob; O'Dowd, Catherine (2002): The Web content style guide. An essential reference for online writers, editors, and managers. London: Financial Times Prentice Hall.

Microsoft Blog: Microsoft SharePoint Team Blog: SharePoint Connector for Confluence - How We Did It. Online verfügbar unter http://blogs.msdn.com/sharepoint/archive/2008/01/10/sharepoint-connector-for-confluence-how-we-did-it.aspx, zuletzt geprüft am 07.08.2008.

Microsoft MSDN Channel 9 (2008): Ward Cunningham - How did you come up with the idea for the Wiki. Online verfügbar unter http://channel9.msdn.com/ShowPost.aspx?PostID=7726%, zuletzt geprüft am 05.08.2008.

Nielson, Jacob: Participation Inequality: Lurkers vs. Contributors in Internet Communities (Jakob Nielsen's Alertbox). Online verfügbar unter http://www.useit.com/alertbox/participation_inequality.html, zuletzt geprüft am 25.08.2008.

O'Reilly, Tim (2008): What is Web 2.0. Online verfügbar unter http://www.oreilly.de/artikel/web20.html, zuletzt geprüft am 09.05.2008.

Paeger, Jürgen (2008): Integrierte Managementsysteme. Online verfügbar unter http://www.paeger-consulting.de/html/integrierte_managementsysteme.html, zuletzt geprüft am 04.05.2008.

Pelz, Waldemar (2004): Kompetent führen. Wirksam kommunizieren Mitarbeiter motivieren. 1. Aufl. Wiesbaden: Gabler.

Probst, Gilbert J. B. (1987): Selbst-Organisation. Ordnungsprozesse in sozialen Systemen aus ganzheitlicher Sicht. Berlin, Hamburg: Parey.

Remer, Andreas (2002): Management. System und Konzepte. Bayreuth: REA-Verl. Managementforschung (Schriften zu Organisation und Personal, 15).

Rüegg-Stürm, Johannes (2002): Das neue St. Galler Management-Modell. Grundkategorien einer modernen Managementlehre - der HSG-Ansatz. Bern, Stuttgart, Wien

Schmidt, Jan (2006): Social Software: Onlinegestütztes Informations-, Identitäts- und Beziehungsmanagement. In: Forschungsjournal Neue Soziale Bewegungen, H. 2, S. 37–46.

Schreyögg, Georg (2003): Organisation. Grundlagen moderner Organisationsgestaltung. Mit Fallstudien. Wiesbaden: Betriebswirtschaftlicher Verlag Gabler.

Schulte-Zurhausen, Manfred (2002): Organisation. 3., überarb. Aufl. München

Schweizer, Peter (2008): Systematisch Lösungen finden. Eine Denkschule für Praktiker. 3., überarb. Aufl. Zürich: vdf-Hochschulverl.

Schwerdtle, Hartwig (1999): Prozeßintegriertes Management - PIM. Ein Modell für effizientes Qualitäts- Umwelt- und Arbeitsschutzmanagement. Berlin: Springer.

sciencegarden - Magazin für junge Forschung (2008): Web 2.0–Social Software der neuen Generation. Redaktion sciencegarden. Online verfügbar unter http://www.sciencegarden.de/content/2007-02/web-20%E2%80%93social-software-der-neuen-generation, zuletzt geprüft am 10.05.2008.

Siebert, Jörg (2006): Führungssysteme zwischen Stabilität und Wandel. Ein systematischer Ansatz zum Management der Führung. Wiesbaden: Deutscher Universitäts-Verlag / GWV-Fachverlage GmbH Wiesbaden.

Sixtus, Mario (2005): Gutenberg reloaded. Wie Weblogs die Medienwelt verändern: Heise.

SPIEGEL ONLINE: Studie: Wikipedia fast so genau wie Encyclopaedia Britannica - Netzwelt - SPIEGEL ONLINE - Nachrichten. Online verfügbar unter http://www.spiegel.de/netzwelt/web/0,1518,390475,00.html, zuletzt geprüft am 04.08.2008.

Stadtwiki Karlsruhe (2008): Hauptseite – Stadtwiki. Online verfügbar unter http://ka.stadtwiki.net/Hauptseite, zuletzt geprüft am 01.09.2008.

Staehle, Wolfgang H. (1994): Management. Eine verhaltenswissenschaftliche Perspektive. 7. Aufl. / überarb. von Peter Conrad ; Jörg Sydow. München: Vahlen.

Streiff, Andres (2005): Wiki - Zusammenarbeit im Netz: Books on Demand.

Szugat, Martin (2007): Social Software. [Blogs Wikis & Co.]. 1. Nachdr. Paderborn: Entwickler.Press (Schnell + kompakt).

Tapscott, Don; Williams, Anthony D. (2006): Wikinomics. How mass collaboration changes everything. New York, NYPortfolio.

Tecchannel (2008): Spezielle Enterprise-Wikis | Professionelle Wikis für den Unternehmenseinsatz. Online verfügbar unter http://www.tecchannel.de/kommunikation/grundlagen/1741654/index7.html, zuletzt geprüft am 07.08.2008.

Tiemeyer, Ernst (2005): IT-Controlling kompakt. 1. Aufl. Heidelberg: Spektrum Akademischer Verl.

TWiki: WebHome < Plugins < TWiki. Online verfügbar unter
http://twiki.org/cgi-bin/view/Plugins/WebHome, zuletzt geprüft am 01.09.2008.

Ward Cunningham: Top Ten Wiki Engines. Online verfügbar unter
http://c2.com/cgi/wiki?TopTenWikiEngines, zuletzt geprüft am 07.08.2008.

Weber, Cedric: Confluence - neuer Stern am Wikihimmel? Online verfügbar unter
http://m.zung.us/2005/12/01/confluence-neuer-stern-am-wiki-himmel/,
zuletzt geprüft am 07.08.2008.

Wiki Patterns: About. Online verfügbar unter
http://www.wikipatterns.com/display/wikipatterns/About, zuletzt geprüft am 03.09.2008.

Wikipedia: Bürokratieansatz – Wikipedia. Online verfügbar unter
http://de.wikipedia.org/wiki/B%C3%BCrokratieansatz, zuletzt geprüft am 10.08.2008.

Wikipedia: Entwurfsmuster – Wikipedia. Online verfügbar unter
http://de.wikipedia.org/wiki/Entwurfsmuster, zuletzt geprüft am 03.09.2008.

Wikipedia: Gartner Inc. – Wikipedia. Online verfügbar unter
http://de.wikipedia.org/wiki/Gartner_Inc., zuletzt geprüft am 02.09.2008.

Wikipedia: Gewinnerzielungsabsicht. Online verfügbar unter
http://de.wikipedia.org/wiki/Gewinnerzielungsabsicht, zuletzt geprüft am 08.09.2008.

Wikipedia: Google Maps – Wikipedia. Online verfügbar unter
http://de.wikipedia.org/wiki/Google_Maps, zuletzt geprüft am 05.08.2008.

Wikipedia: Hype-Zyklus – Wikipedia. Online verfügbar unter
http://de.wikipedia.org/wiki/Hype-Zyklus, zuletzt geprüft am 02.09.2008.

Wikipedia: Kollaboration – Wikipedia. Online verfügbar unter
http://de.wikipedia.org/wiki/Kollaboration, zuletzt geprüft am 04.08.2008.

Wikipedia: Maslowsche Bedürfnispyramide – Wikipedia. Online verfügbar unter
http://de.wikipedia.org/wiki/Maslowsche_Bed%C3%BCrfnispyramide, zuletzt geprüft
am 13.08.2008.

Wikipedia: Spielwiese – Wikipedia. Online verfügbar unter
http://de.wikipedia.org/wiki/Wikipedia:Sandbox, zuletzt geprüft am 25.08.2008.

Wikipedia: Systemtheorie – Wikipedia. Online verfügbar unter
http://de.wikipedia.org/wiki/Systemtheorie, zuletzt geprüft am 11.08.2008.

Wikipedia: Taylorismus – Wikipedia. Online verfügbar unter
http://de.wikipedia.org/wiki/Taylorismus, zuletzt geprüft am 11.08.2008.

Wikipedia: Transparenz (Politik) – Wikipedia. Online verfügbar unter
http://de.wikipedia.org/wiki/Transparenz_(Politik), zuletzt geprüft am 07.09.2008.

Wikipedia: Brockhaus Enzyklopädie – Wikipedia. Online verfügbar unter
http://de.wikipedia.org/wiki/Brockhaus_Enzyklop%C3%A4die#Zuk.C3.BCnftige_Entwic
klung, zuletzt geprüft am 31.08.2008.

Wikipedia: Dynamik – Wikipedia. Online verfügbar unter
http://de.wikipedia.org/wiki/Dynamisch, zuletzt geprüft am 31.08.2008.

Wikipedia: Facebook – Wikipedia. Online verfügbar unter
http://de.wikipedia.org/wiki/Facebook, zuletzt geprüft am 12.05.2008.

Wikipedia: Flickr – Wikipedia. Online verfügbar unter http://de.wikipedia.org/wiki/Flickr,
zuletzt geprüft am 12.05.2008.

Wikipedia: GNU General Public License – Wikipedia. Online verfügbar unter
http://de.wikipedia.org/wiki/GNU_General_Public_License,
zuletzt geprüft am 07.08.2008.

Wikipedia: Integriertes Managementsystem – Wikipedia. Online verfügbar unter
http://de.wikipedia.org/wiki/Integriertes_Managementsystem,
zuletzt geprüft am 04.05.2008.

Wikipedia: MediaWiki – Wikipedia. Online verfügbar unter
http://de.wikipedia.org/wiki/MediaWiki, zuletzt geprüft am 07.08.2008.

Wikipedia: Memex – Wikipedia. Online verfügbar unter
http://de.wikipedia.org/wiki/Memex, zuletzt geprüft am 09.05.2008.

Wikipedia: Soziale Software – Wikipedia. Online verfügbar unter
http://de.wikipedia.org/wiki/Soziale_Software, zuletzt geprüft am 06.05.2008.

Wikipedia: TWiki – Wikipedia. Online verfügbar unter
http://de.wikipedia.org/wiki/TWiki, zuletzt geprüft am 07.08.2008.

Wikipedia: Web 2.0 – Wikipedia. Online verfügbar unter
http://de.wikipedia.org/wiki/Web_2.0, zuletzt geprüft am 06.05.2008.

Wikipedia: Web 2.0 - Wikipedia, the free encyclopedia. Online verfügbar unter
http://en.wikipedia.org/wiki/Web_2.0, zuletzt geprüft am 08.05.2008.

Wikipedia: Wiki – Wikipedia. Online verfügbar unter http://de.wikipedia.org/wiki/Wiki,
zuletzt geprüft am 05.08.2008.

Wikipedia: Wikitext – Wikipedia. Online verfügbar unter
http://de.wikipedia.org/wiki/Wikisyntax, zuletzt geprüft am 22.08.2008.

Worldsites Schweiz: Die beliebtesten Social Network Communities in Deutschland.
Online verfügbar unter http://news.worldsites-schweiz.ch/die-beliebtesten-social-
network-communities-in-deutschland.htm, zuletzt geprüft am 02.09.2008.

Wortgefecht.net: Michael Gisiger: Maslow und das Web 2.0. Online verfügbar unter
http://www.wortgefecht.net/social-%20media/maslow-und-das-web-2-0/,
zuletzt geprüft am 13.08.2008.

Zielke, Katja (2004): Qualität komplexer Dienstleistungsbündel. Operationalisierung
und empirische Analysen der Qualitätswahrnehmung am Beispiel des Tourismus. 1.
Aufl. Wiesbaden: Dt. Univ.-Verl.

Zollondz, Hans-Dieter (2001): Lexikon Qualitätsmanagement. Handbuch des modernen Managements auf der Basis des Qualitätsmanagements. München: Oldenbourg (Edition Versicherungsmanagement).

Anlagen

Anlage 1. Fragebogen der Onlineumfrage als Printversion:

Wikis als Managementsystem

Wikis als Managementsystem

1. Wikis als Managementsystem

05Entscheidung: Wie wird über den Einsatz neuer Software entschieden?

Bitte erläutern sie gegebenenfalls Ihre Auswahl.

Bitte **nur eine Antwort** aus folgenden Möglichkeiten wählen
- ☐ Geschäftsführung
- ☐ Bereichsleitung
- ☐ Abteilungsleitung
- ☐ Projektbezogene Auswahl
- ☐ Mitarbeiter entscheidet selbst

Bitte schreiben Sie einen Kommentar zu Ihrer Auswahl

---

* 10WikiJANein: Werden im Unternehmen bereits Wikis genutzt?

Bitte **nur eine Antwort** aus folgenden Möglichkeiten wählen
- ☐ Ja
- ☐ Nein
- ☐ Weiß nicht
- ☐ nicht offiziell (Entwicklerwikis)

[Bitte beantworten Sie diese Frage nur, falls ihre Antwort 'nicht offiziell (Entwicklerwikis)' oder 'Ja' war bei der Frage '10WikiJANein ']

15WIKIJA: In welchen Abteilungen wird das Wiki bereits eingesetzt?

Bitte erläutern sie gegebenenfalls Ihre Auswahl.

Bitte alle auswählen die zutreffen und einen Kommentar dazuschreiben
- ☐ Unternehmensweit
- ☐ Forschung / Entwicklung
- ☐ Produktion / Fertigung
- ☐ Lager / Versand
- ☐ Buchhaltung / Controlling
- ☐ Marketing / PR
- ☐ Service & Support (intern)
- ☐ Kundendienst / Kundenservice (extern)
- ☐ IT
- ☐ Personal
- ☐ andere

16WIKINEIN: Für welche Abteilungen können Sie sich den Einsatz eines Wikis (ebenfalls) vorstellen?

Bitte alle auswählen die zutreffen und einen Kommentar dazuschreiben
- ☐ Unternehmensweit
- ☐ Forschung / Entwicklung
- ☐ Produktion / Fertigung
- ☐ Lager / Versand
- ☐ Buchhaltung / Controlling
- ☐ Marketing / PR
- ☐ Service & Support (intern)
- ☐ Kundendienst / Kundenservice (extern)
- ☐ IT

1 von 3

97

Wikis als Managementsystem

☐ Personal

☐ andere

[Bitte beantworten Sie diese Frage nur, falls ihre Antwort 'Ja' oder 'nicht offiziell (Entwicklerwikis)' war bei der Frage '10WikiJANein ']

25WIKIJAZWECK: Wür welchen Zweck wird das Wiki bereits eingesetzt?

Bitte alle auswählen die zutreffen und einen Kommentar dazuschreiben

☐ Wissensmanagement

☐ Projektmanagement

☐ Qualitätsmanagement

☐ Führungsinformationssystem

☐ Dokumentenmanagement

☐ Versionsmanagement

☐ Kommunikationsplattform

☐ Intranet

☐ andere

27WIKINEINZWECK: Für welche Bereiche könnten Sie sich den Einsatz eines Wikis (zusätzlich) vorstellen?

Bitte alle auswählen die zutreffen und einen Kommentar dazuschreiben

☐ Wissensmanagement

☐ Projektmanagement

☐ Qualitätsmanagement

☐ Führungsinformationssystem

☐ Dokumentenmanagement

☐ Versionsmanagement

☐ Kommunikationsplattform

☐ Intranet

☐ andere

30 Bewertung: Bitte Bewerten Sie diese Eigenschaften im Bezug auf ein Wiki

Bitte wählen Sie die zutreffende Antwort aus

	positiv	eher positiv	neutral	eher negativ	negativ
Transparenz	☐	☐	☐	☐	☐
Einfachheit	☐	☐	☐	☐	☐
Kosten	☐	☐	☐	☐	☐
Motivation	☐	☐	☐	☐	☐
Editierbarkeit	☐	☐	☐	☐	☐

2. Persönliche Daten

* 0001: Bitte nennen Sie ihr Alter.

Bitte **nur eine Antwort** aus folgenden Möglichkeiten wählen

☐ 18-25

☐ 25-30

☐ 30-40

☐ 40-50

☐ über 50

☐ Sonstiges

* 0002: Bitte nennen Sie ihr Geschlecht.

2 von 3

Wikis als Managementsystem

Bitte <u>**nur eine Antwort** aus folgenden Möglichkeiten wählen</u>
- ☐ männlich
- ☐ weiblich
- ☐ keine Angabe

3. Firmenangaben

* 0001: In welcher Branche sind Sie tätig?

Bitte <u>**nur eine Antwort** aus folgenden Möglichkeiten wählen</u>
- ☐ Wissenschaft
- ☐ Dienstleistungen
- ☐ Industrie
- ☐ Banken
- ☐ Medizin
- ☐ IuK-Technologie
- ☐ Baugewerbe
- ☐ Verwaltung
- ☐ keine Angabe
- ☐ Sonstiges |

* 0002: Bitte nennen Sie ihre Firmengröße.

Bitte <u>**nur eine Antwort** aus folgenden Möglichkeiten wählen</u>
- ☐ 1-10
- ☐ 10-100
- ☐ 100-500
- ☐ 500-5000
- ☐ 5000-10000
- ☐ 10000 oder mehr Mitarbeiter

* 0003: Welche Position innerhalb des Unternehmens bekleiden Sie?

Bitte <u>**nur eine Antwort** aus folgenden Möglichkeiten wählen</u>
- ☐ Geschäftsführung / Eigentümer
- ☐ Vorstand
- ☐ Bereichsleitung
- ☐ Abteilungsleitung
- ☐ Projektleiter / Projektmanager
- ☐ Consultant
- ☐ Vertrieb
- ☐ Entwicklung
- ☐ keine Angabe
- ☐ Sonstiges |

4. Abschluss

eMail: Wenn Sie an den Ergebnissen der Umfrage interessiert sind, dann hinterlassen Sie bitte Ihre E-Mail-Adresse.

Bitte schreiben Sie Ihre Antwort hier

Kommentare: Sie möchten uns noch etwas sagen? Hier ist der passende Platz!

Bitte schreiben Sie Ihre Antwort hier

Vielen Dank für die Beantwortung des Fragebogens.